publication supported by

Figure Foundation

parsing courage

Unconquerable

JOHN ROSS

"UNCONQUERABLE"

The Story of ~~~~~~ John Ross, ~~~~ Chief of
the Cherokees, 1828 -1866

by

John M. Oskison
~~~~~~~~~~~~~~~~

John M. Oskison
Vinita, Okla.

"Unconquerable"

The Story of John Ross, Chief
of the Cherokees,
1828 - 1866

UNCONQUERABLE

The Story of John Ross,
Chief of the Cherokees,
1828–1866

John M. Oskison

Edited and with an introduction by
Lionel Larré

UNIVERSITY OF NEBRASKA PRESS   LINCOLN

Frontispieces: Title page of the original manuscript, with a portrait of John Ross (under his name, Oskison had typed, between brackets and quotation marks, the word *Tsalagi,* which means *Cherokee* in the Cherokee language, before he crossed it out), and title of the manuscript, handwritten by Oskison.

The University of Nebraska Press is part of a land-grant institution with campuses and programs on the past, present, and future homelands of the Pawnee, Ponca, Otoe-Missouria, Omaha, Dakota, Lakota, Kaw, Cheyenne, and Arapaho Peoples, as well as those of the relocated Ho-Chunk, Sac and Fox, and Iowa Peoples.

Université
**BORDEAUX
MONTAIGNE**

Library of Congress Cataloging-in-Publication Data
Names: Oskison, John M. (John Milton), 1874–1947, author. | Larré, Lionel, editor.
Title: Unconquerable: the story of John Ross, Chief of the Cherokees, 1828–1866 / John M. Oskison; edited and with an introduction by Lionel Larré.
Other titles: Story of John Ross, Chief of the Cherokees, 1828–1866
Description: Lincoln: University of Nebraska Press, [2022] | Includes bibliographical references and index.
Identifiers: LCCN 2021057676 | ISBN 9781496230966 (hardback) | ISBN 9781496231482 (paperback) | ISBN 9781496232120 (epub) | ISBN 9781496232137 (pdf)
Subjects: LCSH: Ross, John, 1790–1866. | Cherokee Indians—Kings and rulers—Biography | Cherokee Indians—History. | BISAC: SOCIAL SCIENCE / Ethnic Studies / American / Native American Studies
Classification: LCC E99.C5 O77 2022 | DDC 305.89/97557092 [B]—dc23/eng/20220204
LC record available at https://lccn.loc.gov/2021057676

Set and designed in New Baskerville ITC by N. Putens.

ACKNOWLEDGMENTS

I am grateful for the help I received from the staff in the Department of Special Collections of McFarlin Library at the University of Tulsa, where the original manuscript of Oskison's biography of John Ross is preserved.

I am also grateful to the reviewers who carefully read the manuscript and approved of its publication. Their constructive criticism and encouragements were crucial. I am grateful also to University of Nebraska Press, especially Matt Bokovoy and Heather Stauffer, for their help and their renewed trust.

And I am grateful to my university, Bordeaux Montaigne University, and research department, CLIMAS, for their financial help that made this publication possible. Finally, thank you to LeAnn Stevens-Larré, Rachel Myers Moore, and Aaron Carr for your careful proofreading.

INTRODUCTION

The History of the "Unconquerable" Manuscript

LIONEL LARRÉ

John Milton Oskison was born in 1874 in Indian Territory to an English father and a Cherokee mother.[1] He grew up in Vinita, in the Cherokee Nation, at a time of profound transformation. In the wake of the Civil War—which left the Cherokees divided and their nation devastated—several railroads were built across their territory, inviting the intrusion of thousands of Euro-American citizens. As a fiction writer, a journalist, and an activist, Oskison described these changes, and the issues they raised for the Cherokees, in numerous short stories and essays in diverse periodicals published mostly between 1897 and 1925, in four novels written in the 1920s and '30s,[2] and in an autobiography left unfinished when he died in 1947. The latter was published in 2012, along with many of the short stories and essays, in *Tales of the Old Indian Territory and Essays on the Indian Condition.*

Oskison also wrote three biographies: one of Sam Houston, *A Texas Titan,* published in 1929, one of Shawnee leader Tecumseh, *Tecumseh and His Times,* published in 1938, and one of John Ross, which remained unpublished until now. During my research for the publication of *Tales of the Old Indian Territory,* I came across the typed manuscript, corrected in places by what appeared to be Oskison's handwriting, of "Unconquerable: The Story of John Ross, Chief of the Cherokees, 1828–1866." It was, and still is, carefully preserved at the University of Tulsa, Oklahoma, in the Special Collections of McFarlin Library. The manuscript was too long to be included in *Tales of the Old Indian Territory.* Yet, the theme of the unpublished book fits nicely within Oskison's oeuvre.

Oskison probably wrote "Unconquerable" between his third novel, *Brothers Three* (published in 1935), and his biography of Tecumseh

(1938). In the University of Oklahoma Press Collection, held by the Western History Collections at the University of Oklahoma, there are documents dated 1933 regarding the rejection of the manuscript by OU Press. An analysis of these documents, and of the reasons why the project was rejected, may be an appropriate starting point to explain today's publication of Oskison's biography of John Ross.

The director of the press at the time was Joseph A. Brandt, who was on friendly terms with Oskison, judging by the tone of their correspondence. The manuscript was reviewed by three readers: eminent Oklahoma historians Grant Foreman and Morris L. Wardell, as well as James Julian Hill, an assistant librarian who would also collaborate with the press on a 1968 edition of Emmet Starr's *Old Cherokee Families*. Foreman had just published his *Indian Removal* (1932) and would publish *The Five Civilized Tribes* in 1934. Wardell would publish *A Political History of the Cherokee Nation, 1838–1907* in 1938.[3]

There seems to have been, among the reviewers, some disagreement about Oskison's manuscript and even some controversy about John Ross, perhaps accounting for some delay in the director's response to the author. In a short letter dated April 7, 1933, found along with all further letters cited pertaining to the "Unconquerable" manuscript in the Oklahoma University Press Collection, Oskison asked Brandt about the status of his manuscript:

> Dear Joe:
>
> The John Ross ms. hasn't been sent to me, has it, and been lost in the mails? It was a long time ago that you said you hoped to get it back to me "next week"! I'm aware that there's nothing pressing, only I should like to know its present status—if you can spare a moment to write.
>
> Beer, beer, glorious 3.2 beer!
>
> Sincerely yours,
> John
> John M. Oskison

Brandt answered on April 13, 1933:

> Dear John,
>
> Separately I am returning to you the manuscript of John
> Ross. I must apologize for not having written sooner but I
> have been ill for the past two weeks and have not been able
> to do so. I have three readers' reports on the book and all
> three like the book. One reader says it is the best exposition
> of the life and character of John Ross that he has ever read.
> This is the opinion of the other two readers but they feel
> that the manuscript should be rewritten to meet our own
> peculiar requirements which might best be described as a
> scientific treatment.

This opening paragraph of the letter summed up the conclusions
of the readers and explains why the press could not publish the manuscript as it was. The most important criteria considered were whether
or not the book was a contribution to the field and whether the scholarship was sound.

To the first question, Grant Foreman answered that "it is, with
qualifications," whereas James Hill wrote that "in its present state the
book is not a contribution to the field." Morris Wardell reconciled
the two in a letter from February 14, 1933: "In a manner it is a contribution to the field, but the material is such that I would question its
being at all worthy of being called even partially scientific. There are
parts here and there which certainly are new, but so written that the
reader must be a student of history and rather thoroughly acquainted
with Indian affairs to know what really constitutes the contribution."
Foreman explained his "qualifications" in a letter, dated February
27, 1933, that he enclosed with the reviewer's form. His reservations
were mostly related to the scholarship and the reference apparatus of
the manuscript, which seems to have been one of Wardell's concerns
too. Foreman wrote: "The book is not documented; there is not one

footnote. There are many quotations and the inquiring reader who looks for this index to scholarship will wonder why citations to authorities and sources are not given." It is true that the manuscript has no footnotes and that Oskison hardly ever cites his sources. He never gives precise references. My work as editor has mostly consisted of referencing the quotations in footnotes and adding explanatory footnotes when deemed necessary, mostly to give basic information about the many characters Oskison mentions. To that end, I have provided an updated reference list that complements Oskison's. I also corrected some of the quotations, as they were not always faithful to the original. I corrected most of them in the main text, using square brackets and crossing out incorrect or added words. Sometimes, however, for the sake of clarity when the quotations were more mangled, I have provided the correct version of the quote intended by Oskison in a footnote.

"On the whole," Foreman wrote to Brandt on March 15, 1933, "I feel that Oskison has got his history pretty accurate though I noted a few little lapses" or "minor errors of fact" as described by Hill. These historical inaccuracies have also been corrected in footnotes. Oskison could have corrected these errors himself had he been willing to submit a revised manuscript. Foreman concluded the scholarship part of his review by telling Brandt that if he could "overlook the absence of documentation, his scholarship is pretty sound." The two other reviewers agreed. Foreman assumed that Oskison neglected the reference apparatus probably because "he at first hoped to place his manuscript with a publisher who would turn out a book for popular consumption," perhaps to one of the New York companies that had published his novels and his biography of Sam Houston.

This may well have been why some very short passages are more akin to fiction than history, which was mainly James Hill's criticism in his letter dated March 15, 1933: "The elements of fiction employed tend to create a false impression of the author's purpose and cast a doubt on his historical accuracy." Hill then proceeds to list the passages to which he refers. They amount to two "reports of imaginary conversations" and three "quotations of imaginary conversation."

Certainly, no archival proof could be found for these conversations, and they may well have been brief manifestations of Oskison's fiction-writing impulse. However, they are too limited, both in form and in content, to invalidate the scholarship that backs up the rest of the book. They would, perhaps, have been controversial if they had been meant to represent some aspect of decision-making about resistance to removal, for example, or neutrality during the Civil War. However, these fictional conversations are not about significant historical decisions and bear no consequence on the accurate reporting of history and understanding of events.

As indicated by Oskison's response to the reviews on May 20, 1933, the function of these fictional passages was likely meant to shape a livelier story for a broader audience than a smaller scholarly one:

> Of course, I see the point of their adverse criticisms. Have I not, in my college days, struggled through such sober, documented, foot-noted, and damn dull tomes as they want me to turn out about John Ross!
>
> I just can't do it—and wouldn't if I could—much as I'd like to have the University Press bring out the book. I feel, after reading the comments of the experts, that I approached the Press rashly to say the least, and to say the worst under false pretenses. But I did try to explain that I am not an historian, and I did call my ms. the *story* of John Ross and of the Cherokees of this time.

After all, Oskison never claimed to be a historian, even when he wrote of Sam Houston, a few years before the biography of John Ross, which he also called a "story" and a "fictionized [*sic*] biography."[4]

Grant Foreman, in his February 27, 1933, letter, actually did think it was "a fine story of John Ross and the Cherokee Indians," actually "the best exposition of the life and character of John Ross that I have seen."

Anthropologist James Mooney, one of the most authoritative sources on Cherokee history, wrote that telling the story of John Ross was, to a great extent, telling the history of the Cherokees: "In this year

[1828], also, John Ross became principal chief of the Nation, a position which he held until his death in 1866, thirty-eight years later. In this long period, comprising the momentous episodes of the removal and the War of the Rebellion, it may be truly said that his history is the history of the Nation" (Mooney 1992, 114).

Indeed, it can be said that "Unconquerable" is a history of the Cherokee Nation, which was also a reservation of the reviewers. Although he otherwise praised the book as far as the story of Ross's life was concerned, Grant Foreman saw a "serious objection" in the fact that

> this is much more than merely a life of John Ross; approximately one hundred pages—from 80 to 180,[5] is the story of Indian Removal—Cherokee Removal. He has told it very well indeed. He has covered much of the same ground that I did though in quite a different way; frequently he uses the same language to be found in my book where we have quoted from the same sources. The question is, would you care to publish a book, no matter how well done, that duplicates to a considerable extent another just off your press.

It is true that several chapters cover the conflict with Georgia and the subsequent removal, however, it is an exaggeration to imply that these pages do not deal with Ross. Oskison represents how Ross, newly elected principal chief, tackled the issues faced by his people, and how he led the Cherokees into resistance. John Ross's papers attest to the obvious fact that the first decade of his chieftainship was very much dominated by the Georgia crisis and the impending removal. A story of Ross could not be written without writing the story of the removal, and, equally, a story of the removal could hardly be written without mentioning Ross. So the problem does not appear to be that Oskison tells a story more encompassing than Ross's personal story, but rather that such a larger narrative, Foreman's own *Indian Removal*, had been published just the year before in 1932 by the same publisher. Incidentally, Oskison did not use Foreman's book as a secondary source, possibly because his research for his own book had been done before Foreman's was published.

Moreover, although Foreman does not consider the possible redundancy of the publications in financial terms, such considerations were likely to be on Brandt's agenda. What Albert L. Hurtado describes of the University of Oklahoma finances in 1937 hints at the fact that the financial situation of the press throughout the 1930s was strained. Citing the University of Oklahoma president, Hurtado writes, "Bizzell worried about the finances of the press. The Depression was on and university funding was inadequate" (2001, 429). Brandt was encouraged to publish Oklahoma books, but these publications were not profitable. Publishing a biography of John Ross so soon after Foreman's *Indian Removal* might not have been a sound financial decision.

The fact remains that, of the twenty-seven chapters of the book, Oskison deals exclusively with private matters only in the first chapter, in which he recounts a particular childhood experience. The other twenty-six chapters reference private matters only sporadically. In these rare passages, Oskison certainly invents dialogues, but he also uses historical references, mainly Cherokee historian Rachel Caroline Eaton's 1914 *John Ross and the Cherokee Indians*, and also Payne's papers and missionaries' accounts. These twenty-six chapters all deal, at least partially, with how Ross was involved in Cherokee public and political life and in the development of the United States. When Oskison tells the story of John Ross, then, not only does he tell about a significant part of Cherokee history, but he also gives a Cherokee perspective on important episodes of United States history. Far from being superfluous, this vantage point adds value to the book.

This book is worth reading, in spite of the scientific reservations expressed by some of the original reviewers, because Oskison produced what was, in pre-Gary Moulton days, one of the very few and thoroughly accurate historical accounts of John Ross accessible to wide audiences. Today, students of John Ross can enjoy Moulton's remarkable biography of the Cherokee chief and his edition of Ross's papers; in Oskison's time, however, few such books were available. The manuscript's bibliography may have its shortcomings, but a closer look reveals that Oskison did in fact rely on all the major relevant secondary sources available in 1933—Eaton, McKenney, Mooney, Parker, Ramsey, Royce, Starr—and significant primary sources—Featherstonhaugh, Gilmer, Lumpkin, Payne, and, of course, Ross's own papers, as well as Cherokee and U.S. government documents. In "The Indian in the Professions," a paper he gave at the first annual conference of the Society of American Indians in 1912, Oskison claimed that throughout his career he had "tried to make myself an interpreter to the world, of the modern, progressive Indian" (Oskison 2012, 399). Considering the state of research at the time that Oskison wrote the book, his accomplishment as an "interpreter" of John Ross to a potentially wide popular audience, without overly sacrificing scientific accuracy, was considerable.

It may be worth noting that the reviewers' reservations as far as Oskison's scientific approach is concerned are all, of course, Eurocentric, in the sense that the reviewers do not envisage the possibility of any other epistemology than the Western scientific method. In the 1930s, Native American studies did not exist yet as a discipline in the way that the participants in the First Convocation of American Indian Scholars at Princeton University, in March 1970, meant it when they "called for the development by Indians of bodies of Indigenous knowledge" (Cook-Lynn 1997, 9). Oskison's methodology may have been disparaged by the reviewers because it was partly grounded in the Cherokee community, not only because he relied on the work by Cherokee historians such as Rachel Caroline Eaton and Emmet Starr, but also on the oral tradition and the collective memory of the people. According to Elizabeth Cook-Lynn, "The intellectual information, the knowledge itself, found in the oral traditions of the indigenes, is grounded in language and geography" (10). If it may be true that Oskison's work relies partly on the indigenous knowledge, as Cook-Lynn defines it, that knowledge was something Wardell and Foreman certainly dismissed. In the 1970s, Native American studies as a discipline "was defined in general terms as the *endogenous* consideration of American Indians or, more specifically, the *endogenous* study of First Nation cultures and history" (11). Oskison's work, as well as the rest of the prolific early twentieth-century Native American intellectual production, occupy a significant but undervalued place in the long account of Native American intellectual history as an epistemology "emerg[ing] from *within* Native people's enclaves and geographies, languages and experiences" and "refut[ing] the exogenous seeking of truth through isolation . . . that has been the general principle of the disciplines most recently in charge of indigenous study, that is, history, anthropology, and related disciplines all captivated by the scientific method of objectivity" (11).

As the reviewers admitted, such a work as Oskison's biography of John Ross was necessary at the time because Ross's image and reputation had to be set straight. In his letter to Brandt on February 27, 1933, Foreman wrote: "I hope it may be published in order that the truth about this great Cherokee chief may be better known and some of the calumnies on his character current in this state may be quieted." One reason for the supposed lack of "scientific treatment," according to Wardell, was that Oskison's take on Ross was biased, which gave Brandt an argument not to publish it in his letter to Oskison on April 13, 1933: "Any book we might publish should definitely be the definitive book on John Ross and not subject to another charge of bias." Oskison was not surprised at the accusation and admitted the difficulty of writing an unbiased biography of such a larger-than-life character in his response to Brandt on May 20, 1933: "I think anybody who undertakes to do John Ross, from whatever angle, will find himself charged with bias—you've either got to like or despise him, and I defy anyone to sit in balanced judgment, God-like, after getting himself soaked in the material." This may well be true, for at least two reasons. First, one essential scientific source of information for a John Ross biographer is bound to be John Ross's own papers, which are very substantial, and biased by nature. Secondly, in spite of controversies, Ross quite simply exists in history as a people's hero who adamantly defended their rights against an unfair colonizing force.

In chapter 23 of his biography of John Ross, the following passage was crossed out, probably by Oskison: "Ross had not been able to save for the Cherokees their beloved homeland; his stubborn resistance had been in part responsible for the horrors of the 'Trail of Tears' along which thousands had died; largely because of him, the first years in the west were filled with strife; his people heard him reviled and threatened as a destroyer of peace, and later charged with enriching himself by diverting tribal funds to his own use, yet they always came away from contacts with him crying exultantly, 'Oh-zay-oo! Oh-zay-oo!'" In light of the controversy manifested by Wardell and Oskison's disagreement on how a biography of Ross should be written, it is significant that Oskison chose to cross out these negative comments about his subject.

Any controversy surrounding Ross in the 1930s might have been contained only within the limits of Cherokee academic circles. Brandt admitted to Oskison in his April 13, 1933, letter that he "did not realize that John Ross was such a controversial subject until my readers reported on the book"—readers who were, in fact, exclusively academic. It is well known that factionalism developed among the Cherokees because of events that occurred mainly while Chief John Ross was in office. It would be quite unfair, however, to blame him solely for these divisions. Between 1828 and 1866, the Cherokee Nation faced forced removal and the reconstruction that it entailed, and was caught between the North and the South during the Civil War, these being only two of the major historical turbulences affecting them. Any social and political body would have had to face divisions and disagreements in such circumstances. And, at the time Oskison's manuscript was being reviewed, in the 1930s, some of these wounds may not have yet completely healed in the Cherokee community, just as the wounds left by the Civil War were not completely healed in the whole of the South. Ross's ambiguous position in the war—oscillating between siding with the Confederacy, neutrality, and siding with the Union[6]—may have still been lingering in the minds of some Cherokees and Oklahoma scholars.

According to Hurtado, University of Oklahoma Press publications could be partly affected by considerations for Oklahoma politics. He mentions the example of "a fiery history of the dispossession of the Five Civilized Tribes that detailed the chicanery and intrigue of certain influential Oklahomans who were still alive" (Hurtado 2001, 431), a book submitted to the press in 1936 by Angie Debo.[7] Joseph Brandt told Debo that the manuscript was "one of the most valuable books ever offered the University Press" (quoted in Schrems and Wolff 1991, 191), and he would eventually publish *And Still the Waters Run* in 1940 at the Princeton University Press, whose directorship he accepted in 1938. Brandt had failed to publish it at OU Press, because President Bizzell "recommended that the press should not publish Debo's book," which he regarded "as inflammatory, and feared legal repercussions" (Hurtado 2001, 432). According to Suzanne H. Schrems and Cynthia J. Wolff (1991), who published a thorough study of the episode, equally important in the decision not to publish "was the threat to Joseph A. Brandt, director of the OU Press, that if he published such a controversial book about Oklahomans, political repercussions, both from within and without the university, could result in the closing of the young, but nationally known, press" (186). The problem was that Debo mentioned by name "important Oklahomans as 'grafters.'" Although Brandt considered the book important, he deferred to President Bizzell's judgement. Bizzell's assistant reviewed the manuscript, and concluded that "it was 'dangerous' to impugn people who had swindled the Indians, especially 'a friend of the University of Oklahoma'" (Hurtado 2001, 431). He also wondered if the University of Oklahoma should "rehash something that [this friend of OU] no doubt would like the public to forget" (quoted in Schrems and Wolff 1991, 193). This reviewer, who was willing to accept that the Oklahomans forget part of their history, was none other than historian Morris Wardell, the very same who reviewed Oskison's manuscript.

Schrems and Wolff also analyze politics internal to the University of Oklahoma which created tension between Brandt on the one hand and President Bizzell on the other. The senior faculty, "appointed by Bizzell to the administrative council," attempted to control university affairs and were ruffled by younger Brandt's progressive ideas when he became director of the press in 1929, to the extent that "they mounted attacks on the O. U. Press" (Schrems and Wolff 1991, 194–95).

Although I found no document establishing that Bizzell ever had anything to do with Oskison's biography of controversial John Ross, one can only infer that Brandt would have had a hard time defending it against Wardell, considering the latter's closeness to the president and fear of controversial issues.

Albeit true that Oskison is rather sympathetic to his subject, just as he was sympathetic to Sam Houston and Tecumseh in his biographies of them, it is not surprising that Wardell accused Oskison of being biased. The two authors apparently had fundamentally different opinions about Ross. In an otherwise laconic but positive reader's report that Oskison produced for OU Press on October 29, 1935, about a manuscript by Wardell entitled "A Political History of the Cherokee Nation," Oskison wrote:

> In the first part, too much weight is given to Arbuckle's arguments and negotiations, and his animus to John Ross is not made sufficiently clear—an attitude inspired, of course, by that of a succession of U.S. treaty-making emissaries. In consequence, John Ross is here presented, in the first part of the ms., I believe unjustifiably, as an able schemer and not as a patriotic, consistent champion of the Cherokees, speaking for 2/3 of the tribe against the 1/3 (backed by the U.S. that had forced the Schermerhorn Treaty) who strove to organize and control the Nation in the West.[8]

Oskison had more to say but lacked room on the reviewing form. He turned the page into landscape mode and added in the margin: "I should like to see, as a part of the appendix material, John Ross's statement of the case of the Eastern Cherokees against the Treaty Party. I feel that too much space is given his opponents."

Oskison was not the only one to sense an anti-Ross bias in Wardell's book. In a review published in 1938, the same year Wardell's *Political History* came out, renowned historian Annie Heloise Abel-Henderson wrote: "That, at the outset, [the author] seems a bit out of sympathy with John Ross is regrettable. To be distrustful of that supremely great chief argues an unfamiliarity with the significant events of the twenties and early thirties. Faith in his continuing integrity is of the very essence of Cherokee nationalism" (1938, 417). The scientific community, at least at the University of Oklahoma and for the political reasons explained above, was obviously divided over John Ross.

Nevertheless, Oskison openly expressed that Ross was not unanimously appreciated by his fellow Cherokee citizens. To explain the consistent opposition from Stand Watie's followers, for instance, he wrote that "it was certainly true that many of the Ross kin held offices, and prospered; Ross preferred that his friends rather than his opponents should be in power, and he was humanly loyal to those who had shown loyalty to him and his ideals" (176, this manuscript).

To conclude this history of the "Unconquerable" manuscript, it is worth noting that Oskison was contacted a few years later, on October 6, 1938, by the new director of the Oklahoma University Press, Savoie Lottinville, who expressed interest in the work:

> Dear John,
>
> In writing to you recently, I failed to ask a question, the answer to which I am interested in, and I am going to take the liberty to do so now. Have you ever done anything with the manuscript material of your life of John Ross? I remember that you submitted it at one time to Joe Brandt, but I had had no information about it after that time. If you have made no plans for publishing it, I should like to consider its possibilities for our list, providing that were favorable with you.
>
> Cordially yours,
> Savoie Lottinville,
> Director

Oskison's response is unknown, but the manuscript does not appear to have been through another reviewing process.

Thus far, I have proposed that this book, in spite of its shortcomings in terms of historical inaccuracies, is valuable as a biography of John Ross and as a history of what is arguably the most tumultuous period the Cherokee people experienced. However, the main reason I decided to exhume this text from the archives is the same reason I published the *Tales of the Old Indian Territory* in 2012. It sheds light on the critical work of an author who deserves more attention from both the public and scholars of Native American studies.

If it is interesting to read this unpublished manuscript today, it is not only because the readers may learn something about Ross. This work may also, in an oblique way, reveal something about its author and his possible attachment to Cherokee—and more broadly Indigenous—nationhood and sovereignty, as Craig Womack defines it at the "intersection of the political, imaginary, and literary" (1999, 26). In an epigraph printed at the beginning of his biography of Tecumseh, Oskison wrote: "This book is dedicated to all Dreamers and Strivers for the integrity of the Indian race, some of whose blood flows in my veins" (1938). This dedication could just as well have been printed at the beginning of "Unconquerable." Most of Oskison's writing career took place at a time when Native American sovereignty suffered greatly under the assaults of federal assimilation policies. Even if "Unconquerable" was probably written just as that began to change—John Collier was appointed Commissioner of Indian Affairs in 1933 and started implementing the Indian New Deal in 1934—the context until then imbued Oskison's writing with a political dimension that is worth keeping in mind and exploring further.

Over the few decades following the allotment of tribal lands, the abolition of tribal governments, and Oklahoma statehood in 1907, "non Indians politically, legally, and demographically surrounded the Cherokees" (Cobb 2007, 466). According to Daniel M. Cobb, the period would culminate with, "by the 1960s, a majority of Oklahomans accept[ing] the fiction that tribal authority had been subsumed by the state and that Cherokee history and peoplehood were, for all intents and purposes, things of the past" (466). Of Oskison's novel *Black Jack Davy* and the works published in the first half of the twentieth century by three other Cherokee authors (Rachel Caroline Eaton, Lynn Riggs, and Ruth Muskrat Bronson), Kirby Brown writes that "read together, these works inscribe a Cherokee national presence within academic discourses that often position Indian peoples as cultural relics *of* history rather than as political agents *in* history" (2018, 4). Had "Unconquerable" been published when Oskison submitted it, it would have considerably contributed to inscribing Cherokee national presence within and outside academia. Considering that, as he wrote in his review of Wardell's manuscript quoted earlier, Oskison believed Ross to be "a patriotic, consistent champion of the Cherokees," one can easily see this biography of John Ross as a Cherokee nationalist text. Oskison wrote at a time "most commonly seen in decidedly non-national terms, as either overly accommodationist or outright assimilationist" (Brown 2011, 79). I have questioned elsewhere Oskison's reputation as an assimilationist (Larré 2013). His choice to write a biography of John Ross, the embodiment of Cherokee sovereignty and resistance, in the heart of a long period (1907–1970s) when the Cherokee principal chief was appointed by the president of the United States, is an act of resistance, in the sense that the book constitutes one of those "sites where the past, present, and future of the nation/national community might be recovered, remembered, (re)examined, (re)imagined, enacted, and critiqued" (Brown 2018, 5). It is an act of resistance against oblivion, against the possible loss of Cherokee nationhood.

According to Cobb, the Cherokees were "wracked by internal tensions" (2007, 467), divided "between those whose social lives revolved around close-knit traditional communities and others who accepted the dominant society as their own" (467). If a "key component of nationhood," as Womack explains, "is a people's idea of themselves, their imaginings of who they are," and if "the ongoing expression of a tribal voice, through imagination, language, and literature, contributes to keeping sovereignty alive in the citizens of a nation and gives sovereignty a meaning that is defined within the tribe rather than by external sources" (1999, 14), Oskison's text was an attempt at reinforcing Cherokee sovereignty, and an act of resistance against a settler-colonialist historiography. At a time when the Cherokees could feel that their "chief for a day," appointed by the U.S. president, did not speak and act on their behalf, Oskison's biography of Ross made sure they would remember the principal chief who had been their best spokesperson.

Moreover, if Oskison's work, among others from the same period, must be seen as anticipating the emergence of Native American studies as a discipline founded in endogenous and indigenous knowledge and epistemological approach, his wish to see it published by a university press, when his other biographies were published by mainstream houses, may be seen as an act of resistance against the exclusively exogenous approaches that were predominant in academia at the time. As he wrote to Brandt in his May 20, 1933, letter, he may have "approached the Press rashly" but he did not claim to be a historian and called his manuscript a story, not a history, of John Ross. Trying to have a story published by a university press, instead of a history, may be seen as Oskison's attempt to subvert Western epistemology of Native American studies and put forward a more indigenous, community-based one. In his letter to Brandt on February 27, 1933, Grant Foreman may have sensed it as he acknowledged that Oskison had "covered much of the same ground that I did though in quite a different way."

As Kirby Brown found out from the audience after a presentation he gave at the Sequoyah History Symposium, held in Tahlequah's Northeastern State University in 2008, some Cherokee people refer to the early decades of the twentieth century as a "dark age" in Cherokee history. After the dissolution of tribal governments and the creation of the state of Oklahoma in 1907, the Cherokees certainly entered a difficult era during which their sovereignty was drastically reduced. However, as Brown points out, the "dark age" may refer to the lack of historiographical enlightenment on the period as well as to the period itself. Indeed, for the longest time, Native American studies have overlooked events and cultural productions of the first half of the twentieth century. So much so that, after such disastrous policies and events as allotment, land spoliations, and the abolition of tribal governments, "even the possibility of Cherokees continuing to imagine themselves as a national community becomes unthinkable" (Brown 2018, xii). What the works of that period's Cherokee authors—especially, one might add, when they seek to assess John Ross's legacy—tend to signal is that not only could the Cherokees imagine themselves as a nation, but also that they may have needed it even more in these dire times.

What John Ross embodied was appealing to Oskison, and might have been appealing to many Cherokees during this "dark age." One-eighth Cherokee, like Ross, Oskison had seen his Cherokee citizenship questioned by the representatives of the Cherokee Nation in front of the Commission to the Five Civilized Tribes (better known as the Dawes Commission). The latter had been created by act of Congress in 1893 and was in charge of drafting a Cherokee roll before allotting the land in severalty. Their ultimate purposes were to open new territories within which U.S. citizens could settle and to end tribal governments. Oskison's application documents are useful to understand the complexities inherent to a definition of Cherokee nationhood. On March 16, 1901, Oskison faced the Commission after he had applied to be inscribed on the final citizens' roll. Oskison was submitted to harsh interrogation from Commissioner T. B. Needles and J. L. Baugh, "representative of the Cherokee Nation." After he repeatedly asked Oskison where he was born, where he resided, and how long he had been away from the Cherokee Nation, Baugh "protest[ed] against the listing for enrollment of the said John Oskison as a Cherokee citizen by blood, because of the fact of non-residence," despite assurance from Commissioner Needles that "the name of John Oskison is found upon the authenticated roll of 1896." The problem for Baugh seems to have been that Oskison spent too many of his twenty-seven years away from Indian Territory. Oskison had not been physically present in the Cherokee Nation for a few years, between 1894 and 1898, while studying at Stanford and Harvard. Since being a "Cherokee by blood" did not seem to be enough, Oskison insisted on his ties to the place where he was born and where he grew up. To the question "Did you always consider the Cherokee Nation your home," Oskison answered, "Yes sir." In a final statement he gave the Commission after Needles and Baugh had pressed him to repeat that he had been away, Oskison insisted on his attachment to Cherokee land as proof of his Cherokee identity, stating:

> All interests I have are in the Indian Territory, Cherokee Nation, and that I have never regarded any other place as my permanent residence. I have been away for educational purposes and that I have never been away except for educational purposes for a longer time that one year and a half; and that as I understand it that my father being away the five years extending from '82 to '87 did not lose his citizenship; that my father has not citizenship personally; that by his being away that the citizenship of his children has not been impaired. (*Applications*)

On that day, final judgment as to his enrollment was suspended and his name placed on "a doubtful card." Citing the Cherokee constitution, Oskison's attorney argued that "the conditions upon which a citizen may lose or forfeit his rights, privileges and immunities as a Cherokee citizen are: 1st. He must remove from the limits of the Cherokee Nation; 2nd. He must take with him his effects; 3rd. He must become a citizen of some other government." He argued that his client had "never left the Cherokee Nation with the intention of becoming a citizen of some other government. He never took any of his effects, except what was necessary for school purposes. And he never at any time declared by word or act that he was or desired to be a citizen of some other government." Finally, on September 11, 1903, two and a half years after he applied, Oskison was granted citizenship by the

Commission, which stated, "The evidence shows that John Oskison is a Cherokee Indian and is identified on the authenticated tribal roll of 1880, and also on the Cherokee Census roll of 1896. The evidence further shows that the said John Oskison has resided in the Cherokee Nation all his life, excepting from 1894 to 1898, during which time he was attending college. He was a resident of the Cherokee Nation at the time of the application herein" (*Applications*).

At a time when people often defined themselves and each other by the blood flowing in their veins, Oskison's Cherokee lineage was acknowledged, but his Cherokee citizenship was challenged on the grounds that he spent a few years outside Cherokee Nation. In the words of Rennard Strickland (1980, 15), referring to the divisions that appeared in the tribe over the question of removal in the 1830s, "Tribal identification was so strong that an eighth-blood Cherokee, John Ross, led the full-blood faction while a full-blood, Major Ridge, led the mixed bloods" to the other side of the Mississippi. The episode of Oskison's application to Cherokee citizenship in front of the Dawes Commission illustrates that for him, as for John Ross, being Cherokee remains a cultural and political choice, more than a biological determination. As Daniel Heath Justice puts it, he "emphasizes the primacy of Cherokee nationhood and political self-determination above the arbitrary distinctions of blood quantum" (2006, 110). One might add that to Oskison—whose job kept him in New York a large part of his life but who always came back to his "old I. T." to write—being Cherokee is an attachment to the land or, as he writes about Ross in the final page of this work, "a passionate devotion to his own soil" (200, this manuscript). Ross's struggle to preserve the Cherokee Nation's geographical and political integrity must have rung true to Oskison.

Another belief of Ross's may have raised the ire of some, although it found a familiar resonance in Oskison. They both dealt with the integration of Native Americans into U.S. society in terms of "amalgamation." Oskison wrote: "Ross was sure that removal would only delay the necessary adjustment of the tribe to American ways. He wasted no thought on the comparative value of Indian and American civilization. In essence, white culture might be better or worse than Indian; good or bad, however, the Indians would have to learn to live according to its precepts. Let the process of amalgamation work the transformation here where it was already well under way" (34, this manuscript).

John Ross grew up at a time when many Cherokees understood they had better try all they could to adjust to the new Euro-American way of life, if only to be able to understand the colonizers' mechanisms of power and control. Born in a mixed family in 1790, he was a teenager when the Cherokees allowed the first Christian missionaries to settle among them under the explicit condition they taught Cherokee children to read and write in English. Within three decades, schools were opened, laws were written both in English and in Sequoyah's syllabary, a constitution was drafted and published in the first Indian newspaper, and a plantation economy was developed, integrating them into the economic fabric of the South.

Later, when the Cherokee Nation was about to burst under the pressure exerted by intruders, the state of Georgia, and Jackson's administration, adjustment as a social philosophy naturally gave way to amalgamation, considered a necessary evil by Ross so the Cherokee people could remain on their land, even if the Cherokee polity could not survive as such. In a letter he sent to Jackson in March 1834, he offered amalgamation to protect the Cherokees from removal as a last resort:

From the peculiar circumstances of the painful grievances under which our people labour, we were induced to . . . present the subject in another view for your further determination, and we would entreat you by every consideration of honor and truth to be assured, that in thus submitting this question, we are influenced solely by a desire to secure the permanent welfare and happiness of our people, who dearly love the land of their Fathers, and are devotedly attached to the Govt. of the United States. Feeble as the Cherokees are, and surrounded by a nation so powerful as the

United States, we cannot but clearly see, that our existence and permanent welfare as a people, must depend upon that relation which will eventually lead to an *amalgamation* with the population of this great republic . . .

Will you agree to enter into an arrangement on the basis of the Cherokees becoming prospectively citizens of the United States . . . ? And will you agree to have the laws and treaties executed and enforced for the effectual protection of the nation on the remainder of its Territory for a definite period? With the understanding that after that period, the Cherokees are to be subjected to the laws of the states within whose limits they may be and to take an individual standing as citizens thereof, the same as other free citizens of the United States [. . .] Such an arrangement as this, would put an end to all conflicting interests—and secure to the Cherokees time to prepare for the important change of their condition, and enable them by means of education to defend their individual rights as free citizens against any fraud or violence before the proper tribunals of the country. It is no more than reasonable and just, that ample time should be extended to the Cherokee people to prepare for so important a change of their political character, in their native land. No nation of people emerging from the natural state of man can ever prosper by an *untimely amalgamation* with a civilized and refined community. (Moulton 1985, 1:283)

Because it was a necessary evil, however, amalgamation should not come too quickly, before people were given the means to adapt to their new social and political status. It is remarkable that, in this acceptance of inevitable amalgamation, there is on Ross's part no value judgment made on either culture. Ross did not believe that the Cherokees should become U.S. citizens because Euro-American culture was superior in any way to Cherokee culture.

Of course, it may sound paradoxical to both defend Cherokee geographical and political integrity and promote amalgamation. However, for Ross, amalgamation allowed the Cherokees to remain on their original territory, including in Georgia, and it did not necessarily jeopardize cultural integrity. Political integrity, of course, was threatened by the U.S. citizenship that he had asked Jackson to grant the Cherokees, but individual freedom and self-determination would be preserved. Again, Ross did whatever he could to navigate dangerous waters, while endeavoring to salvage as much as possible.

Similarly, during a period when Indians were still sometimes considered "savages" to "civilize," Oskison, notably as an activist in the Society of American Indians and a member of its Executive Committee, promoted what he called amalgamation (SAI 1912, 8).[9] He saw it as a different form of integration than mere assimilation. For him, it did not signify a rejection of everything Indian, but a union of Indians and European Americans in one common society, a way to provide the Native Americans with the place they deserved in U.S. society, and "to deny the past-ness of Indian presence and to carve out space for Indian participation in the present" (Nelson 2014, 639). To reach that objective, the founders of the Society of American Indians believed that Native Americans had to organize themselves in a pan-Indian movement in which their own voices would be heard better than through existing organizations with mainly Euro-American members and speakers, such as the Indian Rights Association or the Lake Mohonk Conference of the Friends of the Indian. Even if the latter sometimes invited Native speakers, Oskison among them, they only had a marginal voice in the organization's conversations.[10] The SAI founders claimed inspiration from Shawnee leader Tecumseh, whose attempt to unite "the entire race or a considerable portion of it" for its "advancement" had been one of the most successful (1912, 3). In their founding documents, the SAI activists lamented that much of what justified Tecumseh's resistance against "the oppression of the red race . . . unfortunately exist[s] today," notably "the natural misunderstanding that exists between races of radically different environments and different stages of ethnic culture" (3). In a document entitled "Objects of the Society," they wrote that "the Association seeks to bring about a condition whereby the white race and all races may have a better and a broader knowledge of the red race, its claims, its needs and its ability to contribute materially and spiritually to modern civilization" (14). Thus, the SAI, like Oskison, thought of itself as "an interpreter to the world, of the modern, progressive Indian" (Oskison 2012, 399). Simply put, it meant to explain to Euro-Americans that Native Americans were not what they thought they were.

The unity of Native Americans that the SAI tried to embody was short-lived and, because of internal divisions of diverse kinds, the organization dissolved in 1923.[11] However, what remained common to all of its members was the strong belief that inappropriate federal policies were obstacles in the way of Native Americans to become independent and self-reliant, a state necessary to their advancement and happiness: "A reservation does not afford a normal condition of human environment, the condition of wardship is not conducive of independence or of development. The paternal system of the Federal Government which now exercises control over about 300,000 native [*sic*] Americans has bred many gross evils, and the Indian of today as a result of that system finds himself unable to assert himself in a natural way" (SAI 1912, 4). Oskison, among others, was a staunch advocate of anything facilitating the conditions allowing Native Americans to become self-reliant and to contribute to society. This is not to suggest, however, that "the responsibility for their state—poverty, ill health, homelessness—falls disproportionately on Indigenous people" (2019, 79), contrary to what James Cox thought I implied in my previous analyses of Oskison's work. According to Oskison and the SAI, Native Americans suffered from those ills because of federal policies in which they had no voice. Native Americans were resourceful, had "distinctive and admirable" qualities (Oskison [1914] 2012, 436), but the paternalistic policies stifled them. Joshua Nelson includes Oskison when he writes of the SAI members that "they looked for ways that American Indians might integrate with American society and accepted that Indian people would have to adapt in some ways to do so successfully," but "they did not believe . . . that this adaptation meant wholesale abandonment of Indian culture and tradition" (2014, 641). They had to be given a chance, by the colonial-settler power, to contribute to the betterment of American society, to use their "distinctive and admirable" qualities for the benefit of a common U.S. society. In the words of Daniel Heath Justice, "Whatever the future holds for Native peoples in the Americas is, to Oskison, as much the responsibility of non-Indians as Indians" (2006, 118). One of the SAI's "high aims [was] to see the development of conditions whereby the Indian as an individual and as a race may take his place as a man among men, as an active member of the great commonwealth, and independent of all support not accorded to any body of people who have achieved a position equal to the most enlightened" (SAI 1912, 14). In order to reach that goal, Native Americans had to be enabled "to meet enlightened races upon an equal footing in all walks of life" (14). They needed to be given the opportunity to go to school in order to understand Euro-American values and how to better employ their Native American values to a society that should be called *American society* instead of *white civilization.* The ultimate purpose of such infiltration, as it were, was self-reliance and economic self-sufficiency, which Oskison believed Native Americans were capable of: "Graduates of the great government schools, and mixed bloods who have penetrated to the universities are taking their places as leaders in the movement toward amalgamation. Born to the Indian prejudice against white influence and ways, then trained to see the point of view of the whites in their colleges and universities, these men are standing by eager to help forward any movement that tends to advance their people toward economic independence" (2012, 357).

Among the Cherokees, this movement toward economic independence, for want of political independence, had been enjoyed personally by Ross the planter and trader, but also strongly encouraged and developed by Principal Chief John Ross, especially during the peaceful period of nation-(re)building that the Cherokees enjoyed in the 1840s and 1850s; that is, between the two disasters that framed Ross's chieftainship. In a way, by means of writing a biography of John Ross, Oskison was able to support those among his Native American contemporaries who struggled against colonial-settler forces to achieve self-reliance and preserve cultural and economic sovereignty within U.S. society. After writing his biography of John Ross, Oskison published a biography of Tecumseh (1938), the nineteenth-century historical figure who had inspired twentieth-century progressive Native Americans to form the Society of American Indians and develop "a race consciousness and a race leadership" (SAI 1912, 9). John Ross and Tecumseh were antagonistic figures, since Ross fought with General Jackson against Creek forces who had joined Tecumseh in his pan-Indian resistance against the United States in the War of 1812. Yet Oskison admired them both, as the passage below, from his biography of Tecumseh, makes clear:

> [Tecumseh's] statesmanship was solidly founded on one issue: the saving of his race from contamination and eventual destruction. In substance, it was the same issue which motivated the long fight of a contemporary but very different chief, John Ross of the Cherokees. By contrast with the flaming, all-Indian Tecumseh, Ross was only one-eighth Cherokee and seven-eighths Scotch—a cool, canny leader with an excellent English education. The descendant of a line of able and upright traders among the Cherokees, Ross became known in Washington and throughout the East for his intelligence, sound sense, and unfaltering devotion to his tribe. Ross tried, too, with the powerful help of eastern and New England statesmen, to prevent the removal of his people from their homes in Georgia and Tennessee. He failed as completely and tragically as did Tecumseh. Jackson was his Nemesis, as Harrison was Tecumseh's. (Oskison 1938, 231)

Daniel Heath Justice (2006) remarked on the connection Oskison established between the two leaders. According to him, it is the tension at the heart of what he calls "the Beloved Path"—a "balance between concessions to a ravenous empire and defiance against being swallowed up completely" (2006, 40)—that "allows Oskison to laud Tecumseh's

FIG. 1. John Mix Stanley. *International Indian Council (Held at Tallequah [sic],
Indian Territory, in 1843)*. 1843. Oil on canvas. Smithsonian American Art Museum.

accomplishments as a freedom fighter and political strategist" at the
same time that he states his fight was "hopeless" (108–9). One may
argue that it is the same tension that allows Oskison to write lauda-
tory biographies of both Tecumseh and John Ross. Oskison, by the
very act of writing these two biographies at a time when "assimilation
and erasure" (38) was all the United States asked of Native American
sovereignty, walked the Beloved Path—"which centers itself within an
enduring Cherokee presence" (40)—of adjusting to Euro-American
values, but never at the expense of Cherokee cultural integrity and
nationhood.[12]

In a way, at a time when Native sovereignty was under attack, Oskison
reconciled the Shawnee chief and the Cherokee principal chief by
representing them, to a world that did "not believe in Indian capacity"
(SAI 1912, 15) to lead and to know what is best for Native Americans,
as progressive, intelligent, patriotic, and independent Native leaders

and national figures. In any case, Oskison expressed in the very last paragraph of his biography of Ross that the latter loomed large in twentieth-century Cherokees' ability to face the new challenges presented them by American citizenship: "Certainly his projection over the troubled and dramatic history of my people is a valid reality. Because John Ross lived and labored for them, the Cherokees preserved an extraordinary race pride and integrity, stepping without fear or difficulty, when the time came to extinguish the tribal organization, into the ranks of American citizenship" (200, this manuscript).

NOTES

1. For Oskison's biographical information, see *Tales of the Old Indian Territory and Essays on the Indian Condition* (Oskison 2012).

2. One of these novels, however, *The Singing Bird*, was published posthumously in 2007. His first novel was *Wild Harvest*, published in 1925, followed by *Black Jack Davy* in 1926. *Brothers Three* was published in 1935.

3. Considered in hindsight, and regardless of the reviewers' arguments analyzed in the next pages, the research interests as well as the publishing histories and plans of these reviewers could be seen as having played a part in the eventual rejection of Oskison's manuscript, seen as redundant with their own work.

4. I reproduce here the full author's note placed immediately after the title page of *A Texas Titan, The Story of Sam Houston*: "This story, although it follows closely the main current of Sam Houston's career, is presented as a fictionized [*sic*] biography."

5. Foreman referred to the manuscript's pages. These page numbers correspond to the middle of chapter 9 and the middle of chapter 20.

6. Two of the most useful works on the Cherokee Nation in the Civil War are *The Cherokee Nation in the Civil War* (Confer 2007), and *The Civil War and Reconstruction in Indian Territory* (Clampitt 2015). Books about the Cherokee Nation and its ordeals from the 1830s to the last quarter of the nineteenth centuries are numerous, but one cannot go wrong with *The Cherokee Nation, A History* (Conley 2005), and William G. McLoughlin, *After the Trail of Tears, The Cherokees' Struggle for Sovereignty, 1839–1880* (Chapel Hill: University of North Carolina Press, 1999).

7. Oskison would later work with Angie Debo on an Oklahoma guide, *Oklahoma: A Guide to the Sooner State* (Norman, University of Oklahoma Press, 1941).

8. Oskison's review of Wardell's manuscript is in Morris L. Wardell Collection, box 63, folder 12, Western History Collections, University of Oklahoma, Norman.

9. I analyze Oskison's notion of amalgamation in "John Milton Oskison and Assimilation" (Larré 2013, 23–25). Oskison deals with amalgamation notably in "The President and the Indian: Rich Opportunity for the Red Man" (1901), "The Outlook for the Indian" (1903), and "The Closing Chapter: Passing of the Old Indian" (1914). All are reprinted in *Tales of the Old Indian Territory*.

10. Oskison became a member of the Lake Mohonk Conference in 1904. In 1905 he was elected member of the Press committee (Lake Mohonk Conference, 1905, 10), where he remained until 1907. At the 1906 annual conference, he gave a talk on "The Need of Publicity in Indian Affairs" (Lake Mohonk Conference 1906, 38–40). In 1915 he was invited to give an address again, entitled "A Bigger Load for Educated Indians" (Lake Mohonk Conference 1915, 174–77). Both texts are reprinted in Oskison (2012).

11. The best among the most recent research about the Society of American Indians is the joint *sail/aiq* summer issue, *American Indian Quarterly* 37, no. 3 (2013). For the divisions, even the factionalism, within the SAI, see in particular Philip J. Deloria's "Four Thousand Invitations" (25–44) and Thomas C. Maroukis's "The Peyote Controversy and the Demise of the Society of American Indians" (161–80).

12. In *Our Fire Survives the Storm*, Cherokee scholar Daniel Heath Justice proposes an analytic methodology for his reading of Cherokee texts "through the two principles that thread their way through Cherokee literary and cultural expressions: the 'Beloved Path' of accommodation and cooperation, and the 'Chickamauga consciousness' of physical and/or rhetorical defiance" (2006, 16). The "Chickamauga consciousness" is embodied by Tsiyu Gansini (Dragging Canoe), a leader of a resistance movement against the violence and encroachment of the United States at the end of the eighteenth century, while the "Beloved Path" is embodied by Nanye'hi (Nancy Ward), who worked for peace between the Cherokee and the Euro-Americans, "plac[ing] peace and cultural continuity above potentially self-destructive rebellion" (30), while "oppos[ing] any sacrifice of land or sovereignty that threatened the Cherokees" (40). It is important to note, however, that these two principles are not opposed to each other, they are "distinctions in *degree*, not *kind*" (31). For example, following the "Beloved Path" implies some form of adjustment to the Euro-American world, but never at the expense of nationhood, which is difficult when the empire does not leave room for compromise: "The difficult nature of the Beloved Path is clear: when the opposition sees any maintenance of cultural identity as a threat, anything less than assimilation and erasure is unacceptable. When the focus centers on the survival and endurance of the People, peace itself can be as much an assertion of defiance as the Chickamauga consciousness of war" (38).

REFERENCES

Abel-Henderson, Annie Heloise. 1938. "Reviewed Works: *A Political History of the Cherokee Nation, 1838–1907* by Morris L. Wardell." *The Mississippi Valley Historical Review* 25, no. 3 (December): 417–18.

Applications for Enrollment of the Commission to the Five Civilized Tribes, 1898–1914. The National Archives. Record Group 75.

Brown, Kirby. 2011. "Citizenship, Land, and Law: Constitutional Criticism and John Milton Oskison's *Black Jack Davy*." *Studies in American Indian Literatures* 23, no. 4 (Winter): 77–115.

———. 2018. *Stoking the Fire. Nationhood in Cherokee Writing, 1907–1970.* Norman: University of Oklahoma Press.

Clampitt, Bradley R., ed. 2015. *The Civil War and Reconstruction in Indian Territory.* Lincoln: University of Nebraska Press.

Cobb, Daniel M. 2007. "Devils in Disguise: The Carnegie Project, the Cherokee Nation, and the 1960s." *American Indian Quarterly* 31, no. 3 (Summer):465–90.

Cook-Lynn, Elizabeth. 1997. "Who Stole Native American Studies?" *Wicazo Sa Review* 12, no. 1 (Spring): 9–28.

Cox, James H. 2019. *The Political Arrays of American Indian Literary History.* Minneapolis: University of Minnesota Press.

Hurtado, Albert L. 2001. "Romancing the West in the Twentieth Century: The Politics of History in a Contested Region." *Western Historical Quarterly* 32, no. 4 (Winter): 417–35.

Justice, Daniel Heath. 2006. *Our Fire Survives the Storm. A Cherokee Literary History.* Minneapolis: University of Minnesota Press.

Lake Mohonk Conference. 1905. *Proceedings of the Twenty-Third Annual Meeting of the Lake Mohonk Conference of Friends of the Indian and Other Dependent Peoples 1905.* Reported by Lilian D. Powers.

———. 1906. *Proceedings of the Twenty-Fourth Annual Meeting of the Lake Mohonk Conference of Friends of the Indian and Other Dependent Peoples 1906.* Reported by Lilian D. Powers.

———. 1915. *Proceedings of the Thirty-Third Annual Lake Mohonk Conference on the Indian and Other Dependent Peoples.* Lake Mohonk Conference.

Larré, Lionel. 2013. "John Milton Oskison and Assimilation." *American Indian Quarterly* 37, no. 1 (Winter): 3–33.

Mooney, James. [1891] 1992. *History, Myths, and Sacred Formulas of the Cherokees.* Fairview NC: Bright Mountain Books.

Morris L. Wardell Collection. Box 63, folder 12. Western History Collections. University of Oklahoma, Norman.

Moulton, Gary E., ed. 1985. *The Papers of Chief John Ross*. 2 vols. Norman: University of Oklahoma Press.

Nelson, Joshua. 2014. "Keeping Oklahoma Indian Territory: Alice Callahan and John Oskison (Indian Enough)." In *The Oxford Handbook of Indigenous American Literature*, edited by James H Cox and Daniel Heath Justice, 638–54. Oxford: Oxford University Press.

Oklahoma University Press Collection. Box 9, folder 10. Western History Collections. University of Oklahoma, Norman.

Oskison, John Milton. 1925. *Wild Harvest: A Novel of Transition Days in Oklahoma*. New York: D. Appleton.

———. 1926. *Black Jack Davy*. New York: D. Appleton.

———. 1929. *A Texas Titan: The Story of Sam Houston*. New York: Doubleday, Doran and Company.

———. 1935. *Brothers Three*. New York: MacMillan.

———. 1936. "John M. Oskison Manuscript of Unconquerable: The Story of John Ross, Chief of the Cherokees, 1828–1866." University of Tulsa, McFarlin Library, Department of Special Collections and University Archives.

———. 1938. *Tecumseh and His Times, the Story of a Great Indian*. New York: G. P. Putnam's Sons.

———. 2007. *The Singing Bird*. Norman: Oklahoma University Press.

———. [1914] 2012. "The Closing Chapter: Passing of the Old Indian." In *Tales of the Old Indian Territory and Essays on the Indian Condition*, edited by Lionel Larré, 429–36. Lincoln: University of Nebraska Press.

———. 2012. *Tales of the Old Indian Territory and Essays on the Indian Condition*. Edited by Lionel Larré. Lincoln: University of Nebraska Press.

Schrems, Suzanne H., and Cynthia J. Wolff. 1991. "Politics and Libel: Angie Debo and the Publication of *And Still the Waters Run*." *Western Historial Quarterly* 22, no. 2 (May): 184–203.

Strickland, Rennard. 1980. *The Indian in Oklahoma*. Norman: University of Oklahoma Press.

SAI (Society of American Indians). 1912. *Report of the Executive Council on the Proceedings of the First Annual Conference of the Society of American Indians*. Washington DC.

Womack, Craig S. 1999. *Red on Red. Native American Literary Separatism*. Minneapolis: University of Minnesota Press.

Unconquerable

CHAPTER 1

Tsani he was called by his Cherokee mother, the name a caressing diminutive. He was seven, rather short for his age, thin and active. His abundant light brown hair was a rumpled thatch for a broad brow; out of intent gray-blue eyes he considered a diverting Indian world; and women would always love him for the humorous upturn of his mouth corners and the suggestion of a snub nose. The slightness of his frame was emphasized by the striped loose woolen hunting shirt he wore.

To playmates he was *Tsan-Usdi*, Little John; a boy of surprising resourcefulness and grit, more serious than the average, less talkative, more apt to notice what was going on and to listen to grown-up talk. His real name was John Ross. Eldest son of Daniel Ross, trader in the Cherokee country, and Molly McDonald Ross, he was in blood one-eighth Cherokee Indian and the rest Highland Scot.[1]

The Ross family was one of perhaps a thousand encamped at Willstown,[2] near the western edge of the tribal lands, close to the Georgia-Alabama boundary and within forty miles of the southern Tennessee border. It was early in July 1797; corn was in roasting ear; and the Cherokees had met at this summer capital for the yearly

1

green-corn dance. It was a time of prosperity and contentment: save in a few Upper Coosa and Chickamauga towns, there had been peace for twelve years, and the tribe had all but recovered from the scourges of war and smallpox, to begin rebuilding on a new pattern their communal clan life.[3]

Days in camp were adventures for little John Ross. He was out of his blanket and the family shelter at the first dawn-greeting whoops of the young men, still called warriors although hunting, trapping, and farming were now their occupations. A dip of the serving gourd into the hominy pot simmering on the banked embers of the camp fire and a hurried gulping of the flavorous food, a drink of cold spring water, then he was off to watch the rousing of the vast camp to life.

A good beginning to a festal summer day whose sun would roll too swiftly across the sky to *unsunhi-yi*, the mysterious darkening land. An active day: first, the squirrel hunters went out, then there were pony races, men wrestled as others watched laughing and shrilling pungent comment, older men squatted in clock-dial groups talking, telling stories, with the sun caught in the folds of their striped turbans; in more secluded spots, the wild whiskey drinkers caused occasional flurries of violence; women in voluminous earth-sweeping skirts and tight calico waists with light shawls about their heads walked rapidly, glidingly from group to group, talking, laughing, squatting in front of cooking fires, shielding faces with one hand while they prepared corn and meat . . .

For Tsan-Usdi, a ball play was the day's climax: sixty of the Wolf Clan young men against sixty Blind Swamp Clan champions. It was furious clean play by tiger-quick and hickory-tough, slim, all-but-naked, sweat-streaming dark bronze youths, their coarse shining black hair tightly banded, each with two short ball sticks in his hands, running, dodging, leaping, crashing with breath taking grunts body against body, across the wide ball field whose goals were set six hundred yards apart. Two intense hours of this, watched by restless children and older people in holiday spirit and attire, chatteringly excited or critically absorbed, and then at a signal ball sticks were dropped and the players raced panting for the relief of the cool stream.

In the water John Ross, and hundreds of other boys, joined them, he a pale sliver of eager flesh among flashing brown bodies. Rapid talk, gasps, shouts, whoops, laughter, splashing; old men on the bank, watching, recalled vividly details of long past struggles on the ball fields of the Holston, at Old Echota and Louden, at towns in the narrow valleys of Carolina before the building of Fort Prince George at Keowee. Their minds reached back to the time of the war chief Oconastata and the great days of the civil chieftainship of Atakul-lakulla, the Little Carpenter.[4]

Lassitude followed, leisurely eating, smoking, visiting. Clothed, spent, tasting luxuriously the creeping reflow of energy into their lean bodies, the ball players lay relaxed, listening to expert criticism of their game, taking from the women little helpings of venison or beef broth, small mouthfuls of corn, sips from gourd dippers. John Ross darted from one to another admiring their toughness, touching their bruises, talking to them in Cherokee; and they answered with a laugh or a jesting word.

Late in the afternoon at the town house, a big flattish dome of bark supported by tall posts and open all around, the chiefs and leading men gathered in council. Dignified, frank, cheerful, chosen for their sanity and wise restraint in dealing with truculent white borderers, they settled to their deliberations easily and without ceremony.

Tsan-Usdi followed them under the dome, silently as a shadow. There was something shadowlike, absorbent in the boy's attitude, sitting with his back against the knee of one of his father's old friends. He became lost in the talk, though much of it he could only vaguely comprehend, his eyes shifting from chief Keanotah to Ocunna, to Pathkiller, to the eloquent Doublehead, to Dragging Canoe, to Ridge, men of furrowed semi-Oriental faces and rather small hands.[5]

Daniel Ross could safely trust his son to remain quiet in that company, for he had always liked listening to the elders. At home, when important men of the tribe came to pose their problems and seek help in shaping the future, Tsan-Usdi would slip in to sit with them. Catching the drift of the talk, he would afterwards carry questions to his mother and to his adoring grandmother, Ann Shorey McDonald, half Indian and a proud teller of tribal history and traditions. It was out of his home environment that the boy's love for the Cherokees and an increasing knowledge of their background, ideals, and hopes had grown. He had become more Indian with each year that passed.

Now, sitting with the old men, his heart held the conviction, which was to be the controlling influence of his life, that his people must forever struggle against the white man.

They talked first of cotton. Their agent, Colonel Silas Dinsmore,[6] sent to them nearly a year before by President Washington, urged them to grow cotton and learn to spin, weave, and dye it and make it into clothes such as the whites wore. He said they could never grow too much cotton; all they produced beyond their own needs they could trade to the whites, who would take it down the Tennessee River, the Ohio, and the Mississippi on boats and send it to other lands. McDonald, Tsan-Usdi's white grandfather, and Daniel Ross had already told them the same thing.

They had good cotton land, lying below the rocky hill-slopes where their destroyed towns used to stand, and a sufficient number of horses. Colonel Dinsmore was a man of sense; his advice must be considered seriously; but could they count upon his promise of the tools they required, ploughs, hoes, and cards for teasing the white staple? They could make their own spinning wheels and looms . . .

They talked also of the Moravian missionaries who wished to send two ministers from stations in North Carolina. Why did those men want to come? To save Cherokee souls? Men deeply committed to their own spiritual faith smiled at that explanation. But they had also promised to teach Cherokee children the white man's language. Good! The tribe needed more men to speak English, like Vann, the Gunters, John Thompson, and Arthur Coodey, mixed-blood descendants of traders and soldiers who had long ago settled in the country, married Cherokee wives. and become members of the tribe by adoption . . .[7]

Still another matter must be talked about, the gravest of all, treaties!

4

Not of ancient treaties did they talk; the Revolutionary War had wiped the slate of the succession of agreements made with colonial authorities, and consistently disregarded by the whites pushing across the border. They discussed the two treaties negotiated with the new government of the United States, the first at Hopewell in 1785 and the second on the Holston in 1791.

In the Indian manner, they reviewed events leading up to these treaties: the first had been a peace settlement, for the tribe had fought on the side of the English, and they had yielded to President Washington's commissioners a great slice of their old domain in return for the promise to keep white settlers off of what remained. The white borderers, however, had paid no attention to that Hopewell treaty; they had pushed over the line and provoked bloody raids and counter raids until General Knox, secretary of war, promised to investigate and, if necessary, negotiate a new treaty.

It was discovered that the new United States government was not strong enough to expel the whites from Cherokee land, so the Holston agreement was forced upon the tribe. In exchange for land occupied by settlers, Washington's agents promised certain things: to fix tribal boundaries exactly and for all time; to pay the tribe a regular annuity; to supply farming tools; and to send interpreters and properly regulated traders to them.[8] After the government men had gone from Holston, the Cherokees found that they had been deceived concerning the extent of the last cession of land, and it was necessary to send a delegation of chiefs to Philadelphia and lay their case before President Washington. That good man was sympathetic, presented to them a golden chain to symbolize the tie that must always bind the races together, but he could not recover the land for them. However, after protracted haggling, he did secure an increase of their annuity from $1,000 to $8,500.[9]

Six years had passed since the Holston treaty, and the Cherokee boundaries were not yet fixed. Three months ago, an agent named Hawkins had come to them, a man of authority over all the southern Indians, and observing that they had obeyed the terms of the treaty and moved back into the mountains of Tennessee, North Carolina, and Georgia, promised to run their lines and keep the whites back.[10] Would he carry out that promise? One of the old men spoke doubtfully; no surveyors were yet at work, and it was known that a white man named Zachariah Cox had lately led a group of settlers upon unsurveyed tribal land south of the Cumberland; if Cox were allowed to stay, then there would come a demand for another treaty and another cession of land.[11]

Land! Land! Indian land! As persistently as a sick baby's wailing, sounded the cry of those whites who seemed to multiply like rabbits and who had, since the days of Walker, Waller, Smith, and Boone, turned always westward with cocked rifles and scorn of Indian titles.[12] That old Cherokee who doubted the good faith of the whites had once heard a missionary say, "God has made of one blood all nations of the earth." But it might not be true? How could an Indian credit Paul's assurance to the philosophers of Athens if he must judge a border man's faith by his works? Men like Cox believed that God meant the whites to inherit the earth. Perhaps Hawkins did, too? He was the agent of the white man's government, and a professed servant of God . . .

On the talk went; the sun set; Tsan-Usdi ran through the twilight to supper carrying a fresh, deep impression of the integrity of his people and their great concern over the future. The color and flavor of that council survived in him over many tumultuous years. Those who had spoken were the elders and aristocrats of an old race, clan leaders rooted in the pleasant valleys and billowing mountains of a domain still extensive though it had been reduced by more than thirty thousand square miles. They had come from homes encircled by dark hills, beyond which rose loftier blue peaks that kindled to flame at sunrise of frosty bell-clear mornings, or were veiled in soft summer haze. They lived prosperously, comfortably; they, whose Cherokee forbears had once been sold into slavery and died under the lash rather than submit to servitude, now owned many negro slaves, runaways from Virginia and the Carolinas and their descendants.

In all the talk of white encroachments and unfulfilled pledges there had been no hint of warlike resistance. Old battles had been referred to, but without heat. Tsan-Usdi had heard white warriors, Weatherford, Montgomery, Grant, and Sevier, named without bitterness, indeed with respect, military leaders who had harried and crushed them, driven them from their burnt towns, fertile fields, and orchards of sweet fruit to live like wild beasts in the mountains.[13] Those days had passed, and to lament them was to waste breath. The wise look ahead, and prepare for the new struggle in the new way.

Then night came, and they danced the ceremonial green-corn dance under the branches of giant oaks whose leaves reflected the light of smokeless dry-log fires. It was a dramatic representation: first, the talk of an old chief reviewing the day's ball play, praising the manliness and fairness of the players and recalling former epic struggles; then the drummers and singers sat down cross-legged well back from the fires; a company of girls dressed in white buckskin, wearing beads and bracelets and gay ribbons, formed in a semicircular double line back to back and sang in low sweet voices responses to the singing and drumming of the seated men; and at length, whooping and flourishing ball sticks, the young men rushed to face the girls and, as the drums beat their low penetrating thunder and old men's voices became urgent and hypnotic, passed through the lines of girls, forth and back, back and forth, time after time . . .

It was a night-long ceremony, and only a little of it could Tsan-Usdi keep himself awake to watch. He carried to his blanket, however, an enduring sense of its beauty and dignity, its significance . . .

Maiden corn, coming into full milk! Corn for delight and nourishment. Corn, symbol of fruitfulness—fructifying corn. Corn silk, corn ear, sapfilled stalk, broad caressing leaves—symbols. Mate! Plant seed, seed as of the corn, cherish her in whom the seed lies, the mother! . . .

Clan law said, "It is forbidden that a maid and a man of the same clan mate lest the issue be weak;" among the Cherokees in those early days there were no deformed, no idiots, and no insane persons.

Next morning, as a surprise, Tsan-Usdi's mother held before his eyes a white boy's new suit of nankeen, and helped him to put it on. Daniel Ross watched the change approvingly, and said, "We must cut your hair now!"

The new clothes were stiff, hampering; the boy did not like them, and ran off wondering why he must wear them and be uncomfortable. He joined his playmates, thinking that perhaps they would admire the new coat, trousers, and boots. But they laughed at him instead, and taunted, *Unaki*! White man! Tsan-Usdi wanted to cry with shame and rage, but he didn't; he wore the nankeen suit all that day—stubborn, proud boy that he was. On the following morning, however, he sought grandmother McDonald and begged for his hunting shirt, leggins [*sic*], breech cloth, and moccasins.

He got them; and it was as though he dedicated himself that day to the Cherokees.[14]

CHAPTER 2

White man's clothing, and school too, were nevertheless inevitable for John Ross; for his sake, soon after the Willstown celebration, Daniel Ross moved his family from the home at the head of the Coosa River in Georgia to a bigger house near Maryville, Tennessee, and got the permission of the Tribal Council to bring in a white man as teacher and set up a school in the front room. There was some opposition from old tribesmen, as there had been at Willstown to the Moravians' project, but it was easily overcome by the progressives who argued that it was more and more necessary to know the white men's language, customs, and laws. The progressive Cherokees were beginning to realize their power.

It was more than a year, however, before Daniel Ross found the man he wanted as teacher—young John Barber Davis, meagerly equipped with books but genuinely in love with learning.[1] With Tsan-Usdi in the improvised schoolroom were his younger brother Lewis and half a dozen children of neighboring families. John set the pace; he was enthusiastic even over the long exercises in penmanship and learned to write a beautifully rounded script; he liked the sound of tall, pretentious words. He and the other pupils had learned to count with shiny black buckeye beans, and to spell out words from the Bible, before Mr. Davis took them.

In that front room school John Ross met Euclid; he studied geography, wondered what really lay beyond the Mississippi River in that vaguely mapped region; there were lessons in ecclesiastical and common history; and the promise, when the mental teeth were more firmly set, of Virgil's Aeneid and the Orations of Cicero. The teacher was insistent upon rhetoric, too, and the desirability of an elegantly ponderous epistolary style. In an early letter, sent off to a young Cherokee friend, David Brown,[2] in the missionary school at Cornwall, Connecticut, John Ross reflected that style:

"To meditate seriously on the conditions of the Indians and to review the miserable fate which has befallen them and swept into oblivion the numerous tribes that once inhabited the country bordering on the Atlantic is enough to make the remnants of those tribes who are now encompassed by the white population shudder. Yet I cannot believe that the Indians are doomed to perish in wretchedness, from generation to generation, as they are approached by the white population, until they shall all be annihilated from the face of the earth."[3]

Here was the forecast of the lifelong passionate concern he was to feel for his people.

His Indian education, of course, was gained outside of any school. With other boys, he set traps and snares, twisted rabbits out of hollow trees with long split-end switches, called wild turkeys with a peculiar device whittled from a turkey bone. He knew how deerskins were prepared for tanning by letting them float in running water until the hair was loosened. With Lewis, he kept his father's sheep safe from panther raids. He knew where the best wild strawberries grew, and whortleberries, haws, grapes, walnuts, and hickorynuts. Out of doors, his ears were always alert for the warning ch-r-r-r-r of gentleman rattlesnake.

From both sides of his family, John Ross inherited physical sturdiness and fine traditions. The story of his father reaches well back into

Scottish history and is involved with the adventures of John McDonald, whose daughter Molly married Daniel Ross.

Of Inverness birth, McDonald was caught in the snarl of the Reformation and exiled from Scotland. He tarried only briefly in London, sailing for Charleston, South Carolina, as a youth of nineteen in 1766. From there he went to Savannah, Oglethorpe's still new settlement, and became a clerk in a trader's store. Being a dependable lad, and shrewd, he was soon sent by his employer on an expedition up the river to barter with the Cherokees for skins and furs. Pushing on across the mountains that form the watershed of the Savannah and also the westward-tumbling feeders of the Tennessee, the young Scot saw the opportunity to set up for himself. He left the Savannah trader, settled at Fort Louden[4] in Tennessee, and married Ann Shorey, daughter of William Shorey and *Ghigooie* of the Cherokee Bird Clan.[5] Thereafter he devoted himself Scotch-honestly to his business, his people, his family, and the service of God.

Following the peace settlement of 1785 between the United States and the Cherokees, McDonald joined the band of irreconcilables led by Chief Bloody Fellow that fled west from Louden to the Tennessee River near Muscle Shoals. They settled at the foot of Lookout Mountain, and established as their capital the outpost town of Sitico, now Chattanooga. McDonald, however, preferred a site for his trading post fifteen miles south of the river.[6]

He was living there when a huge flatboat, laden with trade goods for the Chickasaw country beyond, was stopped by Bloody Fellow, who found on board an enemy named Mountain Leader. True to his name, Bloody Fellow was for killing Mountain Leader and the whole intruding party, taking the cargo and sinking the boat; thus would they most effectively warn back white civilization from their retreat.

More cautious counsel prevailed. Do not, said the chief's advisers, risk bringing soldiers against us by killing the two white men on the boat; or at least wait until we can hear what the trader McDonald says. McDonald was sent for. He found a Mr. Mayberry of Baltimore in charge of the boat, and with him was twenty-year-old Daniel Ross, whose family had emigrated to America from Sutherlandshire soon after McDonald left Inverness. Young Ross was alone in the world, his father having been killed while serving under General Washington soon after his mother died at Baltimore. He had a small interest in the Mayberry cargo.

These facts McDonald learned, then spoke sternly to Bloody Fellow: "Let the boat go; they are honest men on a friendly mission. Any injury done them will be a personal affront to me!" Because the Indians knew McDonald as a wise and just man, they released crew and cargo and even invited Mayberry and Ross to stop with them and set up as traders. Ross, influenced by McDonald, accepted.

Since 1690, the Cherokees had been lucky in the matter of traders; from the beginning an able, resourceful, and trustworthy line of Scotch and Irish commercial adventurers had sought them out. Like McDonald, they had proved upright and honest in the literal Indian sense; they married Cherokee women whom they loved and respected, to whom they taught their ways and religion; and naturally they and their children gained strong influence in the tribe.[7]

Traders among the Indians were men of imagination and sympathy. Were? They still are! The successful ones come to wield, by degrees, the power of tribal chiefs; living close to the Indians, they know their families, understand their political complications; the words they speak are given serious consideration in the councils. They *know*, where the government agents too often only guess. They trust the Indians, and prove themselves worthy of trust.

Because McDonald vouched for Ross, the Cherokees accepted him, brought pelts and furs and whatever fruit of the woods and mountains he would take in exchange for cloth, tools, flour, rifles, and ammunition. When he had been with them a year, he married McDonald's quarter-blood daughter, Molly.

With his marriage, Daniel Ross became automatically an adopted member of the tribe, as McDonald had done before him by taking as wife the half-blood Ann Shorey. His marriage marked the real beginning of his long and prosperous career as trader; and for more than twenty years he ranged the Cherokee country, extending his journeys to every limit, establishing connections far beyond the Sitico band and working himself into the affairs of the tribe.

Such was Tsan-Usdi's heritage and background. Good blood on both sides, drawing from Father Daniel and Mother Molly sound health and a wise spirit.

The new century came in. John Ross was ten. John Adams, succeeding Washington, had for three years maintained the first president's fair and friendly attitude towards the Cherokees, though he had been hardly more effective in protecting them from the intrusion of white settlers. Another election was near, in which Thomas Jefferson was to be made president.

Daniel Ross thought it would be desirable to send his sons John and Lewis to the Academy at Lovely's Spring near Kingston, a busy entry port on the Tennessee River nearly a hundred miles west of Maryville. It would be good for the boys, since they were destined to carry on his business, to gain contact with the swelling stream of emigrants from Virginia and Maryland flowing on towards Nashville, spreading over the rich Cumberland valley and beyond to Kentucky. The brothers would stay with a merchant friend, Mr. Moore of Kingston, and help in the store during their spare hours.

They studied in the evenings by the light of fat-pine torches and candles—when candles could be procured. The Academy offered Rollin's *Ancient History*, Locke's *On the Human Understanding*, and Paley's *Moral Philosophy*; and the boys joined a Friday debating club. At Mr. Moore's table they had good corn bread to eat, bacon, greens, and stewed wild fruit.

While the boys, especially John, did credit to the Academy by enthusiastic application to study, the perennial campaign of the whites to persuade the Cherokees and other southern tribes to move back and make room for them was in progress. To assist the land seekers, President Jefferson sent, in the summer of 1801, the commissioners James Wilkinson and Andrew Pickens to the Cherokee country. No survey of the tribal boundaries had yet been made, and when the chiefs Doublehead and Bloody Fellow met the government men they found to their bitter disappointment that none was intended. Instead, the commissioners demanded a further cession of territory!

"No!" cried Doublehead indignantly, while Bloody Fellow said, "If I had known why you came, I would have done the same as Chief Glass and refused to meet you."[8]

Finding it impossible to treat with the tribe, Jefferson's emissaries made a tour of the Cherokee country and included with the report of their failure to negotiate a treaty of cession observations on the Indians' manner of living and progress:

"It is with singular pleasure we have witnessed the advance of this people in the arts of civilization, the acquirement of individual property by agricultural improvements, by raising stock; and domestic manufacture seems to have taken strong hold on the Nation."

For the encouragement of the eager whites, they added: "We believe a few years' perseverance in the beneficent plan which has produced these results will prepare them to accommodate their white neighbors with lands on reasonable terms."[9]

Here was the foreshadowing of a policy destined to harass the tribe and try the strength and courage of John Ross over two generations.[10]

Hawkins had warned the government that pressure for Indian land and the jubilation of the frontiersmen over the election of Jefferson who, they believed, would support white demands, had alarmed the Cherokees. It was hard for an Indian to understand this strange fierce craving for land and yet more land in a seemingly limitless expanse of unsurveyed territory stretching on and on towards the sunset! Hawkins wrote that while "the wheel, the loom and the plough are in pretty general use," the Cherokees were not yet ready to own their lands as individuals and become citizens of the States. Many still feared being forced into too close neighborhood with the whites; this fear was so real that some had consulted him "on the propriety of looking out west for an eventual reservation where the Nation already has a settlement of near one hundred gun men."[11]

That little settlement of Cherokees in the Arkansas Territory had lately been formed by the members of the tribe who were bitterly opposed to what they believed to be a destructive civilization leading to white domination. Unwittingly, that refugee handful bred the germ of the policy presently to be adopted by Jefferson: the removal of the Indians beyond the Mississippi. A mere whispered suggestion at first, it grew in the following quarter of a century to an angry roar of conviction.[12]

As a Virginian, Jefferson had an understanding sympathy with the demands of the westward trending whites. He took office soon after the beginning of a period of tremendous national expansion. Spanish claims east of the Mississippi were to be extinguished following the withdrawal of the French after the Louisiana Purchase. The western boundary of the United States was being pushed far towards the Texas plains. On behalf of the government, Jefferson conducted a successful controversy with Georgia by which he saved for federal exploitation a great oblong of territory between the Coosa and the Mississippi. Georgia had claimed it under the vague charter from King George II to Oglethorpe in 1732, but the colony had become involved in the Yazoo Grants complications and the state, in the agreement with Jefferson in 1802, was glad to turn over to the Washington government the task of settling these conflicting claims.[13]

For the Cherokees, the significant item in that agreement of 1802 was the promise made by the United States in return to extinguish Indian title to all lands within the limits of Georgia as soon as it could be done peaceably and on reasonable terms. *Peaceably and on reasonable terms*; that condition must be kept in mind in following the course of John Ross's long struggle against a determined Georgia and a vacillating United States.

Thus Jefferson became committed to the removal policy; moreover he was anxious to push it in order to silence the loud critics of the purchase of the Louisiana Territory, who asked why good money had been paid for that waste land [*sic*]. Jefferson could now reply that it would be the ideal home for the southern Indians standing in the

way of white settlers moving towards the Mississippi. He went so far as
to draw up the rough draft of a constitutional amendment providing
for the removal there of all tribes living east of that river, but it was
never submitted for action.

After three years at the Academy, John Ross was called home by the
death of his mother.[14] Serene, gentle, loving Mother Molly lying starkly
silent in the darkened front room! It is said that the Scots are unemo-
tional, and that Indians are notable Stoics; labels are easily applied. The
particular Scotch-Indian boy called Tsan-Usdi, however, was crumpled
by grief. He told, but only long afterwards, how he was stricken by
a shivering coldness at the heart, how something in his breast hurt
almost intolerably before he could weep. The light of his life had
gone out; no one now to call him Tsani, talk to him of the great future
that was ahead. He clutched desperately, chokingly at the clay image
that had been his mother, and knew how the prolonged high note of
the Cherokee women's death wailing could sharply pierce the heart.

As best he could in his own grief, Daniel Ross comforted his children. John, nearest because Molly had loved him best, he took on
extended trips through the Indian country: to Willstown, down the
Coosa, across the lower districts, to Oostinaleh, Turkey Town, Broom's
Town, back through the Upper Cherokee towns to Qualla in North
Carolina. Sometimes they were out together for months, staying a day
here, two days there, a week at another place, entering Indian homes
as old friends and familiars. They visited Glass, Pathkiller, Toochalar,
Hicks, Ridge, the Vanns, full bloods and mixed bloods; they stayed
at little cabins in mountain valley clearings as well as in commodious
plantation homes ringed about with slave cabins.[15] The boy was an
attentive listener, an observer, speaking seldom in company but always
absorbing facts and impressions. In the five years that followed he
came literally to know the whole tribe.

He saw a people moving swiftly forward on the road to civilization
in the white man's sense. New fields came under cultivation and small
fields grew larger; ramshackle shelters were replaced by stout log

cabins; cattle and horse herds multiplied; more and more men were using ploughs, driving wagons; they were turning to blacksmithing, milling, ferrying, and toll-road building; and even among the conservative mountain men who clung to the rifle and beaver trap for occupation, hunger had become a legend.

During those years, he saw the establishment of a Cherokee tribal government that in rough outline matched the white man's. It was a step in which all were greatly interested, taken after much discussion. At Broom's Town, the great September council of 1808 adopted a penal code: a hundred lashes for horse theft, fewer for less grave offenses. A real police force was set up consisting of a captain, a lieutenant, and four men in each of the eight political districts of the Nation. Two years later, twenty-year-old John Ross was present at the council which abolished the ancient sanction of blood revenge, the feud habit. Courts were created to deal with every form of lawlessness and to settle civil disputes.[16]

Young Ross developed a tireless, powerful body, proof against weather, uncertain meals, difficult mountain journeys. Short of stature, he remained always Tsan-Usdi, Little John, but he had all the strength and quickness of the tough Highlanders from whom he descended. His physical fitness attracted the men and women of the tribe; still more they liked him for the way he listened with quick understanding, smiled sparingly, took to heart their problems, and as time went on, brought them increasingly wise solutions.

Good for the Cherokees, and for the Ross trading enterprise, was this up-curving new-patterned life. Better than the old ways, when the hunters and trappers worked out of the sixty-four closely built towns hedged by the narrow strips of communal orchards and fields of corn, beans, squash, and such other staples of food as the women could raise. Those old towns had nearly all been destroyed in the protracted years of warfare between the Indians and whites, and with the coming of peace their head men advised against rebuilding. It would be better to scatter, develop family homes and fields, find individual ranges for stock, become more individual in every way; learn, indeed, to live like the whites with whom in time they must inevitably mingle. That counsel was learned from traders and agents like Dinsmore and his successor, a wise ripe New Englander named Return Jonathan Meigs.[17]

But not every Cherokee, of course, agreed. On his journeys John Ross saw the tribal rift over this question widen until in the spring of 1808 a delegation of progressive Upper Cherokees went to Washington to ask the president to divide their lands from those occupied by the Lower Cherokees, who resented the new tribal laws and rejected the trappings and tools of "civilization." The progressives asked for the allotment of their portion of the lands in severalty and for the privileges and duties of American citizenship.[18]

Jefferson regretted that he could not meet this demand. Only Congress could authorize the change and, since it was altogether unlikely that Congress would do it, he advised the whole tribe to remove west of the Mississippi. The president was insistent; he sent back to the Cherokee Nation an agent to choose representatives from both Upper and Lower Cherokees and conduct them on a journey of exploration of the Arkansas country to which a few of their brothers had already gone. Adroitly chosen from the discontented, these investigators returned with highly favorable reports. There was a great stir, much talk, and many announced their intention to go west. Before practical steps could be taken to start the exodus, however, Jefferson's second term ended; and President Madison was not in favor of wholesale removal.

An increasingly powerful influence against removal were the missionaries, able and clear headed men who foresaw the day when the ambition of the Upper Cherokees to incorporate themselves into the body of Americans could be realized for the whole tribe.

While Ross was still a boy, the firm establishment of the missions had been accomplished. First to come were the Moravians, Abraham Steiner and Gootlieb Byhan, who established themselves at Spring Place two years after they had been granted permission to preach if they would also open a school. They had at once begun holding services in the house of a half-blood, Vann, but took no steps towards setting up a school. At the Council of 1801, therefore, it was ordered that unless they began teaching within six months they must leave the Nation. Whereupon, with Vann's help and the assistance of agent Meigs, the school building was erected and instruction begun, Vann donating a part of his fine farm as a site, and lodging the two churchmen.[19]

Next, at about the time John Ross left the Academy, the Presbyterian, Gideon Blackburn, opened a mission school at Maryville. By his energy, integrity and common sense, by the example he set as a diligent worker with hands as well as brain, he made himself a beloved counselor of the tribe.[20]

Then, in 1816, came Cyrus Kingsbury from the recently created Baptist American Board of Foreign Missions, of New England. As spiritual descendant of John Eliot who, a hundred and forty years before had a served circuit of fourteen Massachusetts Indian villages and made 1,100 converts, he set up a station at a Chickamauga town near Lookout Mountain and called it Brainerd, in honor of a long dead zealous worker among the Indians.[21]

These men were the successors of a picturesque French Jesuit, Christian Priber, who had long since briefly illuminated Cherokee history. A cultured, courageous priest, Priber had adopted the tribal customs, learned the language and, in the short span of five years, won the chiefs and medicine men to the idea of an Indian monarchy. Before he was arrested by the British as a secret emissary of the French Government, he had persuaded the Cherokees to make their chief medicine man emperor; the capital of the empire he established at a town in Tennessee called Great Tellico; he had himself appointed as the emperor's secretary, and in that character conducted correspondence with the Colonies. Dying in a Georgia prison in 1741, he earned his martyr's crown. The Indian empire dissolved into a romantic and rather appealing memory.[22]

From the beginning, therefore, had been set the high standard of missionary effort that vitally affected Cherokee history and Ross's career.

CHAPTER 3

Early in life John Ross had come to realize that treaties between the
United States and the Indian tribes, always for the cession of land to
the whites and always including solemn guarantees that the remainder should belong to the Indians "as long as trees grow and water
runs," were easily broken promises on the part of the government.
Apparently the white man had no conception, in the Indian sense,
of the significance of the pledged word; if he wanted land and an
Indian treaty barred his way, he took it by peaceable nullification of
the treaty if feasible, and, if not, "by the sword, which is the best right
to all countries!"[1] This knowledge was distressing, but the fact must
be faced; the Government's bad faith was simply one element of the
problem of race survival that must be handled with the rest.

Between the week of the green-corn dance of 1797 and the day he
quit the academy, John Ross saw the pressure of white settlers upon
the United States government increase sufficiently to force three
revisions of the Holston treaty, each taking from the Cherokee additional tracts of land. The cessions were obtained by whatever devices
government commissioners could contrive. To the treaty of 1804,

for example, the Cherokees discovered that a secret paragraph had been attached bestowing bribes of valuable tracts of land individually on two chiefs, Doublehead and Tolluntuskee, in violation of the Cherokee law forbidding any but communal ownership of the soil; and so seriously was this menace to tribal integrity regarded that the people met in council and condemned the two chiefs to death. Tolluntuskee escaped to the west, but the sentence was carried out in the case of Doublehead.[2]

The 1804 cession was followed by another in 1806, the white commissioners contending that it was necessary in order to correct the boundaries of the first. It was not surprising that agitation for flight from these avaricious and elbowing intruders grew among the pessimistic Cherokees. Against them stood the clearer sighted, who saw that any retreat could be but a postponement of the merger of Indian life with that of white America. These progressives proposed to stand by their homeland and there effect the inevitable amalgamation on the best terms they could make.

As John Ross reached manhood there came an interval of relaxation from aggressive pressure. For the moment, the government was more concerned with keeping the Indians loyal in the impending war with Great Britain than with sending them west. Tecumseh, able Shawnee chief pledged to the British, with his fanatical brother, the Prophet, was working for a great Indian confederacy strong enough to roll back the white tide. The vision of such a combination was fascinating to many Indians of the southern tribes, including those Cherokees to whom white ways were hateful.[3]

To nullify British propaganda, the secretary of war instructed Indian agents to bind the tribesmen to the United States in every possible manner. Gifts to chiefs and influential men were distributed, and huge silver medals struck, to be hung ceremoniously about the necks of those who had served the government.

For the Cherokees, this wooing of the savage was assigned to Agent Meigs. He was able to report that there was no doubt of the loyalty of the ninety per cent of the tribe living under his agency, and to the rest who, led by Brown, Rodgers, Tolluntuskee, and others, had gone out to the Arkansas, Meigs promised to send a persuasive pleader.[4] His choice fell on a mixed-blood interpreter who, loaded with gifts, started west with a well-equipped party. Nearing the Mississippi and hearing exaggerated tales of recent earthquake destruction in the country about New Madrid, this man turned back in alarm.[5]

Meigs must find another ambassador at once. John Ross was at the time visiting his son Timothy. Meigs knew him well, liked and trusted him; there was in the youth a sound and appealing quality; his background was good; and young as he was in years, he had already proved that he was able to win the confidence of influential leaders. Meigs called John into the house; between the man of seventy-five and the nineteen-year-old youth passed probing questions and ready answers; and at length:

"Will you prepare to go at once if your father is agreeable?"

The young man's eyes lighted. A service for the tribe, his mother's people, his people! Of course, he was eager to go.

Daniel Ross consented, and the start was quickly arranged. On Christmas day of 1809, accompanied by John Spier, a stout half-blood, Kolsatchee, an old full-blood, and a drifting Mexican called Peter, homesick for the Rio Grande, young Ross pushed off from Rossville Landing on the Tennessee in a crude "clapboard ark" laden with gifts.

As the craft floated down the river it attracted the eye of Isaac Brownlow, a frontiersman almost as well known in Tennessee as was his brother, Parson Brownlow. Calling the expedition to shore to "git the hang o' things," Brownlow said it was a dang shame that a supposedly sensible man like Meigs would let a youngster pole off on a long and dangerous trip with an outfit like that! Brownlow was a borderer, with no love for the Indians, but he was taken by Ross's courage and impressed by his levelheadedness; and he had as well the frontiersman's instinctive desire to guard his none too numerous fellow adventurers from unnecessary peril.

"I'll go with ye a ways an' see how that ol' ark behaves," he decided;

and for eighty miles he drifted down the river alongside the yawing flatboat. Then he insisted that Ross should exchange it for his own riverworthy keelboat. "Mine's wuth more 'n yours," he said, "but I'll take an order on the Gove'ment for the difference. Maybe an order won't be wuth a tinker's damn, but danged ef I wouldn't ruther lose the price o' my craft than see ye go furder in that crazy thing!"

In the sixty days that followed, Ross and his companions lived a schoolboy epic. They were fired upon by over-nervous white settlers who mistook them for hostile Indians; they were chased by Indians in canoes who believed that they were invading whites; pulling toilsomely up the unknown and difficult reaches of the Arkansas River, after long weeks of drifting with the currents of the Tennessee, Ohio, and Mississippi, they wrecked their boat one wild night and lost nearly all its cargo. Finally, through the late February cold and sleet, with what remained of the gift packages on their backs, they finished the journey on foot, wading streams and swamps, living on game, covering two hundred miles in eight days.

At the end of the trail there was rest for John Spier, Kolsatchee, and Peter, long sleeps and plenty to eat. But for young Ross, intent on his mission, there was no rest. At once he sought out Brown, Rodgers, and Tolluntunskee, the head men of that Arkansas band Cherokees, delivered the few gifts and medals that had been saved, repeated the messages of good will from the government, answered their questions, met their arguments, and listened patiently to the long hours of reminiscent talk that followed.

The outcome of the conferences was that the western band agreed with their brothers in the east concerning the British; they would stick to the Americans. Satisfied of this, Ross secured horses and an escort for the return overland to Rossville. Within four months the round trip of nearly two thousand miles was accomplished, and his report made to Meigs. Then Ross went back to helping in the trading activities of his father.[6]

Those four arduous months ripened him amazingly, gave him self-confidence, extended his knowledge. He began to take over, with his brother Lewis, more and more of the details of business from his father. The changing seasons brought him into ever closer relations with the tribesmen. The springtimes sent him off on long journeys with packtrains burdened with goods to trade for pelts; and as the trafficking went on, he gave sound advice about planting, urged the growing of more cotton, suggested the building of sawmills and gristmills and better houses. In midsummer he met the runners on the tribal paths carrying, as summons to the year's green-corn dance, their little bundles of short "calendar" twigs. One twig was to be thrown away each day by the recipient, and the last dropped upon the ceremonial fire at the moment of arrival. He had known these runners when he and they were children; meeting him, they stopped for a minute their untiring jog-trot, relaxed against a tree, accepted tobacco from him, gave him in return pinches of *wissatoe*, parched corn meal, or a handful of dried peaches, all their fare on the long trails. The great council of the tribe was held in October, at the beginning of the Indian new year. John Ross attended as a matter of course, mingling freely, talking little but listening always. When winter came, snow blocked the mountain paths, making the work heavy, but trading outposts must somehow be supplied with the goods brought in during the fall over the roads and traces winding up from Savannah and the sea. Not least amongst these goods were the medicines which were taking the place of brews anciently supplied by the medicine men, whose prestige had passed.

Meanwhile the threat of war between America and Great Britain was growing more definite. The Indians knew it and talked of it in their councils and at home. The leaders hoped that it would not involve the tribe, however; it was none of their business, this quarrel of the white nations. The dispute lay quite outside their understanding.

Beyond the Cherokee borders the strain grew ever more intense. Tecumseh visited the southern tribes, followed by the fiery, eloquent Prophet, preaching hatred of Americans, foretelling the destruction of the white race on a predetermined day by an unnamed, mysterious scourge. The Prophet gained some followers amongst the Cherokees, and sent them out to distribute "calendar" bundles of red sticks, which should date the beginning of that concerted revolt of red against white which was to follow the cataclysm and restore to its first owners all the country clear to the Atlantic.

Ross talked to the fanatics; he could name and number them all. He watched them start for the high mountain top from which, said the Prophet, they were to witness the annihilation of the whites—and not alone the whites, but all those Indians too who refused to seek sanctuary there. He saw them return, disillusioned, to their abandoned homes and fields when the Prophet's day of judgment had passed uneventfully. Without comment, he gave them credit at the Ross trading posts for needed supplies.

The war, when at last it broke, did involve the Cherokees, against their will. The Lower Creeks, their neighbors on the southwest under the leadership of a strong mixedblood chief named Weatherford, were won by Tecumseh and the Prophet to the English cause. Because the Cherokees would not join them, Weatherford's warriors attacked the towns along the Coosa. These raids of Creek "red sticks" rendered impossible the Cherokee policy of neutrality; and when the energetic Tennessee militiaman, Andrew Jackson, organized his force to go against Weatherford's fanatics, he had a regiment of Cherokees amongst his Indian auxiliary troops.[7]

Ross was adjutant of that regiment, chosen because of his familiarity with writing and the keeping of records. Older men of Indian blood were in active command, Gideon Morgan as colonel, Richard Brown as lieutenant colonel, James Brown, Ridge, McNair, Saunders, and Shoe Boots as captains, but none was more deeply involved in the actual fighting.[8] Witness the record of the final decisive battle of Horseshoe Bend:

Weatherford's finest warriors, a thousand desperate men, had chosen a strong position with the swift water of the Tallapoosa River at their back, their camp and women and children in the bend, and a cleverly traversed log breastworks across the neck of the horseshoe. Along the curving riverbank, concealed by overhanging foliage, lay the Creek canoes. Jackson's Tennesseans attacked the formidable breastworks, battering at it ineffectively with rifles and one small cannon. Across the river along the outer rim of the horseshoe were posted the Cherokees and other Indian allies. Sharp eyes amongst them spotted the hidden canoes, and strong swimmers were called upon to cross and bring them away. John Ross was one of those who succeeded; and he was with the landing force that fell upon the Creeks from the rear, diverted them, and gave Jackson's men, among them the intrepid Sam Houston,[9] opportunity to swarm over the log barrier and, in the next two hours of bloody body-to-body fighting, annihilate the Creek force.

That battle broke the power of Weatherford. Historians have said that it was the daring and resourcefulness of the Indian auxiliaries that made victory possible for Jackson. It is certain that out of that victory grew Jackson's fame as a military genius, his promotion to the highest rank in the army and, eventually, his election to the presidency.

What was the Cherokee's reward? Twenty years after the battle of the Horseshoe, the Cherokee chief Janaluska, who had fought there, said, "If I had known that Jackson would some time drive us from our homes, I would have killed *him* that day!"[10]

CHAPTER 4

John Ross came back from the Creek campaign unscathed in body, matured in character, quickened by the eager impatience of the lover. No cheers, processions, showers of confetti met the returning hero; prowess and valor in battle was by the Indians taken for granted, like endurance in the hunt and skill in the ball play. But Quatie, full-blood daughter of a Bird Clan chief, may have welcomed him a bit more warmly because he had proved himself a worthy warrior.

Under the young man's inherited reserve burned the flame of Highland ancestors. He was approaching the age of twenty-four; Quatie was twenty-two, slender, slightly taller than he, with extraordinarily alive black eyes; ardent and lovable, and an aristocrat. It was a match based on love and approved by both families. Not long after his return, they were married; Tsan-Usdi and Quatie or, as the names were recorded by the preacher-missionary who united them, John Ross and Elizabeth Brown.

It was a happy marriage, a fortunate union of two strong lines. In the home, Quatie was tenderly dominant, true wife and with something of the Indian mother feeling too towards her man, but she yielded

27

to him in those larger matters that were concerned with the tribe.
Through her, he was drawn closer to the full-blood people. She helped
him to understand the ancient *tribal* bond, better to comprehend a
political organization growing out of family, clan, and race claims on
the affections. Beyond her husband's expanding fields and the walls
of their home, her eyes took in the whole Cherokee scene. Devoted
to her household, to the children she bore, domestic, frankly passionate, she could yet grasp the whole people's problems. Her father had
been one of the first tribal judges chosen under the laws of 1808.[1] She
might have been of an ancient Levantine stock, there was in her that
Oriental, matriarchal quality.

His marriage strengthened Ross with the new and more modern
leaders who were replacing old chiefs like Ocunna, Black Fox, and
the venal Doublehead.[2] When, therefore, early in the winter of 1815–
16, a delegation was selected to go to Washington and present the
Cherokee claims for the correction of the boundary line between the
Creek Nation and their own, he was named as one of the five.

Ross was by far the youngest of that embassy, and rode as special
protégé of the eldest, Major Ridge of the graying hair, the courtly
manner, fastidious dress, and a social charm that made him, though
he must speak through an interpreter, a favorite in Washington drawing rooms. Cunnessee was the other full-blood of the party; and he,
like the mixed-bloods Lowry and Walker, had been educated in white
schools.[3]

It was a type of Indian delegation new to the capital, not a bead nor
a feather amongst them; a distinguished group, of whom the *National
Intelligencer* newspaper spoke with approval as "men of cultivation
and understanding; their appearance and deportment are such as to
entitle them to respect and attention." Pioneers in method they were,
too, for they brought with them saddlebags bulging with testimony
and the knowledge of how to use it.

The hearings were held before Secretary of War Crawford. General
Jackson, under whom the disputed survey had been made, appeared
and defended its correctness with all the fiery assurance of his nature.

But his eloquence could not prevail against the presentation by Ross, speaking for the Cherokees, of the detailed evidence gathered from old tribesmen who had traced for him the true boundary almost yard by yard. Crawford gave his decision for the delegation, rousing Jackson to violent protest and making of him a lifelong enemy.

The return of the delegation was in the nature of a triumphal march; in the tribe, Ross's personal prestige was enormously strengthened by the success of the mission.

He spent the spring and summer at home, engaged with his brother Lewis and Timothy Meigs, who had become a partner, in expanding the Ross trading enterprises. He finished building a roomy two-story house in the midst of his enlarging fields near the agency, and provided quarters for the increasing numbers of slaves. Late in the fall he set off for Savannah with a long packtrain of skins and furs, and from there took ship for Baltimore. In that city, and later in New York he spent the winter disposing of his cargo and buying the goods he required for his stores. More important to the career that lay ahead, however, were the friendships he made with men of business and political influence in the east. To them he unveiled the truth about his people, their ambitions and needs. Later, they were to rise to a fervid championing of the Cherokee cause, marked by fiery oratory, excited public meetings, and substantial material support.

Ross was hurried home by the newspaper report that President Monroe had yielded to the demand of the Tennessee congressional delegation to free their state of its Indian population. Commissioners were named to treat with the Cherokees on the basis of removal beyond the Mississippi, the now familiar proposal against which Ross and the other progressives had determined to fight. A Tribal Council was to meet in May, and the commissioners were due in June.

He rode to the council with Judge Brown, influential member of the National Committee, the upper branch of the tribal legislature. They talked of the problem the council must face, the framing of a policy for dealing with President Monroe's representatives. On the way, others joined them, discussion grew more serious and seemed to center about Ross. Before they reached the Amohe council ground, Brown, the full-blood, threatened with a glint of humor in his eye:

"Son, when we get to the Council, we're going to put you into purgatory!"

"Purgatory? What do you mean?" Ross was startled.

"Well, we're going to put you up for member of the Committee— same thing!" Behind the old man's smile was a reflection of his confidence in the young man, and his affection for him.

"I see; yes—" Ross fell suddenly silent; he knew that Brown must be sure of his choice; henceforth, he must stand as a responsible leader among the people. It was a challenge both to his spirit and his intelligence. He hoped that he could meet it. None knew what the outcome of the tribe's inevitable struggle for survival would be, but he could at least resolve to bear with courage his share in the battle.

Early in the session Major Ridge, speaker of the council, the lower body of the legislature, who presided over the General Council, announced Ross's unanimous election to the committee. He spoke proudly of the young man.

Ross was twenty-seven years old, stocky, his face beginning to set in the mold that in old age so resembled the New England cast of an Emerson. He was more serious, more settled in character than was suggested by the slightly uptilted nose and the rather fluffy, unruly brown hair. He faced the long test, fifty years of uninterrupted connection with the official government of the Cherokees, with an extraordinary physical vitality as well as a fortunately extended mental preparation.

A long road ahead! Fifty years of singlehearted effort on behalf of his people, of tireless contriving, stubborn battling, patient endurance, passionate pleading. He was to know intervals of triumph and peace, and others more frequent of bitter disappointment and sharp grief; victories, half victories, defeats more glorious than victories. He was to face banishment, a weary and sick old age, final vindication.

CHAPTER 5

Ross's first test as an official representative of the Cherokee Nation was against able opponents: Monroe's commissioners, Andrew Jackson, Governor McMinn of Tennessee, and General David Meriwether.[1]

These three arrived at the agency on the June day they had named, but found there only a dozen or so Cherokees who had returned from a visit to the Arkansas, and had already declared for removal. For two weeks, the commissioners, assisted by agent Meigs, strove to bring together a sufficient number of Tennessee, Georgia, and North Carolina Indians to open negotiations. But as the people had already, at the May council, pronounced against removal they saw no reason for discussing the question further.

Then Ross, appealed to by the commissioners, used his influence to bring the chiefs and head men in. "Come," he said, "and repeat to the President's men what you have decided so that they may take your words back to Washington."

When a hundred or more leaders were assembled, sitting under the council dome behind Principal Chief Pathkiller, the virulent, tousle-haired Jackson made a talk to them: A crisis in Cherokee history demanded action; those Cherokees who had already removed west of the Mississippi were pressing the Government to establish the boundaries of their Arkansas reserve; the government, however, would not make the survey until all the others who expected to remove should declare themselves, for after the western limits were fixed no more would be admitted.

Jackson promised governmental aid to all who would emigrate, "one rifle gun and ammunition to each, also one blanket and one brass kettle, or, in lieu of the brass kettle, a beaver trap, which is to be considered as a full compensation for the improvements which they may leave."[2] Jackson could never give up the belief, gained in the Creek campaign, that all Indians were savage nomads, could not comprehend the Cherokee ambition for civilization. Thinking to frighten them into the mood for removal, he added that all who elected to stay in the east must become citizens of the United States. "As free men," he said, "you must now make your choice. Those who go west will go to a country belonging to the United States"—quite ignoring in this statement the fact that the government had not yet obtained from the Osage Indians release of their claim on that portion of the Arkansas territory. "There," he went on, "your father the President can never be urged by his white children to ask their red brothers the Cherokees for any of the land laid off at that place for them." As a matter of fact, the president's white children did within ten years demand, and secure, the removal of the Arkansas Cherokees from that very land!

Jackson further outraged the men listening to him by declaring that the United States had never recognized Cherokee ownership of their eastern lands, but only the right of occupancy for hunting purposes.

In answer, Pathkiller and others repeated what had been decided at the Amohe council: the Cherokees would never willingly give up their homeland, and few wished to go to the west. "We will give you our words in writing," Pathkiller said, and named John Ross and Ross's brother-in-law, Elijah Hicks,[3] to put the answer on paper. They cast it in the form of a memorial to the president, setting forth the strong desire of the great majority to remain on the land of their forefathers, where the tribe was moving forward rapidly in the way of white civilization; they were no longer merely hunters and warriors, and did not wish to revert to that state.

The writing was signed by sixty-seven chiefs and head men and handed to the commissioners. They paid no attention to it, however. They had not come to get Cherokee opinion, but to express the government's wishes. Under Jackson's lead, the commissioners drew up a treaty of removal, which was signed by fifteen Arkansas Cherokees and twenty-two others, none of standing or authority in the tribe; and that document was borne off to Washington as an authentic expression of the Cherokee Nation.[4]

According to the Jackson theory, the western exodus was to be prompt and general; thousands taking up their rifle guns, blankets, and brass pots, and streaming towards the fair lands of the Arkansas. But in fact all the arguments, cajolery, threats, and intimidation used during the following year by government agents, by Governor McMinn in person, and by a few Cherokees like Toochelar and Chisholm, who had been converted to the notion of removal, succeeded in enrolling only seven hundred for the Arkansas. However, a breach had been made which, in the next twenty years, was to widen and cause much bitterness.[5]

At the fall council of that same year, 1817, Toochelar was deposed as assistant chief, Charles Hicks was named in his place, and the spurious Jackson treaty was formally repudiated.[6] In the words of John Ross, the council declared, "We consider ourselves a free and distinct Nation, and the Washington Government has no polity over us further than a friendly intercourse in trade."

A more virile force was rising in the Cherokee ranks. It expressed itself admirably in Ross. The Indians were not mere vassals, to be ordered hither and yon by the white man's government! Their old fatalistic attitude was changing. Though Ross had grown to maturity in the environment of traditional communal life, and had drawn from his mother's breast the philosophy of an old race schooled to bow to the decrees of a fate represented by superior physical strength, he was able to resist its sad teaching. He had read: "Now there arose a new king over Egypt which knew not Joseph . . . and made their lives bitter with hard bondage . . . And the people took their dough before it was leavened, their kneading troughs being bound up in their clothes upon their shoulders . . . And a mixed multitude went up also with them" out of Egypt.[7] Were the Cherokees, like the children of Israel, to fly before the hard-knuckled and bearded modern Egyptians seeking their land? Fly to a wilderness where beaver, deer, and wild turkeys were said to abound and the thunder of buffalo herds sounded in the wind?

Easy to yield! But the Cherokees must not yield. Ross was sure that removal would only delay the necessary adjustment of the tribe to American ways. He wasted no thought on the comparative value of Indian and American civilization. In essence, white culture might be better or worse than Indian; good or bad, however, the Indians would have to learn to live according to its precepts. Let the process of amalgamation work the transformation here where it was already well under way.

As a new leader coming to power in the tribe, Ross proposed to fight for the people's homes, not with rifle and knife, with odds of a hundred to one against the tribe, but with the resources of diplomacy.

He told the Cherokees that Jackson was right in saying that they were free to go west. He would not oppose the propagandists of removal; rather, let them test their strength. When the trickle of emigration ceased, however, it was time to secure the annulment of the fake treaty carried away by Jackson, McMinn, and Meriwether; and for this purpose he asked for the appointment of a strong delegation to present their case to Washington. Twelve men were chosen to go with Ross.

While he waited for his fellow delegates to prepare for the journey, there befell Ross an experience that augmented his influence in a most useful quarter. He received a call for help from Brainerd Mission.

Somewhere in the Nation was a little Osage boy who had been taken captive in a counter raid of western Cherokees and handed over to an eastern Cherokee, then visiting in Arkansas, who had brought him home and sold him to another Indian. A small girl, said to be his sister, had also been taken. She was in the Brainerd school, and Mr. Kingsbury was anxious to have the boy as well. On consulting Agent Meigs, he was told, "If anyone can find the boy, John Ross can."

It was a mission that strongly appealed to Ross. His practical mind foresaw another Indian raised to understanding of the white man's way; and he was glad to aid Kingsbury, who had proved to be the same type of useful, energetic, and sympathetic worker as Gideon Blackburn. Besides, the tang of the romantic in the search appealed to the Highland strain in him.

Securing from Agent Meigs authority to take the boy, Ross set out on horseback with two Indian companions. Guided by chance words, they rode 250 miles over doubling and twisting trails before coming to the remote cabin of the boy's "owner." They hid their horses in a wood, crept to the house, and saw the little Osage boy playing, naked, in the dooryard. Taking him suddenly in his arms and smothering his outcries with a hand over his mouth, Ross ran back to the horses, and the kidnappers galloped off for Brainerd. Kingsbury won the confidence of the boy, enrolled him in school, and conferred on him the name of John Osage Ross.[8]

Thus, characteristically, Ross supported the missions in the Cherokee Nation with faith and works. He was inheritor of a belief in a just and helpful God, not an awesome Being of fanatic thunderings. The God of his tradition was one with that Spirit Power of the old Cherokees, to whom they prayed:

Hear me, oh Being! I have purified my feet from the dust of the earth on which I am a dweller until they are fit to bear me to the high place, even above the treetops, where I may meet thee undisturbed by the things of the world and look straight at thee and behold thee clearly. My heart, oh Being, you have loved; let it not slip from thy hand!

35

Missionaries were, to be sure, God's spiritual helpers, but in John Ross's mind they were even more certainly helpers of the Cherokees on the road to a civilization based upon reading, writing, arithmetic, productive farms, smithies, looms, mills, and weathertight houses. With that theory, fortunately, the missionaries agreed, and in the next twenty years of struggle against the ever-growing passion and power of those who sought the tribe's removal, Ross had valiant backing from them and the widely ramifying influences behind them.

The twelve who went to Washington were of both the older and newer generation, but all of the modern, progressive pattern. Ross was made leader; with him rode the elders, Walker, Brown, and Judge Martin, and such young men as Lewis Ross and Elijah Hicks. With facts backed by crisp argument, they presented their case to Secretary of War Calhoun; they submitted accurate figures of the emigration since the signing of the counterfeit Jackson treaty; and, convinced, Calhoun made a new treaty with them.[9]

The new treaty ceded eastern Cherokee land equal in area to the territory occupied by the western band, and provided for the equitable division of the tribal annuity between the two sections of the Nation. The United States agreed to discontinue removal propaganda, and drive white intruders from Cherokee land.

Ross's purpose to speed forward his people on the white man's road was expressed in the provision that a small block of valuable tribal land should be sold, the proceeds to be used for promoting education. He wanted good tribal schools, and believed that the people were ready for them. Already, two Cherokee boys, Major Ridge's son John, and Killekenah, who had taken the name of his white benefactor, Elias Boudinot,[10] president of the Continental Congress and one of the organizers of the American Bible Society, were studying in the mission school at Cornwall, Connecticut. Six years before, a circular letter from the chiefs to the governors of Tennessee, Georgia, and North Carolina had revealed that many of the youth of both sexes had acquired "such knowledge of letters as to show the most incredulous that our mental powers are not by nature inferior to yours, and we look forward to a time when it may be said, 'This artist, this mathematician, this astronomer is a Cherokee!'"[11]

Progressive tribesmen were becoming zealots for civilization, looking to Ross and the hard working missionaries for direction. At Brainerd, which President Monroe promised to visit on his western tour of 1819, there was eagerness for books and tools; a year after its founding, fifteen of the pupils could read the Bible in English; the boys could plant an acre of corn before breakfast; the girls were interested in sewing, knitting, spinning, and cooking as well as in books, and "among them are some gentle young women who would not disgrace more polished society." A mischievous and difficult youth named Wicked Jack was persuaded to attend; he soon caught the general enthusiasm and, appropriately, changed his name to John Crawfish. Lank, ragged, long haired John Arch tramped to the school from a hillside cabin 150 miles away and offered to trade his rifle for suitable clothing for the classroom, but "so wild and forbidding was he in appearance the missionaries shrank from receiving him until he almost forced himself in." Arch was later one of the ablest interpreters of the tribe.[12]

Old John Saunders, full-blood and illiterate, declared that he could sit up all night just for the pleasure of listening to his boys read the Bible. Learning had been established even in the minds of the old hillmen as the new magic which would preserve the Cherokees.

It was the beginning of a new age, and John Ross was its prophet.

CHAPTER 6

On his return from Washington, Ross was made president of the National Committee, succeeding a conservative. At his insistence, the fall council decreed that white schoolmasters, blacksmiths, millers, saltpeter and gunpowder manufacturers, turnpike keepers, ferrymen, and mechanics "are hereby privileged to reside in the Cherokee Nation under the following conditions: their employers must secure a permit from the National Committee and Council for them, and be responsible for their good conduct; and they will be subject to removal for misdemeanor."

In the same week, the council authorized additional stores, confirmed certain builders in the proprietorship of a toll turnpike, required white men who took Cherokee wives to marry them before a minister, gave the Cherokee wife of a white man control of family property, thus confirming tribal custom, imposed fines on white men who deserted Indian wives, required monogamy of whites married to Cherokees, and strongly recommended it to all Indian husbands—in 1825, universal monogamy was established.[1]

To understand the hell through which Ross toiled in the twenty years from 1819 to 1839, it is necessary to set off against the foregoing picture of a forward striding people this other, drawn by one of the tribe's most implacable enemies, George W. Gilmer of Georgia.[2] In his old age, when the fight to remove the Cherokees was a remote memory, he wrote:

"The curious are puzzling themselves with conjectures about the intent of the Almighty in making such beings [as the Cherokee Indians]—whether they are the descendants of Adam and Eve, and if they are, when and from whence they came."[3]

Gilmer could not believe that Indians were really human, repeating as truth every damning story, every ancient libel spoken of them by hostile borderers. He insisted that in order to appreciate the motives and acts of Georgia's public men "it is necessary to know what sort of people Indians were." He was Ross's contemporary, and must have had in mind the tribesmen with whom Ross grew up.

Gilmer charged that travelers, missionaries, and government agents could not be trusted to tell the truth about the Indians; "Their appearance, manners and habits strangely affected the imagination of all those who talked or wrote about them . . . According to their accounts, some of the chiefs were as crafty as Ulysses, others as brave as Achilles, and here and there one as eloquent as Demosthenes." The truth, as revealed to Gilmer, was that they were "the least worthy of remembrance of any beings."

"The men," he asserted, "did no manual work, therefore their shoulders were never rounded nor their backs bent [. . .]. Indian women were the least inviting of their sex; they lost ~~in drudgery~~ [by drudging] what the men gained in comeliness by freedom from ~~toil~~ [it] . . . Their hair was coarse, like the hair of a horse's tail. They greased it with rancid bear's oil—too offensive for any other beings to bear—to keep down the increase of vermin. They effected the same object for their children['s heads] by ~~the~~ aid of their teeth. Men and women went with unwashed hands, faces, and bodies, except when they cooled themselves in the streams in warm weather."

Because of the scarcity of salt, said Gilmer, "most of their food was eaten in the state preferred by buzzards . . . Their beds were of badly dried skins, whose perfumes added to the other vile smells about their cabins . . . They had no genius for invention . . . stone axes and hickory clubs were their tools for work and weapons of war."

Of their spiritual faith he said: "Their gods they worshipped ~~only~~ when they desired to do evil . . . They were the least obedient [of all men] to the divine command ~~to~~ [—] do unto others, etc. . . . If anyone became dependent, he died . . . Their master passion was revenge, which they indulged in as their greatest luxury. [. . .] They lolled about their cabins smoking and looking at the clouds[. They] talked but little and that little of what happened yesterday and today. [. . .] They seldom asked questions [—] not because they believed in the adage, Ask me no questions and I will tell you no lies—for they loved to act by trick, deceit, and stratagem; but from the absence of [the] desire for information. They were called eloquent, because they followed the vagaries of their imagination in speaking, without investigating facts, or elucidating principles; [—] heroic, because their insensibility enabled them to bear torture without complaining; [—] hospitable, because they laid up no provisions for the future, and consumed what they had without care; [—] and dignified, because they were calm and indifferent when others would have been excited."

The Indian's concept of heaven, according to Gilmer, was not a place "free from sin and sorrow" but a land "where plenty of game would be had;" their warriors were addicted to the habit of thrusting "light-wood splinters into the bodies of their prisoners," setting them on fire and dancing around the victims until they expired.

As a sort of climax to the Gilmer indictment, the Indians were pictured as unresponsive to melody, "unmoved by [. . .] the exalted strains of the organ." They preferred to dance to "the striking of sticks, or the rattling of pebbles in terrapin shells."

This sheer savage, insisted the man who served two terms as governor of Georgia, was the typical full-blood Cherokee; he wrote that the Indians "have remained what they [ever] were, and always will be, until they finally pass away—the most thoughtless, do-less, least loving and least lovely, of [human] beings."

What was the truth, Gilmer's conception, or Ross's? What *is* truth? Gilmer was not only twice governor and congressman from Georgia but an educated man and a church-goer; he applied the final pressure against the Cherokees of Georgia, blazing with indignation against the temporizing policy of the United States and threatening secession and war with the federal government unless troops were sent to drive the Indians out. Certainly he believed himself to be truthful.

What was the truth as disclosed in the lives of the Cherokees of Gilmer's day? Here are some items:

As far back as 1814, a full-blood Cherokee named Young Wolf wrote a will, in scrambled English, revealing the spirit of progress fostered by men like Ross. "In the name of God," he began, "I being in real good sense at this present time do make my last will and testimony . . . To my mother that raised me, I leave a black horse a three year old which The Crawler has in the army . . . By my being careful and by my own industry I have gathered a smart chance of property, and my first start was from my herding my brother's cattle I received one calf which I took my start from, except my own industry and with cow and calf which I sold, and bought 2 sows and 13 pigs. Some time after, I was able to purchase 3 mares and the increase of them since is amounted to 30 more or less, and from that start I gathered money enough to purchase a negro woman named Tabb, also a negro man named Ceasar."[4]

A picture, and a history, this will of Young Wolf; and a segment of truth about the Cherokees of his time.

In 1820, the Cherokee Council, dominated by the full-bloods, divided the Nation into eight governmental districts, in each of which a local council house was built where court sessions were held twice a year; and district judges and peace officers were chosen. A code of laws was adopted regulating taxation and debt, road building, and the liquor traffic—the first prohibition legislation enacted in America. Tribal affairs were already under the control of a National Legislature, with its upper and lower branches, and there was a National Treasurer.[5]

Out of their conviction that the Nation could successfully transform itself only by maintaining tribal integrity, the council of 1820 imposed the death penalty on individuals who should sign away Cherokee land without authority from the Committee and Council acting together. This was done to prevent repetition of the tragic farce engineered by Jackson in 1817.

A national school system, and library, were proposed as fruit of John Ross's thinking and as a sign of the tribe's confidence in his wisdom.

A year later, in 1821, occurred among the Cherokees one of the really significant forward steps in human history. A man named Sequoyah completed a ten-year period of study and experiment by announcing a syllabary of 86 characters so accurately adapted to the Cherokee language that within a few days any tribesman could learn to read and write it. Out of his "lolling and smoking and looking at the clouds," as Gilmer put it, this lame middle-aged Cherokee, knowing no English, duplicated the achievement of Cadmus!

Gilmer notwithstanding, Sequoyah was a man of talent. Lamed in hunting, he had become a silversmith; his syllabary, that rendered literate nearly the whole Nation within a few years, was perfected during his spare time.

There exists a full-blood Cherokee's contemporary history of the life and achievements of Sequoyah, translated into English by another full-blood, and passed upon for its accuracy by a committee of the Cherokee Council in the days when Gilmer was passionately insisting that all Indians were hopeless barbarians. At a gathering of friends one evening in 1809, said the Cherokee historian, "the conversation turned upon the ingenuity of the white man in contriving ways to communicate on paper. Some of the party remarked how wonderful it was to think that simply by making marks on paper, and sending the paper to another, two persons could understand as well as if talking together face to face; and how these things were done, it was impossible to conceive.[6]

"Sequoyah then remarked, 'I can see no impossibility in conceiving how it is done. The white man is no magician. It is said that in ancient times when writing first began a man named Moses made marks upon a stone. I too can make marks upon a stone. I can agree with you by what name to call those marks, and that will be writing and can be understood.' He then took up a small whetstone, and with a pin from his sleeve scratched marks upon the whetstone and said, 'Thus can I make characters, as Moses did, which every one of you will understand.'

"The young men burst into a laugh. They bantered him upon his scheme to make stones converse; told him he would find those stones very unentertaining company . . . and advised him to get his reason back . . ."

That challenge Sequoyah met by years of persistent experiment, first with characters to represent words and then, when he found that this would require too many, with characters standing for separate sounds that would combine to form words. "After vast labor and study, he had completed 86 characters, and with these he began to frame sentences. In the course of this long and silent study, every one was troubled about the strange whim he had taken into his head. His friend, Turtle Fields,[7] now came to pay him a visit. 'My friend,' said Turtle Fields to him, 'there are a great many remarks made upon this employment which you have taken up. Our people . . . think that you are wasting your life. They think, my friend, that you are making a fool of yourself, and will no longer be respected.'"

Sequoyah's reply was: "If our people think I am making a fool of myself, you may tell our people that what I am doing will not make fools of them. They did not cause me to begin and they shall not cause me to give up."

When he had settled upon the syllabary, Sequoyah "made several copies of it, and sent for some of his neighbors, and gave them the copies and taught them how to use the alphabet; so that shortly it got about and several persons found that they could form words and note them down and read them off again; but they did it very slowly, more as if counting or spelling than as if they were reading. Among those he taught, he particularly devoted himself to a little daughter of his own."

The Cherokee historian describes his own view of a test of the syllabary by Sequoyah and his daughter:

"'Eyorkah,' he said, 'say over my alphabet by heart, as I hold up the characters.' The little girl, she was five or six years old, raised her head and spoke out the sounds as rapidly as the characters could be shown.

"'Yoh!' I exclaimed in astonishment. 'It sounds like the Creek language.'

"'But the sounds, put together, make Cherokee words,' he said, and then he held up the characters again while the little girl called them over, and I saw that they formed words. I left him very much surprised at his discovery, and convinced that there was something in it."

So practical did the silversmith's discovery prove that the missionaries abandoned the effort to form an alphabet of Roman letters adapted to the Cherokee language and took over Sequoyah's characters for the printing of leaflets and books. They had them cast by a Boston type founder; they imported a press, paper, and an experienced printer; they secured illustrative cuts, and issued a small primer. John Arch,[8] the once wild hill youngster, made a manuscript translation into Cherokee of a portion of the gospel of St. John. It was copied out hundreds of times by the newly literate, who could read in their own tongue. "For the prince of this world cometh, and hath nothing in me." They were wont to remember this when, later, they defended John Ross against the slanders of his enemies.

Young David Brown, Cherokee, ordained as a preacher, returned from the Cornwall school and translated the whole of the New Testament and, pending its printing, passed the manuscript around until it had been read by scores. Literally thousands who knew no English learned to read and write their own language within a year of Sequoyah's announcement; the whole Nation, said one who observed the effects of his zeal, seemed to have become a great Indian academy, old men and children as well as the middle aged and youths taking up the study. As soon as one learned, he was anxious to teach someone else; every cabin became a school.

A weekly newspaper with a long name meaning *The Cherokee Phoenix*, using both Indian and English type, was started under the editorship of the full-blood Killekenah (Elias Boudinot), home from the Cornwall school with a young Yankee wife.[9] His salary of $300 a year as editor and translator was paid from the tribal treasury; Isaac Harris, the printer, received $400 a year.[10] The little four-page weekly was distributed free to the people from their own post offices and district court-houses. It carried to Indian homes accounts of council proceedings, news of dealings with the government, missionary items, discussions of affairs in Congress, political articles, and general culture essays clipped from New York, Boston, and Philadelphia newspapers, and the Washington *National Intelligencer.*

Text books, hymn books, presently the complete Bible, were issued in Cherokee; the printing shop, under the fostering care of the missionary Samuel Worcester, whose early years had been spent setting type and pulling a hand-press lever, was the busiest spot in the Nation. Another white printer was secured, and Boudinot required an assistant editor. Until tribal funds could be found to meet the added expense, Ross paid for them out of his own pocket.

In 1822, Sequoyah went west to the Arkansas band to teach his syllabary, and an active correspondence in Cherokee began between the head men of the two sections. Sequoyah elected to settle in the west. At the fall council, a silver medal bearing appropriate inscriptions in both Cherokee and English was voted him, along with the more practical grant of an annuity of $200. Ross saw to the striking of the medal and its forwarding; he wrote the council's formal letter of appreciation, and from subsequent correspondence with Sequoyah obtained descriptions of the territory that was urged upon the eastern Cherokees as a refuge.[11]

It was a time of ferment, of swift growth. John Ross lived in a stimulating activity. As president of the National Committee, he shouldered much of the executive work of the government. Nearly always on the wing, like a restless bird, he received from the Indians a new name, *Ghuisgui*, the Cherokee word for the proud plumed egret. More than anyone else, even more than the progressives, Hicks, Ridge, Situwakee, Vann, Martin, Whitepath, and Kelechulee,[12] he stood for education and industry. He was a spur, a gadfly; all Cherokees must learn to read and write, dress like the whites, surround themselves with the comforts and conveniences enjoyed by whites.

In 1825, he had a careful census made of the tribe and its material possessions: 15,142 Indians; 1,726 negro slaves; 12 schools; 62 smithies; 18 ferries; 40 cotton gins, saw mills, and grist mills; 17,531 cattle, 7,563 horses, and 47,732 hogs; 2,486 spinning wheels and 752 looms. He even had the many flocks of sheep and goats counted. He listed the seventy-two families that owned stout six-horse wagons fit for the long freight hauls from Savannah and from Knoxville. He wanted these facts in order to equip himself for the fight, growing ever more grim and determined, against removal.

CHAPTER 7

Turn back to Gilmer's entry upon the Cherokee scene. The time was 1822, the place Washington, the man a representative in Congress from Georgia and chairman of a select committee appointed to report on the question: Was the United States attempting in good faith to carry out the agreement of 1802 to extinguish Indian titles within the limits of the State?

Gilmer's committee answered emphatically, No! He cited as evidence the fact that in other states than Georgia larger cessions of land had been obtained in the last twenty years.

Yielding to Gilmer's demand, Congress appropriated $30,000 to meet the cost of another effort to negotiate the Cherokees and Creeks out of Georgia. Secretary of War Calhoun sent General Meriwether and Commissioner Campbell, both Georgia men, to do the dickering. News of this action coming to the Cherokees, the council met and resolved unanimously: "Not one more foot of land will we yield . . . But upon any question not relating to a land cession we will receive the United States Commissioners with friendship and cordiality, and will ever keep bright the chain of peace and friendship which links the Cherokee Nation with the United States."

Ross had copies of this resolution sent to Calhoun and to the commissioners, and wrote courteously that Meriwether and Campbell might as well spare themselves the trouble of coming and the United States the expense of a hopeless mission. His letter was disregarded, however; the commissioners appeared in the Nation, to remonstrate and then threaten the chiefs with the anger of "the Great Father at Washington, who will shake you off if you persist in your obstinacy." Blindly, the government agents continued to use these outworn forms of speech to the modern leaders of the tribe! A little later, an army man, Major Armstrong, visited the Nation and after a conference with Ross and certain others, wrote to the secretary of war: "The education and intelligence of the greater part of the leading men induced me to abandon the Indian style of addressing them . . . I therefore proceeded with them as men of business."

The pleadings and scoldings of the commissioners had no effect; they returned to Washington to report failure; and for a year no further attempt was made to oust the tribe from Georgia. It seemed to be another case of the irresistible force meeting the immovable obstacle. But the white man, covetous of the land to which the Indian owners clung with the desperate conviction that somehow their rights would be confirmed, would not have it so. The present lull could be only a respite in the struggle, as Ross well knew.

With his friends in the eastern states and in Washington, and the New England backers of the missionaries, he conducted a voluminous correspondence. His letters were packed with facts, with statistics of tribal progress. He was backfiring against the hot blaze fanned by the aggressive Georgians.

Ross's appeals stirred energetic men to action: The record of the increasing number of Cherokee boys sent to the Cornwall school was published abroad by the Rev. Herman Daggett, principal, and examples of their work, their letters to the school's benefactors and to President Monroe were exhibited, as were letters from the young

Cherokee woman, Catherine Brown, graduated from Brainerd and now a teacher. At Washington was organized the ponderously titled American Society for Promoting the Civilization and General Improvement of the Indian Tribes within the United States; its patrons were John Adams, Jefferson, and Madison, its vice presidents the Vice President of the United States and the Cabinet members; among the honorary members were John Jay, Generals Charles and Thomas Pinckney, Henry Clay, and Andrew Jackson (!); and in the list of directors appeared the names of William Wirt, Francis Scott Key, and the Rev. John Haeckwelder.[1]

One of the Society's special Cherokee correspondents was old Charles Hicks, Toochelar's successor as assistant chief. His English was uncertain, but his knowledge sure. He wrote: "It may with propriety be said that the Cherokees had already, in stimulus spirits, entered the manufacturing system in cotton clothing in 1800, which had taken rise in one Town in 1796 and 7 by the repeated recommendations of Silas Dinsmore, Esq., which was given to the chiefs in council during his residence of the three years of his agency."

The time had certainly come when the Cherokees needed help; in the year following the fruitless visit of Meriwether and Campbell, agent Meigs, full of years and honor as a true friend of the tribe, died, and ex-governor McMinn,[2] no friend at all, took his place. Calhoun, relentlessly pressed by the Georgia delegation in Congress, sent Meriwether and Campbell once more join McMinn in an effort to induce removal. He gave them a fund of $35,000, to be used "discreetly."

They appeared at the General Council of October 1823—a notable meeting, ending dramatically.

The three, together with a Georgia congressman, made a formal and somewhat pompous entry upon the council grounds. Agent McMinn ceremoniously presented his colleagues to the chiefs, the Committee and Council in joint session. Major Ridge, as speaker of the council, welcomed them in stately fashion, his words being impressively interpreted. Campbell responded, congratulating the Cherokees on the progress which they had obviously made.

Then no more words from the commissioners! This time they proposed to play a waiting game, try privately to create among the members of the tribal legislature a sentiment favorable to removal, and discover how best to use their $35,000. Two days later, however, Ross came to them with the council's written demand for a statement of their instructions. They hesitated for a while, then disclosed their purpose and began negotiations. At Ross's suggestion, the council asked that all communications should be made in writing; "a novel procedure," said Campbell, "this correspondence in writing conducted with a government regularly organized, composed of Indians!"

Argument began.

Said the commissioners, in effect: The white neighbors of the Cherokees are so cramped in their settlements that they are being driven to distant regions, whilst the Cherokees have more land than they need. This is intolerable, for the Great Father of the Universe intended the earth equally for his white and red children.

Said the Cherokee head men: As to the intentions of the Great Father of the Universe, we have no means of knowing what they are. We oppose removal because we will do better here than in the west. That portion of the tribe who have already emigrated have suffered severely from sickness, war with the Osages, and other calamities; and many now in the west would return to the east if they could do so (John Ross had brought Sequoyah's letters to that effect to the council.) If we had ever wanted to go west, we should have gone long ago. We love the soil on which we were born and which continues to nourish us. The limits of our Nation have been narrowed until we can no longer afford to cede any more land; most of what remains is mountainous and unfit for cultivation. Our experience has shown us that no partial cession will satisfy the white man, therefore we will never again part with a foot of our land.

Logic and unshakeable determination marked the attitude of the Cherokees. The commissioners became petulant, then cajoling, then angry and threatening. Ignoring the terms of the Hopewell peace treaty of 1785, they told the Cherokees that they had forfeited title to the lands they inhabited by fighting against the colonists in the Revolutionary War! They also renewed Jackson's contention that the Indians were mere tenants at will. As a last resort, they tried bribery, and a bungling job they made of it!

Out of all the fifteen thousand and more Cherokees, the commissioners could not find a suitable agent for their purpose, and so selected a visiting Creek chief named McIntosh, who was well known to the Cherokees as a "beloved brother." He had attended their councils for years, and was, so far as the Cherokees knew, an honest man; they were not aware that he had already shown an itching palm in secret negotiations between the Creeks and government agents.

In the third week of the council, McIntosh acted. He was no wily diplomat, and he went straight to the point in a written communication to Ross: Would Ross give him in confidence his "real views" on the proposed treaty of removal? If Ross could bring himself to favor it, McIntosh promised, on behalf of the commissioners, to hand him $2,000; and the same amount would be paid to Hicks, and to Isaac McCoy, clerk of the council, for their support. "No one shall know it, you receive that present. I will get you the amount before the treaty is signed; and if you have any friend you want him to receive, he shall receive." McIntosh admitted that he was to get $7,000 for his share.

Ross wasted no words on McIntosh, but called together his closest associates and laid the letter before them. They were furious. Ross waited for them to cool, then planned with them for the most effective use of the document. In the evening McCoy and Major Ridge were confidentially assured by McIntosh that the bribe was offered with the sanction of the commissioners; and to them McIntosh proposed that he be invited to address a joint session of the Cherokee Committee and Council, where he would speak in favor of the removal of all the southern tribes. If, he said, Ross and his associates agreed with his plan and told the people that it was hopeless to contend longer against Georgia and the United States, then old Pathkiller, Principal Chief, could be won over. He attempted to dazzle Ridge and McCoy by telling them what he and a few others had gained in treaty negotiations between the government and the Creeks, "all knowledge of which is buried in oblivion."

Later that night, Ross heard Ridge's and McCoy's report; and the three set the stage for next morning's meeting. A call was sent out for a general gathering fifteen minutes after the blowing of the sunrise bugle; "special and important business" was to be discussed; and McIntosh had a pressing invitation to attend.

Beaming, primed for the talk he expected to make, the Creek chief was received with the usual outward courtesy, but was soon made uneasy by the grim faces of those who knew his heart. Speaker Ridge, opening the council with some solemnity, called upon Ross to speak. He rose and said gravely, slowly: "My friends, five years have elapsed since I was first called upon to serve on the National Committee. Your approbation of my conduct is manifested by the succeeding reappointments which you have bestowed upon me."

He then turned his eyes upon McIntosh and cried: "An honorable and honest character is more valuable than the lucre of all the world; I would rather live as poor as the worm than to gain wealth and have my reputation tarnished by the acceptance of a pecuniary bribe!" He paused for a few moments, then: "It has now become my duty to inform you that gross contempt is offered my character as well as that of the General Council. This letter which I hold in my hand will speak for itself. Fortunately, the author has mistaken my character." Handing the letter to Clerk McCoy, he sat down.

Sentence by sentence, McCoy read the Creek's words and translated them into Cherokee. He ended, and in the shocked stillness that followed old Pathkiller got up, "tall, erect and dignified, his flashing eyes alone revealing his deep emotion." Astonishment and grief, he said, "hurt me in here"—he tapped his breast—because this Creek brother, whom they had trusted as an honest chief and loved as friend, had shown himself willing to betray his brothers, the Cherokees, for a handful of gold! . . . The council must deal with him.

McIntosh attempted to speak, but his voice was lost in a tumbling surge of angry protest. Ridge and Ross, standing together, quieted the excited Indians; then Ross put a motion to bar forever from time forth Chief McIntosh from Cherokee councils. As the shout of assent rose, the Creek hurried from the assemblage to saddle his horse and gallop away.

In the council's notice to the Creeks advising them that McIntosh could never again be received by the Cherokees, no reference to the attempted bribery was made, but Ross added a line: "The commissioners have departed this day without a foot of land." It was left for the indignant Creeks, when that tribe was forced out of Georgia and McIntosh's duplicity became known, to kill him for his treachery to his own people.

In their report to the War Department, the United States commissioners merely mentioned the fact that a delegation of Creeks headed by McIntosh had visited the council; and in comment on the failure of negotiations with the Cherokees said that there was a better chance of succeeding with the Creeks.

CHAPTER 8

In the early winter of 1823–24, four men rode from the Cherokee Nation to Washington. A small delegation this time, the pick of the tribe. Oldest was Ridge, nearing sixty; then George Lowrey,[1] between forty-five and fifty, three parts Indian and one part white, with a fair English education; John Ross had passed his thirty-third birthday during the sessions of the October council; and the fourth was Elijah Hicks, not yet thirty, a half-blood of good education who had married Ross's sister Margaret. They were all moderns and well to do; they rode good stout horses, to buck the snowdrifts of mountain valleys; they were well dressed, even a bit elegantly considering the state of the roads; and they carried ample changes of linen along with copies of tribal documents. Ross was their leader and spokesman.

They rode on a novel mission. The time had come, Ross insisted after Meriwether and Campbell had departed, for the Cherokees to abandon their defensive attitude. They must show themselves aggressors in the fight to retain their homes. So far as the council had defined their instructions, the delegates were to demand from President Monroe relief from commissions asking land cessions and agitating for

54

removal. Also, they were to seek support in Congress for their cause. Lobbyists; certainly a new role for Indians![2]

On the weeks-long trip there was time for extended talks casting back over the history of the tribe and dissecting its problems.

The Indian has a special love and talent for sketching historical background in talk. Ridge, sitting before a fire in a private parlor of one of the "public stops," stooping now and then to take a live coal in his work-calloused fingers with which to light his small earthenware pipe with its long slender cane stem, would re-create old scenes, reanimate characters who had long ago passed from the scene.

There was the vanished Echota, on the Nolichucky River, once a town of refuge, identical in purpose with that of the three cities named by Moses on the east side of the river Jordan, to which "the slayer might flee which shall kill his neighbor unawares and hated him not in times past, and that fleeing into one of these cities he might live." Under the ancient Cherokee law, Echota was a sure asylum, for a time; but if in that time the slayer's family and clan could not make satisfactory settlement with the victim's people then the slayer must go out and meet the avengers. Ridge told how the doomed man would come forth, running and imitating the sound of a cock turkey, the "gobble-gobble!" of the lone fighting man . . .

They talked of the famous half-blood woman Ghigua, or Nancy Ward, known variously to their grandfathers as Beloved Woman, Pretty Woman, or Wise Woman. Her mother was a sister of that powerful, dapper little chief Attakullakulla, whose diplomacy, joined to Oconastata's war leadership, rendered the Cherokees the strongest tribe south of the Ohio; her father a British army officer. Nancy Ward had fought as a warrior beside her first husband, Kingfisher, taking the rifle from his dead hand. Because of this, and also because of her proved wisdom, she was given the power of life or death over those of her people charged with murder, and over captives. She was the only woman ever permitted to speak in council. "And," put in the practical Ross, "don't forget that it was she who first brought cows to the Cherokees!"[3]

A great figure, Nancy Ward, a matriarch of legend . . .

Back of known history and into the mists of tradition their talk swung; "The old people used to say that when the Cherokees came to this country they found moon-eyed people, unable to see in daylight; a kind of white people; some say Little People, maybe dwarfs. Nobody knows the truth." Major Ridge remembered that in his boyhood a legend was recited at the green-corn dance concerning the migration of the tribe from the place of the rising sun where lived huge snakes and water monsters . . .

They speculated on the tradition that the big earth mounds north of the Ohio had been raised by the Cherokees . . .

They discussed the rich store of tribal myths: How the earth, and the first people, were created, how fire was brought to man by the redbird, and those sad or comic Indian animal stories which were passed along from Cherokee-owned slaves to the negroes whose recitals were the source of Joel Chandler Harris's gorgeous tales . . .[4]

Ridge touched upon the history of inter-tribal wars, campaigns against the Wyandots and Delawares, who boasted that they had driven the Cherokees out of that land in the east. "Do you think they really did?" Ross asked, and Ridge answered in slow liquid Cherokee, "It might be so; I never heard an Indian say he was so stout but that some other fellow could not lick him!" No man, no people, was invincible; one might fight to the end, and after that—? It was an old man's thought, not one for Ross to hold . . .

They revived the dim story of De Soto's journey up from the sea and through the Cherokee towns in 1540, when his armored men were led over the Savannah trail by Cofitachiqui, captive Indian "queen."[5] At their first appearance, those gleaming white men frightened the people so that they fled into the mountains. They came back hesitantly, were friendly and helpful. "What," Ross asked, "were these small fat dogs the Cherokees were said to have given the Spaniards to eat? The dogs that didn't bark!" Ridge laughed, "They were 'possums, of course. The Spanish men got from our people turkeys also, and mulberries . . ."

"Do you know why that man De Soto came all that way to our

country?" Ross answered, "Yes, for gold! Thank God, he did not discover enough to tempt him to return." It had been a profitless venture, though some of the Spanish gold hunters had pushed as far west as the buffalo country, bringing home a dressed skin "as thin as a calf's hide and the hair a soft wool between the coarse and fine wool of a sheep" . . .

Down the years coasted their talk, to the coming in 1690 of Cornelius Dougherty, that adventuring Virginia Irishman who was the first white man to take a Cherokee wife and live with the tribe. Then came Sir Alexander Cummings, whose visit was induced by a dream vision of his English wife. A fine young swashbuckler was Cummings. Landing at Charleston, he got from a merchant, John Stewart, letters to the chiefs who traded with Stewart, and, in company with Ludovic Grant, a trader of Tellico, traveled to Keowee town and stopped with Joseph Baker, another Cherokee trader. A council was sitting at Keowee, to which Cummings invited himself; he attended bearing cutlass, rifle, and a pair of pistols in defiance of the rule that arms must not be brought into the council house. It was night, and the councilors sat around a big fire. Cummings announced himself, then proposed the King's health; and, he boasted in a letter home, "if any of the Indians had refused the toast, I would have taken a brand from the fire that burned in the middle of the room and set fire to the house. I would have guarded the door and put to death every one that endeavoured to make his escape, so that they might all have been consumed in the flames"![6]

Afterwards, Cummings grew to love the Cherokees, and in 1730 took a delegation of seven chiefs, "with the great tribal king's crown of five eagles's tails and four scalps" to his King in London. Of course, the Cherokees never had a king, but such hocus-pocus pleased the courtiers of George's court. "Maybe," taunted Ridge, grinning and turning to Ross, "they will call you king some day, if you go across the water!" . . .

In these evening firelight talks, Ridge and Lowrey with toddies and pipes and Ross and Hicks with neither because they were of the same mind with the missionaries concerning such indulgencies, the four reviewed the roll of the tribe's great men. Six generations back, these were the men sent to make peace with the Carolina colonists: Corani, Kalanu (The Raven), Tlanuwi (The Hawk), Nellawagitchie, Caunasaita of Keowee, and Canacaught (The Conjurer).[7] Twenty years later, in 1705, that peace was ruthlessly shattered by a Carolina governor who granted commissions to various adventurers "to set upon, assault, kill and destroy, and take captive" as many Indians as they possibly could. His savagery brought strong protests from the saner colonists, who complained to the king: "The trade for skins and furs, whereby we held our chief commerce with England is ruined, and turned into a trade of Indians or slave making, whereby the Indians to the south and west of us are already involved in blood and confusion." It was at that time the whites discovered the Cherokees never could be made slaves . . .

Guns had first come to the Cherokees in 1700; fifteen years later, they had enough guns and ammunition to hold raiding expeditions in check and to undertake counter raids. Then whole colonies came against them, to beat them to the ground and force new treaties, always involving land cessions.

They had been buffeted between the English and French, who pushed up from the original settlement at Biloxi, a purgatory that lasted for many years. They had learned to like the French better than the English: witness Priber, and Timberlake, a British officer, returning from a peace mission after the French and Indian war of 1754, said that he "found the Nation much attached to the French, who have the prudence, by familiar politeness—which costs but little and often does a great deal of good—and conforming themselves to their ways and temper, to conciliate the inclinations of all the Indians they are acquainted with, while the pride of our officers often disgusts them . . . They did not scruple to own to me that it was the trade alone that induced them to make peace with us." . . .[8]

So the talk went on, not only by wayside fireplaces but in their rooms at Brown's Hotel in Washington while waiting patiently for audiences with President Monroe and Calhoun. They discussed treaties. Treaties!

During the years of Ridge's manhood there had been twelve, each whittling off a slice of Cherokee territory: treaties signed at Hopewell, Holston, Philadelphia, four at Tellico, Washington, the Chickasaw Council House, the Cherokee Agency, and the last at Washington in 1819; they knew them by heart.

Treaties, war, and smallpox, like the plagues of Egypt, had devastated them. Ridge's grandfather had known the first terrible smallpox scourge of 1738, coming to the tribe across Carolina from a slave ship and killing nearly half of them. "Our people," said Ridge, "knew only that it was a strong sickness, and they treated it by taking steam baths in the sweat huts and then plunging into cold water! The medicine men could do nothing, and threw away their herbs. Ah, the wailing over the dead! Then those who wailed fell down. Sometimes the warriors did not die; they got well, but when they looked at their pitted faces in the looking glasses of springs they were ashamed and killed themselves; some blew out their brains, some cut their throats with knives, some fell upon sharp-pointed canes, and some were so mad they threw themselves into the fires and burned to death!"[9]

But it was not all talk and idling as they waited for appointments at Washington. Ridge, Lowrey, and Ross had friends there, as also in Baltimore, Philadelphia, New York, and Boston, whom it was important to see; and young Hicks was taken with them on those visits. They attended assemblies in hotel parlors, danced with congressmen's ladies in narrow skirts of satin, high-waisted bodices and elbow-length silk gloves so fine that a pair could be imported in the shell of an English walnut, with hair combed high, dainty ribbon-tied slippers, and all as fragrantly scented as a redbud thicket in spring. The Cherokee visitors, like the other men, wore blue tail-coats with gilt buttons, black knee breeches, fine stockings and pumps, ruffled shirts, chokers, and vast white cravats; carriage clothes!

On the floor of the House, with such friends as Edward Everett of Massachusetts, Bates of Maine, or Johns of Delaware, they saw ladies mingling with the congressmen during the intermissions and, while the sessions were on, leaning over the balcony railing to take oranges, sweetmeats, and notes from the ends of long poles thrust up by members. Congress had the color, if not the dignity, of a Great Council of the Cherokees!

The president would not see the Indian delegates; harassed by the insistent Georgians, half believing that removal, though unjust to the Cherokees and a confession of the bad faith of the government, was the only solution of their troubles, Monroe avoided an interview. He sent word to Ross that all business between the delegates and the United States must be conducted through the secretary of war. Calhoun himself, fair minded, was nevertheless weary of the arguments he would have to hear. They had been repeated so often! He received the four coldly, listened glumly to Ross's explanation that they had come to make clear once for all the tribe's determination never again to cede a foot of land.

Calhoun, reviving the twenty-year-old argument, pointed out that the United States was committed by the agreement with Georgia to remove Indians from that state; and he added the likewise familiar observation that it was incompatible with the American political theory to tolerate "the continued existence of a so-called Indian Nation within the limits of a State." Ross replied that the Indians certainly had the prior claim to their territory; and once again reminded the secretary of war that the United States had agreed to extinguish Indian titles in Georgia only when it could be done "peaceably and on reasonable terms."

Calhoun offered the west as a refuge from "annoying encroachments of civilization." Ross answered that the Cherokees did not want to flee civilization, but on the contrary, learn to adapt themselves to its requirements as soon as possible. "It is true," he said, "that we are not yet ready to abandon communal life and become tax-paying citizens of a State. But that time will soon come. We are moving forward rapidly—" and here the facts and statistics with which he was armed were wheeled into action.

Calhoun submitted the gist of the debate to Monroe, who forwarded copies of the document to the Georgia congressmen and the governor, George M. Troup, a wealthy planter who had been elected in the fall of 1823 on the issue of getting rid of the Indians.[10] The angry Georgians insisted that their congressmen protest against the United States's diplomatic interchanges with the Indians; such weakness would only result in fastening them more firmly than ever on Georgia soil. Governor Troup answered Calhoun, doubting that the memorial and arguments submitted by Ross were Indian productions, specifying:

"The last letter of the Cherokees to the Secretary of War contains internal evidence that it was never written by an Indian." Just how an Indian of Ross's education and background should write, Troup did not say, but he evidently shared Gilmer's belief that the Cherokees were mere savages. He pressed this point until Ross prepared an answer which was read in the House and published in the *National Intelligencer.*

"It is with unfeigned regret and pain we discover the sentiments which are expressed by the Governor of Georgia in his letters to the Secretary of War . . . We cannot but view the design of these letters as an attempt, bordering on a hostile disposition towards the Cherokees, to wrest from them by arbitrary means their just rights and liberties, the security of which is solemnly guaranteed to them by the United States . . . We assert, under the fullest authority, that all the sentiments expressed in relation to the disposition and determination of the Nation never again to cede another foot of land are positively the production and voice of the Nation; and what has been uttered by us in the communications which we have made to the Government since our arrival in this city is expressive of the true sentiments of the Nation agreeably to our instructions, and that not one word has been put in our mouths by a white man. Whilst we profess to be complimented by this blow at our intelligence, we cannot in justice allow it to pass without a flat contradiction. That 'last letter' and every other letter was not only written but dictated by an Indian."[11]

President Monroe finally decided to uphold the Cherokee contention, and sent a message to the Georgians in which he said that while he favored removal the very words of the government's agreement with

Georgia were a recognition of Indian titles. Removal was not incumbent on the government until it could be accomplished peaceably and on reasonable terms, a thing that at this time could not be done.

Representative John Forsyth[12] of Georgia took direct issue with the president. Repeating the accepted Georgian fiction that the Cherokees had only a right of occupancy, he declared that if the state could not now acquire the tribal territory within its borders peaceably then force must be used! If the United States would not apply that force, Georgia would. If the government chose to stand aside and see the Cherokees annihilated, and white citizens killed in the process, so much the worse for the government.

The lists were set: John Ross and some 17,000 Cherokees against the state of Georgia, with the embarrassed federal government wavering between the two.

CHAPTER 9

Considering her history, Georgia's attitude was surprising. Founded as a refuge for the persecuted and unfortunate of Europe by the great-hearted Oglethorpe, she had nevertheless in three generations become notable as an oppressor of the weak. From such stock as meek Salzburger Lutherans, Piedmontese Jews, indigent English, and drifting colonists from Carolina and Virginia, had been developed the truculent Troup, Gilmer, Forsyth, Lumpkin, and the land-greed citizenry of Georgia who endorsed their clamorous demands. These were epitomized by one "Atticus" who, in 1825, wrote an open letter to the people:

"What a miserable evasion is the excuse of the General Government for not complying with her contract, that . . . she had not seen the time in twenty-three years when it was in her power to effect it on 'reasonable and peaceful' terms! . . . There is not an honest man in the State who believes it. What! not able to fulfill a contract in twenty-three years! Do they not believe if Georgia had undertaken to extinguish the Indian title herself she would not have accomplished it in that time?" Indignant "Atticus" was undoubtedly right on that point.[1]

He went on to charge the Washington government with hypocritical tenderness towards the Indians, with attempting to hide its bad faith behind a "sweet-smelling savor of morality," with encouraging the Indians to improve their lands and thus hatch amongst them the notion of independence, and with encouraging that absurd Cherokee embassy whose head dared to break a quill with the secretary of war, "indulged by that dignified sage in the courtly humor of writing philippics against Georgia and mouthing a great deal about the arts and sciences, their dripping blood and the graves and bones of their fathers and all that pathetic nonsense."

As Ross's mandate of leadership became clearer—though old Pathkiller was chief, the Scotch Cherokee was looked to for guidance through the thorny maze of negotiations with Washington—the mass of opposition grew portentous. A rift had been made even in Ross's own family; his brother Andrew had been induced to sign the spurious treaty which Jackson took to Washington in 1817.

In May 1824, Georgia's congressmen obtained an appropriation for sending still another commission to negotiate the Cherokees out of the state. They would give the government one more chance to use diplomacy before Georgia troops took over the job! Governor Troup spoke the warning:

"A state of things so unnatural and fruitful of evil as an independent government of a semi-barbarous people existing within the limits of a State cannot long continue, and wise counsel must direct that relations which cannot be maintained in peace shall be dissolved before an occasion shall occur to break that peace."

He was preparing for the next step in his program.

Ross faced the enemy squarely; at the age of thirty-four, he was growing a bit more grim of face, ever more guarded in talk, voluminous but exact in writing; in the rich, resounding style he had learned from Mr. Davis and the public men of Washington, he sent out long letters packed with facts and arguments, building up a following of influential opinion in the east. His appeals to men like William Wirt, Chancellor Kent, and Senator Freylinghausen were widely published, as were his discussions of the necessary steps to be taken in blocking the removal campaign in Congress.[2]

He would come home from these battles in Washington wearied in body and sick of soul. Chicaneries, wire pulling, bad faith of politicians at the capital could but pile up discouragement. On the shifting sand of white men's promises he strove to erect the tower of refuge for his people that again and again crumbled. But at home he received a desperately needed heartening. Firm prop and intimate counselor was Quatie; caring for the children, superintending the plantation in his absence, giving support to school teachers and missionaries, she stood as a beloved symbol of the tribe.

So often she watched him ride out to this new sort of battle! Her warrior, on a stout horse pacing soberly down the tree-shaded drive, his solid back straight under the blue coat, hair slightly gray, the physical body fading to nothingness in the distance but the real man always a living presence in her heart. She understood his devotion to her, knew that she lived in him as verily as any healthily functioning organ of his body; had it been feasible, he would have taken her to Washington, to the dinners and assemblies, to visit at the houses of his friends in Baltimore, Philadelphia, New York, and Boston. Sometimes, intimately, she called him "Sonny," as though he were only another of her children; or again, with laughing lips, "Daddy," and in the seriousness of later years, "Chief."

Through his descriptions, she could follow him into the world of strangers where men were moved by oddly complicated motives and many women seemed to have no occupation beyond winning the attentions of men, displaying their charms, and inviting gallantries. And if they should attempt to cosset her man? Quatie knew how he would question them with a glance, speak a rather pompous, guarded sentence, abash them with the smiling shrug she had seen him use.

When the two were together how life was quickened! All that was seen, heard, and felt had a magnified significance, even the children's chatter at the long family dining table, or the mere barking of dogs chasing foxes through the timber. They were two wise, happy, trustworthy people. As the load on Ross's shoulders grew heavier he bore it with something of a swagger because of the fine confidence of his wife and others near him. Quatie was a strong woman, quite as capable as Nancy Ward had been to stand beside her warrior to the end; and this is exactly what she did!

Troup pressed steadily to clear Georgia of its Indian population. His first overt act was to request the legislature to pass a law excluding from the Cherokee country, which he persisted in describing as Georgia territory, every white inhabitant not specifically authorized to remain there by either the state or federal government. By this move he meant to get rid of the missionaries, teachers, craftsmen, printers, and the rest, who were not only practical helpers of the Cherokees on the road to civilization but their strong partisans in the struggle to save their homeland.

The missionaries were most objectionable, for they knew the Indians best and were most firmly rooted in their confidence. From their eleven stations, in 1825, the workers of the American Board, the Moravians, and the Presbyterians journeyed all over the Nation. With Worcester helping at the tribal printing shop, supervising not only the issue of religious tracts but Ross's letters and the pro-Cherokee writings of eminent men in the east, and with men like Elizur Butler and Butrick preaching, teaching, and carrying on by personal example a flaming crusade of individual and tribal betterment, the Georgians' fear that if civilized the Indians would be more firmly than ever fixed to the soil demanded drastic action. White teachers like Isaac Proctor, and the printer Harris, too, must be got rid of.[3]

Troup meant to drive them out; and it would also be desirable, he told the legislature, to extend the state's laws over the Cherokee Nation.

Troup sent surveyors into the Nation to lay off the route of a proposed canal. They were turned back by order of the Cherokee Council which, in Ross's words, declared that "no individual State shall be allowed to make internal improvements within the sovereign limits of the Nation." A bold defiance, but Troup, who was for the moment intent upon the simpler problem of getting rid of the Creeks and Seminoles, allowed the Cherokee case to hang fire.[4]

Ross farther met the new Georgia offensive with a move he had planned in 1823–24 in the talks with Ridge, Lowrey, Hicks, and white friends of the east. This was the adoption by the Nation of a modern constitution. Before the assembled council of 1826, he reviewed tribal progress: farming, fruit growing, and stock raising occupied practically every family; cotton, wheat, oats, and corn were plentiful—hog buyers of Georgia following their slow droves up through the Cherokee country to shipping points on the Tennessee River everywhere found ample supplies of corn for sale. The Chero-kee were exporting cotton to New Orleans in their own boats, and their live stock were being sold in Georgia and Tennessee markets. Their blacksmiths, carpenters, and silversmiths were busy at their trades. They were operating sixteen saw mills, thirty-one grist mills, and eight cotton gins.

Accompanying this material wellbeing were the rapidly multiplying schools and churches, some with native teachers and ministers. The Nation would be ready shortly for the projected Cherokee Academy, National Library, and Museum; in one district alone there were upwards of a thousand good books, and eleven periodicals were subscribed for and read. Everywhere was order, respect for tribal laws. The next step must be the modern constitution.

The call therefore went out for the convention to meet at New Echota in July 1827, signed by Ross and Ridge and approved by Chief Pathkiller. Detailed instructions for choosing delegates were issued: at each of three precincts in each of the eight districts all "free and full-grown male citizens" would choose ten candidates; and this primary was to be followed by a balloting for three from among the ten.

Under the spur of the tireless Ross and his progressive associates, the election was held in proper order, with clerks to record the votes.

In Chickamauga District the primary named as candidates Ross himself, Richard Taylor, John Baldridge, James Brown, Sleeping Rabbit, John Benge, Nat Hicks, Sicketowee, James Starr, and Daniel McCoy.[5] Then at the designated precinct polling places,[6] the voters chose Ross, Baldridge, and Sleeping Rabbit to be their voices in the convention. In the remaining seven districts, similar procedure sifted the names of the other twenty-one delegates from the seventy candidates.

So there met at New Echota, in the month when, during Ross's boyhood, the green-corn dance had been held, three trusted men each from the districts of Chickamauga, Chatooga, Coosawatee, Amohe, Hickory, Etowah, Taquoe, and Aquohee; full-bloods and mixed-bloods; among them were Ooclenota, Situwakee, Kelechulee, Deer-in-Water, The Tough, Sour John, Chips, Soguwakee, two of the Vanns, three Ross brothers, Walker, Duncan, Timson, Gunter, Downing.[7]

Between the time of calling the convention and its assembling, Pathkiller died, Charles Hicks succeeded him for a brief two weeks before his own death, whereupon the office of chief fell jointly to Ross, president of the National Committee, and Ridge, speaker of the council. A young man and an old man, mixed-blood and full-blood, but both walking in the path of progress. Ross was chosen president of the convention.

A momentous hour! The tribe's challenge to those who called them savages.

Businesslike regulations governing the sessions were adopted; a warning bugle would be blown, and fifteen minutes later the delegates were to be in their places. The organization completed, Ross proposed the Constitution of the United States as model, changed where required to meet local needs. The preamble of the adapted charter was a defiance of Georgia's claims.

"We, the Cherokee people, constituting one of the sovereign and independent nations of the earth and having jurisdiction over its territory to the exclusion of the authority of any other State, do ordain this Constitution."

Under it, the existing executive and legislative organization was continued: a Principal Chief and Second, or Assistant, Chief; a National Committee of two members from each district; and a National Council of three from each district. The tribal judiciary system was enlarged to include a supreme court as well as district courts; and district police organizations were strengthened.

Land was to remain communal property, improvements thereon only to be recognized as individual wealth. White men married to Cherokee women were given every right of Indian citizenship except that of holding office. Missionary influence was revealed in the article, "No person who denies the being of God, or a future state of rewards and punishments, shall hold any office in the civil department of this Nation." On the other hand, no preacher could hold the office of Principal Chief, or sit as a member of the General Council.

If approved by the people, the new constitution was to become effective on October 1, 1828, the beginning of the traditional Cherokee new year. It was so approved in a popular referendum three weeks after the convention adjourned.

This answer to the Georgians who persisted in calling the Cherokees a semi-barbarous people provoked a curious rebuttal from Troup and his legal advisers: They cited Article IV of the Constitution of the United States providing that "new States may be admitted by the Congress into this Union, but no new State shall be formed or erected within the jurisdiction of any other State . . . without the consent of the State concerned as well as of the Congress." Upholding the thesis that Georgia had lawful jurisdiction over Cherokee territory, they denied the right of the Cherokees to form a government within the limits of Georgia. The flaw in this reasoning being that Georgia had no proper claims to jurisdiction over the tribe or the Cherokee lands.

So earnestly did Georgia press the point, however, that the House of Representatives asked the Judiciary Committee and the Committee on Indian Affairs to inquire into the legality of the "Cherokee Republic." Also, a fresh appropriation of $50,000 was voted for another effort to remove the Indians from Georgia.

Removal propaganda, stimulated anew by agents financed by this appropriation, resulted in a brief rebellion against the new Constitution and the modernism it implied amongst the remaining Cherokee reactionaries; these "red sticks," led by old Chief Whitepath, agitated for the rejection of the white man's ways, his religion and laws, a return to ancient tribal customs, and flight west. It was a vain, rather pathetic gesture. It could but fail; under Ross and other progressives, the Cherokees had come too far along the destined path to be turned back by the fanatics. Whitepath's following soon dropped away.

News of the constitution making went out to the world, arousing an extraordinary amount of interest and comment. Letters picturing life in the Nation written by men and women allied to the tribe were circulated far and wide. Harriet Gold, the Cornwall, Connecticut, girl who had defied her family and the wrath of the community by marrying young Boudinot and going with him to his home and job as editor of the *Cherokee Phoenix*, wrote home:

"My dear husband is all that I could wish him to be, and my sisters need not think it is saying anything against their husbands to say that I have excelled them all!" Later, her father, Judge Gold, drove with his wife from Connecticut to New Echota to visit Harriet and his son-in-law, and reported to his brother that he found them living in a "large and convenient framed house, two storeys, 30 by 40 feet on the ground, well done and well furnished with the comforts of life. They get their supplies of groceries, teas, clothes, paper, ink, etc. from Boston, and their sugar, molasses, etc. from Augusta. They have 2 or 3 barrels of flour on hand at once."[8]

Judge Gold visited many parts of the Nation and became acquainted with most of the leading families. He and his wife were guests of Lewis Ross and Joseph Vann; he described Ross's house as an elegant white-painted structure "as neatly furnished as almost any in Litchfield County, Connecticut," and said that Mr. Vann had "about six or seven hundred acres of the best land you ever saw and negroes enough to manage it and clear as much more as he pleases; raised this year about 5,000 bushels of corn, and it would make you feel small to see his situation!"

There were two tiny granddaughters, whom Mrs. Gold described as "handsomer than any children I have seen in the north . . . Harriet says she has never yet seen the time she regretted coming here . . . that she envies the situation of no one in Connecticut."

The Golds were at New Echota during the nearly three weeks of the fall council, "a truly interesting and pleasant place," laid out on a level stretch of valley in one hundred lots of one acre each with a public spring in the center "twice as large as our Sawmill brook." From the door of his daughter's house, Judge Gold could see six new frame dwellings and the council house. Besides, there were the new and convenient *Phoenix* printing shop, one permanent store, and three others opened to accommodate the people attending the council. "The stores in the Nation," the Yankee visitor wrote, "are as large as the best in Litchfield County, their wagons of 6 horses go to Augusta and bring great loads . . . I have seen 11 of them pass Mr. Boudinot's house in company."

In his son-in-law's home, the judge met "much good company," and learned that Boudinot "is as much respected as any man of his age." His paper, too, "is respected all over the United States, and is known in Europe; he has about 100 newspapers sent him from the different parts of the United States by way of exchange, so you perceive we have an interesting stand, where we have the news from all quarters of the globe."

Judge Gold called at the home of Major Ridge's son John, that other full-blood youth who had studied at the Cornwall school and brought away from Connecticut as bride Mrs. Northrop's daughter, the marriage inspiring a local rhymester to this disparaging comment:

> The reverend Vaill we would not blame—
> On Sabbath next he published them;
> But reverend Smith feared not the law—
> He married this lady to be a squaw![9]

The Golds found John Ridge's "squaw" well content with her lot; her husband "is clerk of the Cherokee Council, and is now serving as clerk of a Creek delegation to Congress for the winter, and will likely get his five or six thousand dollars, as he did before."

John Ross, leader and exemplar of the tribe, the Golds did not see, for he was in Washington with a delegation battling as always against the forces of removal.

CHAPTER 10

Ross now became Principal Chief. He was chosen at the election of 1828 and appropriately assumed the duties of the office at the time the new Constitution went into effect. He had triumphed six to one over his opponent, William Hicks, who had been seen too often in the company of agents of the United States and Georgians engaged in removal activity, to hold the confidence of responsible men of the tribe.[1]

Head of the Nation in both name and fact, Ross stood as though stripped and armed for battle, cool, practical, confident. He had been successful both as merchant and planter; near the tribal capital, New Echota, he had his big two-story house; his slaves worked wide and expanding fields. As a leader he had proved himself by years of effective service. His shrewd common sense, his laconic but convincing speech, the immense forward strides the people had made in the ten years since he was condemned to "purgatory" by Judge Brown and his fellow committeemen, testified to the far-sighted wisdom of his actions. He had visualized a prosperous and happy Indian republic, and believed passionately that it was not an idle dream, but a demonstrable reality.

The one great danger threatening it was Georgia's hostility, but, having justice on his side, Ross felt certain of ultimate victory.

Past thirty-eight years of age, he was still on the rising curve of physical and mental vigor. He was graver in manner than ever before, not pompous but notably dignified; he was more meticulous in dress than ever, as fastidious about his linen as any aristocrat he met.

But he was also the dreamer and, like Priber, able to capture the Indians' imagination; in him his people sensed the humble seeker within his own soul for the truth; the questioning line of the brow, the gray-blue eyes asking confidence and deepening at times in wistful musings, the idealism reflected in the sensitive and slightly parted lips, all had significance to them. Women liked him. They talked to him in Cherokee without restraint, as to a brother; and he answered them seriously, for the women were important in tribal affairs, had always been so.

A few weeks after Ross was made chief, Andrew Jackson was elected president.

Bad news for the Cherokees, remembering the spurious treaty he negotiated in 1817. Good news for Georgia, however; and her legislature promptly enacted two measures intended to paralyze the Cherokee government. By the first, all tribal land in Georgia was annexed to certain northern counties, while the second extended the State's laws over the Cherokees after June 1, 1830. By now Gilmer had succeeded to the Governorship, following Forsyth and Troup. These three, together with Wilson Lumpkin, who was presently to succeed Gilmer both as congressman and governor, pursued the task of hounding the Indians with unremitting zeal. They were serving their state's interests, they were playing good politics, and perhaps they hoped that exile would be really good for the Indians. At any rate, with Jackson in the White House, they felt that the consummation of their efforts could not long be delayed.

Before the Georgia legislation should become effective, Ross called a General Council, which declared the state's laws invalid. The people approved a memorial which Ross prepared, protesting to the retiring president, John Quincy Adams, against Georgia's claims and contrasting them with the declaration in the state's Constitution of a belief in liberty and the rights of man. The memorial restated the old arguments and recalled old guarantees by the United States.

Once more Ross headed a delegation to Washington, hoping to secure from Adams a relief from Georgia's oppression that it would be more difficult to get from Jackson. He was put off with evasive words, for Adams had no intention of taking up the vexed question in the last days of his administration.

On the remote chance that the new government might help them, the delegation lingered on to watch "Old Hickory" ride to the Capitol and hear him promise in his inaugural address to observe towards the Indians a just and liberal policy and give such humane and considerate attention to their rights and needs as was "consistent with the habits of our Government and the feelings of the people." Those final thirteen words were menacing to the Cherokees, but immensely heartening to the Georgians.

More than a month passed before Ross could secure an interview even with the new secretary of war, Major Eaton; Jackson flatly refused to see him. Speaking for the president, Eaton said that he could promise a reservation in the west where the Cherokees would be undisturbed "as long as trees grow and water runs"—the same old promise in the same old words. Ross had once again to listen to the stage-Indian talk loosed upon feathered chiefs: "If you will go to the land of the setting sun, my brothers, you will be happy; there you can remain forever in peace and quietness." Hunt the wild deer, be sons of the forest, et cetera.

Ross pertinently cited the serious troubles of those Cherokees who had already moved west in response to the government's urging and promises: repeated clashes with the aggrieved Osages, increasing intrusion of white settlers, and already one enforced removal from their original reservation in Arkansas, just as they had got well started in the development of homes, farms, orchards, and herds. The promised "peace and quietness" had passed utterly delusive, the pledge of eternal tenure had not held for twenty years!

Ross's facts and arguments made not the least impression on the new administration, nor did the prayers and pleadings of the Cherokees' powerful friends in and out of Congress. In this particular, Andrew was certainly the original "Stonewall" Jackson!

The delegation came home in May 1828.[2] Ross called a special session of the General Council, presented the report of their failure, and drew up still another memorial—this one to Congress, asking protection from the threat of Georgia's new laws.

Jackson's attitude presented a perfect reflection of the opinions of Troup, Forsyth, Gilmer, and Lumpkin. Like Gilmer, Lumpkin in his old age published his autobiography. Concerning his role in the tragedy of the Cherokees, he declared "in the presence of Almighty God and before all mankind" that he had felt himself justified. His acts were based on this profession of faith:

"I believe the earth was formed especially for the cultivation of the ground, and none but civilized men will cultivate the earth to any great extent . . . Therefore I do not believe a savage race of heathens found in the occupancy of a large and fertile domain of country have any exclusive right to [the] same from merely having seen it in the chase, or having viewed it from the mountain top.[3]

"Wherever a wild and savage race becomes so far reduced by a civilized people as to be considered subdued and unable to contend in battle with a [the] Christian nation, immediately it becomes the duty of the superior race to look upon the inferior as children—minors—[and] incapable of protecting and providing for themselves; and consequently, [that] benevolence, humanity and religion require the superior, with unanimity [magnanimity] and liberality, to take these *orphans* [*and minors*] by the hand, and do them all the good that the circumstances will allow."

Do them good!

It is pertinent, for the proper understanding of this remarkable statement, to inquire into the Lumpkin works as illustrating the Lumpkin faith:

In the most troubled period of Cherokee history, from 1827 to 1840, this eminent citizen of Georgia spent four years as a representative in Congress, four years as governor, eighteen months as an eight-dollar-a-day agent of the United States for effecting Cherokee removal, and finally as United States senator helping to foil the desperate efforts of Ross to halt the exodus of his people.

"I frankly admit," he wrote, "that my plan was, from the beginning, not to be '*palsied*' by the will of the Indians. I resolved upon carrying into effect such measures as I believed to be best for the happiness and welfare of these people whom I viewed comparatively as children, not competent to judge and decide on the measures best calculated to promote their interest." He contended that "all the intelligent Cherokees, except Ross and those under his influence" agreed with his judgment. That was perhaps true, but then Ross and "those under his influence" constituted ninety per cent of the Nation!

Lumpkin's estimate of Ross is a curious tribute: "From my first acquaintance . . . I was sensible of his superior cultivation and intellectual advantages. He is a well educated man—converses well, writes well, and is a man of soft, easy, gentlemanly manners, rather retiring and reserved; seldom speaks unadvisedly. In all the common duties and intercourses of life, he has always maintained a good moral character. His position in life, from first to last, has afforded him every facility to gain information and add to his stock of knowledge."[4]

Lumpkin actually knew so little about the Cherokees that he wrote of the chief as a king; he thought there was a hereditary succession of kings which Ross had broken, and that he maintained himself by merely seeming to obey the will of the people while imposing upon them his own desires, and by the corrupt use of money. This last charge was merely fantastic, considering that the entire tribal income, derived as it was from annuity payments, was only $6,667 a year, that former Attorney General Wirt and the eminent lawyer John Sergeant were fighting the Cherokee battle through the Supreme Court of the United States for retainers of but $200 each, and Chancellor Kent was preparing his exhaustive opinion in support of their arguments for a fee of $50. Wirt, Sergeant, and Kent, incidentally, were described by Lumpkin as Ross's "fee-d stipendiaries."[5]

He continued: "I pity the ignorance of good men who feel as if they were doing God's service while they are writing and publishing eulogies on the character of John Ross . . . If he could have shared the fate of Haman, or have been banished to New England, Hayti, or anywhere else where the Cherokees could have been relieved from the curse of his presence and influence, [they would have been fifty per cent better off than at present]."[6]

Unfortunately, Lumpkin was a thorough representative of Georgia opinion; to the strong was given the right to subdue the weak, and upon the strong God had conferred the mandate to treat the victims as seemed in their opinion best. No legal quibbling over justice or titles for the Lumpkin men!

Then was revealed the most powerful of all reasons for getting rid of the Cherokees: white prospectors, intruders upon the tribal lands from Georgia, discovered gold!

This precipitated, as gold discoveries have always done, a mad scramble. Ward's creek, flowing into the Chestatee River from the Cherokee country, came alive with camps, provisioned by pack trains grub-and-tool-laden; pick men, pack peddlers, whiskey sellers swarmed in; the rifle and shovel stood side by side in the hastily built brush and bark shelters; in the light of log fires, bearded and sweat-sour men gathered after dark to reaffirm their right under Georgia law to stake claims; they went further, and denied the right of the Cherokees to work their own gold field: "By God, it's Georgy land, an' the Injuns ain't got no proper claim to it!"

So settling that matter to their own satisfaction, they passed the whiskey jug, roaring forth a song popular with the Georgia guardsmen, those hard fisted state troopers who were eager to drive the Indians out and, if necessary, defy the federal government in so doing:

> A man whose name was Johnny Sands
> He married Betsy Meg.
> Although she brought him house and lands
> She proved a cruel Peg!

This was in the late summer of 1829. Gilmer was governor and, while the Georgia law was not to be extended over the Cherokee Nation until June 1, 1830, he issued a warning to all, whites and Cherokees alike, against taking gold from the land, sending companies of the guard to enforce the decree. The whites, understanding the governor's intentions, paid no attention to the warning and remained at work undisturbed, but any Cherokees, many of whom were as eager as the whites in the search for gold, who followed this example, were arrested and taken away in chains.

Ross promptly sought protection for them. The United States agent, agreeing that the white miners were unlawfully intruding, sent federal troops to Ward's creek. But when their commander found that he would have to fight both the miners and the Georgia guard in order to clear the field he simply refused to act. His refusal is understandable: there were more than three thousand miners, while Georgia guard itself outnumbered his force, and President Jackson was definitely committed to the theory that the state was sovereign over all lands lying within its mapped boundaries. Yet Pathkiller and other Cherokees, less than ten years before, had heard the same Andrew Jackson say: "Friends and brothers, I have never told a red brother a lie nor deceived him. The intruders on your land, if they return, will be sent off. If you cannot keep intruders from your lands, report it to the agent, and on his notice I will drive them from your lands."

But now? According to the present Jackson, the Cherokees were the intruders on Georgia land!

CHAPTER 11

Jackson against Ross. The powerful, harsh-willed president of the United States against a soft-spoken little Highland-Cherokee, chief of some 17,000 Indians. Hard steel against steadfast diplomacy. A red-headed, ruthless realist opposed by a God-fearing zealot whose heart and soul were wholly pledged to battle for his people. Impatience, quick fury, matched against cool, persistent demands for rights plainly guaranteed by "solemn" treaty; violent demands upon Congress for removal met by long, closely reasoned memorials and protests which continued to acquaint the world with the *facts*.

A difficult, unequal struggle. Ross must confront both Jackson and the harrying forces of Georgia. He must hearten his own people. He must eke out the pitifully small funds in the Cherokee treasury to retain lawyers—not only Wirt, Sergeant, and Kent, but local counsel to defend Indians arrested and imprisoned by Georgia sheriffs; and he must use every resource of propaganda to build up throughout the United States and in Congress a reserve of pro-Cherokee sentiment strong enough to save his Nation.

Ross had come home from Washington in May 1829, after the fruit-less efforts to get to Jackson and the cool reception by Secretary of War Eaton, to plan with his council further steps for saving the Cherokees from the impending Georgia laws. On his heels, Jackson sent General William Carroll, candidate for governor of Tennessee, as a secret emissary to stimulate removal sentiment. Carroll was instructed to conceal his official character from the Cherokees, and win converts by distributing presents to the children of the head men and to the chiefs, and to pay out money (but not more than $2,000!) to the poor-est Indians. By such means it was hoped he would gain a following in the tribe that would enable him, later, to negotiate a treaty with them.[1]

It proved a futile gesture. By the fall, Carroll reported that his mission was hopeless; the Cherokees were too intelligent, "too well posted on current news of the day," to be kept in ignorance of his real purpose or to be won over by the childish methods he had been instructed to use. He also reported that the tribe had advanced far towards the white standard of civilization and that they had been encouraged, by reading extracts from eastern newspapers reprinted in the *Cherokee Phoenix*, to believe that at the next session of Congress they would get relief from Georgia's encroachments.

When Congress met in December, Jackson at once sent in a message urging removal legislation, contending that by remaining in Georgia the Cherokees were flouting the rights of a sovereign state. Regard-ing the new Cherokee constitution, he asserted that this attempt to establish an independent government within the limits of a state could not be countenanced.

The tone of the message was belligerent. Instantly the friends of Ross both in and out of Congress took up its challenge. For three weeks it was the principal theme of Senate discussion. Sprague of Maine, Asher Robbins of Rhode Island, with other anti-Jackson Sen-ators, joined Freylinghausen in upholding the Cherokees against Forsyth of Georgia, White of Tennessee, and McKinley of Alabama, who appealed to sectional prejudice and defended Georgia's course

on the states' rights theory. In the House, Storrs of New York and
Bates of Maine faced Lamar and Lumpkin. Afire with indignation,
Storrs exposed the hypocrisy of those who pretended that removal
from comfortable homes, cultivated fields, schools, and churches to
a wilderness threatened by warlike tribes would be a blessing to the
Cherokees. He scourged Jackson for presuming to tell Congress what
it could do, and for seeking to annul treaties which he himself had
helped to negotiate.[2]

Protest memorials poured in upon Congress from scores of public meetings and individuals: Governor Knight of Rhode Island; the
citizens of Delaware in mass meeting at Wilmington; the people of
Brown County, Ohio; those of Maine; Burlington County, Rahway, and
Woodbridge, in New Jersey sent numerously signed petitions; the ladies
of Pennsylvania forwarded a huge memorial, supplementing that of
the inhabitants of Pittsburgh; Henry Clay spoke and wrote in behalf
of the Cherokees; John Sergeant's hot denunciation of the repeated
wholesale spoliation of the tribe was widely printed, as was the speech
of Edmund Pendleton of New York supporting the memorial of the
citizens of Duchess County, and Wirt's opinion on the illegality of the
Georgia laws. It was a flood, loosed by Ross's persistent and convincing
propaganda, and it seemed vast enough for a time to overwhelm even
the whip-cracking president and force Congress to decisive action.

Georgia's representatives in Congress raved, shouted that the state
was being grossly misrepresented and vilified; she was "the evening
chant and the matin song of all calumniators in the Union, who
have taken the Cherokees into their holy keeping"; "no epithet is too
strong, no reproach too foul to cast upon her for having followed the
example of ten other States in the exercise of jurisdiction over the
Indians within their territory."

The fact that by Georgia's agreement with the United States the
Cherokee lands could not be annexed until the federal government
succeeded in extinguishing Indian titles "peaceably and on reasonable
terms," carried no weight with the Georgia congressmen.

From the people of Georgia came the charge that this wave of

sympathy for the Cherokees was due to northern fanatics and "pretended philanthropists paid for their services out of the Cherokee
treasury." A widow's curse indeed that meager treasury must needs
have been to meet all the expenses of the tribal government, of lawyers,
and of delegations to Washington, as well as to corrupt scores of hundreds of "pretended philanthropists" who were fighting for the tribe!

But the charge, absurd as it was, gave Jackson an idea: the tribal
income was derived from annuities, granted in exchange for land
ceded by treaty; could a means be found of stopping its flow into the
Cherokee treasury, tribal resistance would certainly be weakened. He
hit on a simple expedient: in the future $6,667 due annually to the
eastern Cherokees should be paid not to the tribe, but to individuals—
which would mean less than forty cents to each!

Now let John Ross find the money to bring delegations to Washington, fee lawyers, print and distribute the pestiferous *Cherokee Phoenix.*
Jackson swore he'd be damned if he would continue to break sticks
for Ross to beat him over the head with!

Ross's whole time was not, of course, spent in stern grappling with
Jackson and the Georgians. He worked at his job as chief with diligence
and conscience, putting it even before the demands of his personal
life. The council of 1828, for instance, passed an act revising the law
governing permits for whites to reside and work in the Nation. In
regular course, it was submitted to Chief Ross for approval or rejection. He had just finished reading it when a slave came to him from
Quatie to say that their last-born child was mortally ill. Ross quivered,
shrank before the tired messenger momentarily, then: "Sit down, rest
yourself; I must write a note before I go back with you."

The note was a brief memorandum to the council, "I cannot approve
this Act; my reasons I will communicate later. I have just been called
to the bedside of my infant child who, I fear, is dying."

Then, on the day after the baby's death, with Quatie silent beside
him for the comfort of his strength, he wrote out this careful veto
message:

"My disapproval is dictated by a sense of justice and equity . . . The law ought not arbitrarily to fix the penalty for failure to secure the required permit; that ought to be left for the courts to determine, for it might often happen that whites would secure temporary employment in the Nation without violating the spirit of our law, owing to the many public roads leading through our country which are daily traveled by citizens of the United States, as well as from the connections which exist between our respective citizens by marriage or by employment . . .

"We will suppose, for example, a family of poor white people traveling along our public roads who should meet with sickness, lose a horse, or encounter some other of the misfortunes to which the human family is subject, so as to compel them to stop a day or two. One of our people finding amongst them a blacksmith, a shoemaker, or some other mechanic, and they being in want of means to get fodder for the horses or a little meat for a suffering family, in order to help such a man employs him to mend a hoe or an axe or make a pair of shoes. Then some vicious neighbor returns this same kind hearted citizen of ours to court for the offense! . . .

"Our law should be founded upon reason and the principles of justice, to suit the convenience of our citizens and the interests of our Nation."

This message, chore of a day in the life of the chief, with its flavor of King James Bible language, is a fair statement of Ross's creed. Reason, justice, equity, the welfare of the people: firm stones on which to build a career!

The council, acknowledging the force of the objections, amended the act. Again he sent it back for revision before approval; he must have not merely good laws but the best that could be wrought.[3]

Tribal records show him attentive to even the smallest problem. One day an aggrieved group bearing the names of Captain Sitting Down, Allbone, Teesunooske, and Hogshooter came to claim pay for their services as tribal police during the year 1821, long past. Ross was able to dig into the records, show them that their engagement had ended with the preceding year, and send them away satisfied. Again, a dispute between neighbors over the boundary between their improvements was brought to the chief, rather than to a court for settlement. Janey Wolf, a widow, with a grievance against two married daughters who wrongfully claimed title to two slave women loaned by Janey, found Ross attentive to her story and sympathetic with her statement. "I am willing to let my daughters keep the women, but I want it so that their increase will be mine, for I do not want to become altogether dependent on my children."

He had enormous patience, loved the semi-Oriental Cadi-like character of his position, was excusably vain of his encyclopedic knowledge of the Cherokees and their affairs, and was completely identified in body, mind, and soul with his Indians. Yet it was said in Georgia that he was without a trace of Indian blood, that he had usurped his power, and used it to enrich himself. Benjamin F. Currey,[4] an unscrupulous special removal agent for the United States, echoed the falsehood in a confidential report to Washington: "He votes at the State elections and acts as chief at Indian councils. He holds rich and valuable reservations within the ceded territory and encroaches with impunity on the agency reservation, where, by the use of his wealth and keeping up a constant system of espionage through the unsuspecting confidence reposed in him by his boarders [Currey meant visitors to his home], he is able to shape the course of nearly all on whom I have to rely in cases of pressing emergency."

So persistent grew the misrepresentations of the Indian character of Ross and the Cherokee legislature that at last the missionaries decided to prepare a detailed report of the facts. Eleven men met: Butrick, Chamberlain, Worcester, Thompson, Butler, Proctor, Ellsworth, and Holland of the American Board; Byhan and Clauder of the United Brethren; and Evan Jones, a Baptist. They named the officers and lawmakers of the Nation and the percentage of Cherokee blood in each; Chief Ross, one-eighth; Major Lowrey, second chief, one-half; Major Ridge and Goingsnake,[5] respectively president of the National Committee and Council, full-bloods; of the sixteen members of the committee, two were full-bloods, seven half-bloods, and seven less than half Indian; sixteen of the twenty-four who sat in the council were full-bloods, seven were half-bloods, and one a quarter-blood.

"The disposal of office," ran the missionaries' report, "is in the hands of the people; the people require patriotism, and the touchstone of patriotism is, 'Will he sell his country?'" In all meetings of the Cherokees, whether in legislative council or general council of the people, full freedom of speech was maintained.

As justifying their rights to report on the facts, these workers explained: "We occupy eleven stations in different parts of the country, one in that part which is considered to have made the least progress in civilization."

Practically every field, they said, was cultivated by the plough. Thanks to Ross's urging and the increasing number of sawmills, every house and cabin was floored with boards. Nearly all the old superstitions, primitive medicine men practices, polygamy, even old habits of dress, had been discarded. While some Indians drank to excess, strictly enforced tribal law made the neighborhood of council grounds and court houses in term time far soberer than were such places among the whites. A hastily compiled list showed more than 200 Cherokee men sufficiently educated in English to transact ordinary business with whites, 132 of them having acquired all of their schooling in the Nation. Certainly more than half of the tribe could read and write Cherokee. Intermarriage had been going on for so long a time that descendants of whites were to be found of the sixth generation. More than 700 Cherokees had been received as members of their churches.

Rather a different picture, this, from Lumpkin's: "A savage race of heathens" basing their claim to their domain on having "seen it in the chase, or having viewed it from the mountain top"!

Removal, insisted the missionaries, would be disastrous. If Georgia should extend her laws over the Cherokees, enforce them, and nullify tribal laws, "some would seek a refuge beyond the boundaries of the United States," but the greater part would stay and endure; and "hard is the task of the philanthropist who would attempt to elevate, or even to sustain, the character of a broken hearted people!"

In an individual report, Worcester wrote: "It is said abroad that the common people would gladly remove, but are deterred by the chiefs and a few other influential men. It is not so. I say, with the utmost assurance, it is not so. Nothing is plainer than that it is the earnest wish of the whole body of the people to remain where they are. They are not overawed by their chiefs. Individuals may be overawed by popular opinion, but not by the chiefs. On the contrary, if there were a chief in favor of removal, he would be overawed by the people . . . The whole tide of national feeling sets, in one strong unbroken current, against removal to the west."[6]

The missionaries were right in saying that the Cherokees had free speech. They had always had it. A solitary Cherokee delegate was brought into the presence of Governor Oglethorpe of the Georgia colony in the days of the tribe's first contact with the colonists. "Fear nothing," said Oglethorpe with a protective gesture, "but speak freely."

"Why do you say that!" the Indian retorted, astonished. "I always speak freely; why should I be afraid?"

It was just as true in Ross's time as in the days of Oglethorpe that when they were dissatisfied they spoke out clearly and fearlessly. Ross never wielded any power over his people that was not granted freely as a tribute to his devotion and sound sense.

CHAPTER 12

While the struggle against Georgia was at its crisis, John Ross's father died. A wise man, a sound counselor, Daniel Ross; even Lumpkin admitted that he was "very shrewd and sensible, of good education . . . and understood the Indian character perfectly."[1] To his son John, he had been a solid rock of refuge. The two had always been uncommonly close, loving and trusting one another, proud of one another, fiercely and unquestionably loyal to one another. The breaking by death of that strong tie was hard to bear; mercifully, the son was engaged to the limit of his power in the battle for the salvation of the tribe amongst whom the father had lived prosperously and happily for almost fifty years.

With Wirt and Sergeant, he was pushing the trial of an injunction proceeding in the Supreme Court of the United States against the application of Georgia's laws to the Cherokee country. He was assisting Chancellor Kent in preparing his opinion in support of the argument against the constitutionality of those laws, "which had no other purpose than the annihilation of the rights guaranteed to the Cherokees by treaty." Wirt's bitter warning that if the Supreme Court should refuse relief the Cherokees must look to some other quarter, "though to what other quarter on this earth they can look with any shadow of hope God only knows!" expressed Ross's own conviction.[2]

To the claim that the tribe's lands lay within the chartered limits of Georgia and were therefore subject to her jurisdiction, Wirt echoed Ross's retort: "They lie exactly where they have lain for a time long antecedent to the existence of that State and, very probably, long antecedent to the existence of the monarchy from which that State derived its charter." Sergeant, with the facts supplied by Ross before him, told the Court that Georgia's legislation made outlaws of the Cherokees; under it, the Indians would be "neither citizens nor aliens, nor competent to be witnesses in courts of justice."

Their arguments were vain. By a three-to-two decision, Chief Justice Marshall and Justice Storey dissenting, the Supreme Court disclaimed jurisdiction in the case.

For Ross, however, the struggle was not ended. Denied the use of the tribal annuity, he must find elsewhere the financial support for its continuance. He borrowed from his many friends; the able lawyers he retained postponed the collection of fees; salaries of tribal interpreters, judges, peace officers, the editor of the *Phoenix* and its printers, were paid with due bills on the empty treasury. Repeatedly Ross appealed to Congress to override Jackson's order concerning the payment of the annuity; and after four years, with the people steadfastly refusing to receive the trifling individual payments, an act was passed directing that the accumulated sum be delivered to "the chiefs or to such a person as the tribe shall direct."

Even then, however, obstructive tactics continued, and another dramatic chapter was written before the money became available:

Despite the act of Congress, Jackson insisted that the mode of payment should be determined by a vote of the Cherokees. At the first test, conducted by agent Currey, 497 declared for payment to the treasury and but 1 for payment to individuals. But, said Jackson's agent, that was not a fair test; too few had voted; and there must be another referendum—some day.

It was while Ross was in Washington that Currey sent out notice of a final balloting on the annuity question at the home of one of the few Cherokees who had been won to the idea of removal—old Major Ridge, tired at last of resisting the incessant pressure of Georgia and the government agents. Returning home ten days before the day set for the voting, Ross was met by a deputation of indignant Cherokees, one of whom cried: "I never before heard of such a thing! It is the same as if a man steal my horse and sell it, then send for me to come and say to him and all the rest, 'For stealing my horse and selling it, I honor you'! Shall I say that? No!"

But Ross told them that the best thing to do would be to go to Ridge's place and vote. He sent urgent messages asking the men to be at an appointed camp near Ridge's home on the evening before the voting. The rendezvous was in Georgia, by whose laws those who went might be arrested for trespass, yet more than two thousand responded. Among them were old men who had covered over a hundred miles on foot. Nothing had been done for their provisioning, and the little bags of parched corn meal they carried and the game they might kill must feed them. Then, making their situation worse, Currey insisted that all their guns should be given up lest they fight the Georgia guard, who were present in some force.

Ross's two thousand, coming orderly into camp under his superintendence, surprised Currey, who delayed the voting as long as possible and made it as cumbersome as he could. He interrupted it to permit a long-winded treaty-seeking agent of the government to speak for three hours and twenty minutes. A blustery cold rain came on, and Ross slept amongst the men without shelter or blanket. Currey prolonged the voting beyond the second day; another stormy night was spent by the two thousand huddled about fires, partially sheltered by bark lean-tos.

If ever a leader's hold on a people was tested, it was there. Every effort was made by Currey, by the Georgia guard, and by a small group of Indians to discourage the Ross men, break down their discipline, create such disorder that the armed Georgians would have an excuse for attacking them. Some of the anti-Ross Indians were made beastly drunk and sent amongst the two thousand cursing and, almost naked, strewing insults; at intervals, drunken members of the guard mounted their horses and rode whooping and firing off their guns, hoping to provoke from the Indians a show of violent protest. Through it all, however, they held themselves rigidly to the course Ross advised: "You endured hardship in order to come here, and now you must not think of anything except the vote on the annuity."

At the end of the third day, Currey had to admit his defeat. The vote was 2,225 for payment to the tribal treasury and 114 against. The accumulated sum was at last handed over to Treasurer Martin.[3]

After June 1830, with the oppressive Georgia laws in effect, the situation of the Cherokees grew more and more difficult. Increasing numbers were arrested for observing their own laws. The exhortations of Major Ridge and his following to quit a losing battle and emigrate aroused bitter resentment; it was necessary for Ross to speak out on behalf of his oldest friend and political mentor to save him from the retributive anger of those who, as Worcester said, would overawe a chief who favored removal. Mistaken Major Ridge might be, but Ross assured the people that he was honest and sincere.

It was necessary, in order to save the machinery and records of the tribal government, to remove the capital from Georgia. Red Clay, in Tennessee, was selected, and for administrative purposes the tribal territory in Georgia was attached to the lesser areas lying within the states of Tennessee, North Carolina, and Alabama. Upon Ross fell the burden of this readjustment.

Georgia's next step was to enact a law requiring all whites residing on Indian Territory within her borders to secure permission from and take an oath of loyalty to the state—another shot at the missionaries whose championing of the Cherokees enraged the Georgians. At first, these men paid no attention to the new law, and Worcester, Proctor, and Thompson were arrested at their stations by the guard and marched off to prison, on foot and in chains. Whereupon a vast clamor arose throughout the United States, and they were released, an excuse being found to save the State's face in the statement that they were agents of the United States in dispensing a national "civilization fund" of $10,000 a year, and so were not subject to the law. It was a quibble, as the missionaries promptly pointed out; upon which Governor Gilmer, agreeing, pressed for their re-arrest unless they complied with the law.

Jackson co-operated by dismissing Worcester from his position as postmaster at his station, so that he might have no shadow of a claim on the United States for protection. He and Elizur Butler, his associate, backed by the American Board, formally defied Georgia; they were tried and sentenced to four years' imprisonment.

Members of Congress were stirred anew to battle on behalf of the Cherokees. Edward Everett sounded this tocsin:

"Here at the center of the Nation, beneath the portals of the Capitol, let us solemnly ~~inaugurate~~ [auspicate] the new era of violated promises and tarnished faith. Let us kindle a grand council fire, [not of treaties made and ratified, but] of treaties annulled and broken. Let us send to our archives for the worthless parchments and burn them in the face of day. There will be some yearnings of humanity as we perform the solemn act; they were negotiated for valuable considerations—we keep the considerations and break the bond. One gave peace to our afflicted frontiers, another protected our infant settlements; many were made when we were weak, nearly all at our earnest request. Many [of them] were negotiated under the instructions of Washington, of Adams and of Jefferson, the fathers of our liberty. They are gone, and will not witness the spectacle, but our present Chief Magistrate, as he lays them one by one on the fire, will see his own name ~~inscribed~~ [subscribed] to a goodly number of them."[4]

The treaties ought to be so destroyed, he added, "as a warning to the Indians to make no more compacts with us . . . We shall solemnly promise, but we shall break our word."

Everett was a steadfast spokesman for the Cherokees, armed with facts supplied by Ross. He took up the question "asked in a highly respectable quarter, 'What has a Cherokee to fear from the laws of Georgia?'" and answered: "He has this to fear: [. . .] men capable of atrocities . . . have but to cross the Cherokee line . . . where the eye of no white man can rest upon them and [they] may burn the dwelling, waste the farm, plunder the property, assault the person, murder the children of the Cherokee subject of Georgia and, though hundreds of the tribe may be looking on, there is not one of them that can be permitted to bear witness against the spoiler.

"It is said that no force has been used against them. No force! . . . There was no force then applied against the Huguenots by the revocation of the Edict of Nantes! They had only to adopt the Catholic faith; and dragoons were sent amongst them to assist in their conversion. There was no force then employed by the British Government towards the Puritans; they needed only to conform to the established church and they would [then] be safe from the visitations of the Star Chamber . . . Sir, law has its seat in the bosom of God, and its authentic voice is the harmony of the world."[5]

Everett had from Ross verified cases of arrests, pillage, and murder of Cherokees resulting from the Georgia laws. He had the copy of the *Cherokee Phoenix* which published its explanation for appearing as only a half sheet: "One of our printers has left us; and we expect another, who is a white man, to quit very soon, either to be dragged to the Georgia penitentiary for a term of not less than four years or, for his personal safety, to leave the Nation . . . Thus is the liberty of the press, guaranteed by the Constitution of Georgia, assured!"

Everett had another copy of the *Phoenix* reporting, a month later: "On last Sabbath, after the usual time of divine service, the Georgia guard arrived and arrested three of our residents, viz. Rev. Samuel A. Worcester, Mr. J. J. Wheeler, one of our printers, and Mr. Thomas Gann, the last two being citizens with Cherokee families. Mr. Isaac Proctor, assistant missionary at Carmel, had the evening before been taken, and came with the guard as a prisoner. On Monday, they were marched to Etowah where, the same evening, were taken the Rev. John Thompson and Mr. William Thompson."

Editor Boudinot had promised, "We shall not give up the ship . . . We have intelligent youths enough in the Nation, and we hope before long to make up our loss." But agent Currey thought of a simple way to foil Boudinot: he had the press, print paper, and type seized and locked in a store-room at the agency.

Ross made formal demand for the return of the *Phoenix* plant, but it was not until *twelve years afterwards* that notice was taken of his demand; then Congress appropriated $2,000 "for payment to the Cherokees for a printing press, materials and other property destroyed"—instruments for self enlightenment which the Cherokees had secured largely through the solicitations of funds by young John Ridge and Boudinot in speaking tours through the east.

Ross had strong allies, but in the government of Georgia he faced a ruthless and confident foe; as early as 1827, when Secretary of War Barbour warned Georgia that the state was transcending her rights by encroachments on the tribal lands and that the United States felt disposed to interfere, Governor Troup had answered:

"Sir, you are sufficiently explicit as to the means by which you propose to carry your resolution into effect. Thus the military character of the menace is established, and I am only at liberty to give it the defiance which it merits. [. . .] From the first decisive act of hostility, you will be considered and treated as a public enemy; and with less repugnance because you, to whom we might constitutionally have appealed for our own defence against invasion, are yourselves invaders; and what is more, the unblushing allies of the savages whose cause you have adopted."[6]

Gilmer and Lumpkin, succeeding Troup, were of the same breed. They also found it safe to defy the federal government; they also persisted in describing as savages the people over whom Ross presided as chief; let Ross and his "fee-d stipendiaries" quote statistics of civilized activities in the Cherokee Nation and cry aloud for justice; matched against the Georgia guard, all the moral force he and they could muster would nothing avail!

Yet Gilmer's autobiography contains this passage, at which even the gods might smile:

"No official act of mine produced so much abuse at the time, or was so little understood, as the punishment of religious missionaries by imprisonment in the penitentiary. An impression was made upon the public outside of Georgia that ministers of the gospel were thus punished for making efforts to Christianize the Cherokees . . .

"Georgia people traveling in other States were everywhere subjected to the mortification of listening to the most malignant strictures upon the conduct of the authorities of the State, and particularly its Governor, who was specially abused by name. In North Carolina, where all the facts ought to have been known, the Presbyterian Synod passed a resolution strongly condemnatory of my conduct. At a Presbytery held in the County of Rockingham, Virginia, the birthplace of my father and mother and where many of my immediate ~~relatives~~ [relations] then resided, a Presbyterian clergyman proposed a similar resolution, though domiciled in the house of my brother-in-law . . . I was an object of dislike to great numbers of my fellow beings, and . . . many of those who thus felt towards me were distinguished by their benevolence."[7]

On one point Gilmer was wrong: those who berated him and branded Georgia's acts as intolerably despotic knew exactly why the missionaries were imprisoned—because of their sympathy with Ross and the overwhelming majority of the tribe that opposed removal.

On behalf of Worcester and Butler, a suit was brought in the United States Supreme Court to nullify the Georgia law under which they had been arrested. Again Wirt and Sergeant made the arguments. This time, the court followed Chief Justice Marshall in declaring the law unconstitutional, and ordered the release of the two men.

A great day for the Cherokees! There was rejoicing everywhere in the Nation. Ross told the council there was hope at last that the tribe might be protected by the United States in the peaceful possession of their homes. He pointed out that the Supreme Court decision had been re-enforced by a recent strong message from Jackson to the people of South Carolina in which it was said, "the laws of the United States must be executed," and "those who told you that you might peaceably prevent their execution have deceived you."

The Indians' joy was shared by their friends throughout the country. Writing from the home of the Rev. Lyman Beecher at Boston to his brother, Boudinot described Beecher's delight when news of the decision came to him: "He jumped up, clapped his hands, took hold of my hand, said, 'God be praised!' and ran right out to tell his daughter and the rest of the family." Harriet Beecher, as a younger girl, must have known Boudinot's wife, for Beecher was a preacher in Litchfield County at the time of Boudinot's marriage to Harriet Gold.

The period of celebration, however, was brief. Gilmer paid no attention to the Supreme Court's order; and Jackson, far from taking steps to have it carried out, remarked cynically: "Marshall has made his decision, now let him enforce it!"

Worcester and Butler remained in prison. Mrs. Butler struggled to carry on the work of the station, mending and sewing for small girls, managing the farm, sitting up far into the night to write letters to her husband and Mr. Worcester for Indian converts and school children, herself asking advice concerning fencing, cropping and harvesting, strengthening and encouraging the two martyrs, praising God that Mr. Worcester was permitted to hold services for the other prisoners.

Gilmer went to Congress, Lumpkin became governor of Georgia, and the lot of the Cherokees grew worse. For the use of the state's congressional delegation, Lumpkin directed the printing of a pamphlet justifying Georgia's course towards the Cherokees, lamenting that she "has been ranked among the despotisms of the East" and that Gilmer had been "placed among the Neros, Dionysiuses and Dracos of infamous memory."[8]

Among the pamphlet's misstatements were that most of the chiefs and leading Cherokees opposing removal "are nearly destitute of Indian blood" and that they had "received and made use of the annuity payments for themselves."

On his side, Ross was desperately seeking means to carry on. Until the annuity money was paid—and none was available in the critical years from 1830 to 1834—he, John Ridge, Boudinot, and the young Cherokee preacher, David Brown, all known in the east and north, spoke and wrote often appealing for funds. Response was encouragingly generous. Interest in the cause increased as their audiences grew. John Howard Payne, at the peak of his fame as playwright and poet, was stirred to action. He came to the Cherokee Nation with a letter of introduction from a complimentary friend to Ross which said that he proposed to write about the tribe in such a strain that "future generations may weep over them and lament the anguish and afflictions which press so heavily upon them."

Unfortunately, Payne never published the story, although with the assistance of Ross and others he collected a vast amount of material for it. Soon after his arrival, and while a guest at the chief's house, he and Ross were arrested by the Georgia guard—both charged with unlawful intrusion on Indian land in Georgia as white men! Payne's papers were also seized. Through the rain and darkness, he and Ross were hustled off to prison. According to a pretty but apocryphal legend, one of their captors learned on the march that Payne had written "Home, Sweet Home," and begged him to sing it; and so movingly did the author render "be it never so humble, there's no place like home!" that the "great gruff men" of the guard broke into tears and, on arrival at the prison prevailed on the warden to let him and Ross go free.

The arrest, of course, was only a bit of malicious annoyance, and Ross's lawyers soon had him and Payne released through regular court proceedings.[9]

CHAPTER 13

Currey too set himself wholeheartedly to the harrying of Ross. He wrote to Washington that the chief was "threatening the peace and safety of the Indian country," while in fact Ross's first message after the Georgia laws went into effect urged the people: "Attend to your farms and domestic pursuits peaceably and industriously, that your wives and children may not suffer with hunger and add to your grief."[1]

To the council Ross reported that the president "has warned us against any hope of interference on his part with Georgia" in the enforcement of her "proscriptive and oppressive laws, under the most degrading circumstances"; nor would he protect the Cherokees from "her jails, penitentiaries, and gallows" for "obedience to our own laws." However, Jackson had promised that "such power as the law gives for your protection shall be used for your benefit, and will not fail to be exercised in keeping out intruders—beyond this I cannot go."[2]

Ross also reported that funds had been raised to retain lawyers, "that our unfeeling prosecutors may be met and bayed at the bar of justice. This measure [course], together with that of sending a delegation to Washington [City] during the session of Congress to plead in behalf of our suffering[s] . . . have had a very salutary and happy effect in counteracting the misrepresentations which are fabricated against us."[3]

Nowhere in Ross's messages, letters or actions was there a hint of violence; he was a man of too sound sense not to know that any attempt at physical resistance by the tribe would be hopeless. His power over the people was such that under fearful provocation he was able to keep them from sporadic outbreaks, though the young men strained at the aggressions of the whites and the old men resented the insults to the honor and integrity of the tribe. They sought to believe, with Ross, that justice must eventually prevail and that, according to prophecy, the meek should inherit the earth.

Enter now the ex-reverend J. F. Schermerhorn.[4]

It was he who, in 1834, interrupted the voting on the annuity payment at Ridge's by three hours and twenty minutes of oratory, Ross numbering those minutes watch in hand. The refrain of that endurance test had been, "Oh, my red brothers, how fervently I yearn to serve you!" The orator had even described how Providence had indicated him for that work. Riding through Tennessee, near to the Hermitage, his horse, he told them, was stricken; it died in Jackson's stables, wherefrom the noble president gave him another and persuaded him to take up the mission of doing good to the Indians.

The fact was that this ex-preacher of Utica, New York, was a hardened negotiator who, in previous dealings with Indians, had shown himself unscrupulous, unhampered by conscience or regard for truth. He was Jackson's last resort man, called in when commissioners like Carroll, Meriwether, and McMinn confessed themselves beaten by the united opposition of the Cherokees. His name was already signed to "treaties" with various unhappy tribes standing in the white man's path, and he spoke from experience when he begged the Cherokees to "take warning from the fate of the tribes of the north and emigrate and live. For if you do not, the bordering States will forthwith turn the screw tighter and tighter till you are ground to powder. And look not for mercy, for the mind of the present ruler of America will not change."

Schermerhorn also gave this advice: "Do you complain of wrongs? Remove and you can retaliate. If the white man here oppresses you, there you can oppress him. If he ~~sticks~~ [slicks, that is 'cheats'] you here, you can ~~stick~~ [slick] him there!" Not conventional Christian counsel, and certainly not counsel that the Cherokees valued.[5]

Payne, hearing this extraordinary talk, said that after it was ended the Indians turned their eyes to Ross and Lowrey, their trusted chiefs, who made their disgust clear; then they rose from the ground where they had been sitting and returned to their camp in silence. "There was no noise except the subdued sound of many voices in earnest conversation; finally they grew more and more indistinct, until they died away into complete silence, and the multitude, worn out by the day's hardships and vexations, slept . . . The sky cleared, the stars came out, and their soft light revealed the outlines of the mountain tops while the valley of the encampment remained in shadow."

Schermerhorn would lead them out of the valley of the shadow to a promised land where they could revert to savagery. In the task he would be ably assisted by his fellow Samaritan, the drunken Currey.

Schermerhorn began definite work towards the desired end by encouraging the formation of a "Treaty Party" among the persecuted Cherokees, and in this he was aided by Major Ridge. The old man's despair of justice, his conviction that further resistance would prove futile—a bowing to fate characteristic of an ancient people—was shared by his son and by Boudinot, whose voice had been strangled when the *Phoenix* was taken from him. These three prominent men were advised by Schermerhorn to bring together as many Cherokees in favor of removal as they could muster and meet with him for the negotiation of a treaty.

Because such a meeting would involve danger to themselves if held in the Nation—the death penalty for unauthorized alienation of tribal land, originally proposed by Major Ridge and endorsed by Boudinot in the *Phoenix*, still being an article of Cherokee law—Schermerhorn took them to Washington and there outlined the terms of a treaty. For their homes, improvements, and their ten million acres of land in Georgia, Tennessee, Alabama, and North Carolina, the United States offered the Cherokees $3,250,000 and a reservation in the west, already partially occupied by those who had emigrated more or less voluntarily. Schermerhorn had promised $5,000,000 before coming to the capital, but a promise was, after all, only a promise.

Ross also came to Washington, and went immediately into battle against the attempted negotiations. His opposition forced Schermerhorn to raise the bid for Cherokee land to $4,500,000; and to include the stipulation that the treaty must be approved by the tribe in General Council before it should become effective. With that last provision agreed to by the Senate, Ross could await the issue with composure; if the people should accept the treaty, he would no longer oppose removal. It was for them to decide, and he was their servant.

Schermerhorn set off hopefully for the Cherokee Nation, carrying an address to the Indians from Jackson: "Listen to me when I tell you that you cannot remain where you now are. Circumstances beyond the reach of human laws render it impossible that you can flourish in the midst of a civilized community . . . I have no motive, my friends, to deceive you . . . What have you gained by adhering to the pernicious counsels which have led you to reject the liberal offers made for your removal? . . . The choice is now before you—may the Great Spirit teach you how to choose. The fate of your women and children, the fate of your people to the remotest generation, depend upon the issue."[6]

During the whole summer and fall of 1835 Schermerhorn tried to secure approval of the treaty. Indefatigably he called meetings, to which the Cherokees refused to come. Desperately he sought to win over individuals who simply did not listen to him. In a letter to Jackson, he suggested that influential men might be bribed by promises of payment at their own valuation for the improvements they must abandon on removal. The letter was turned over to Secretary of War Lewis Cass, who answered that the treaty, if concluded at all, must be procured fairly, with bribes to no one, high or low! Cass added that he would so far favor Schermerhorn as to keep his letter out of the department's files.

Jackson's agent might have been less hopeful if he had known about the stream of Indians that flowed to Ross's home the day before the meeting of the fall council which was to act formally on the proposed treaty. The chief and his family, who had been driven out of the Georgia house and plantation, now lived in a little log cabin near the new tribal capital at Red Clay, Tennessee. There the visitors who had come to hear his opinion gathered, squatting against the walls, the trees in the yard, sitting on the top rails of the little garden enclosure, perched anywhere and everywhere, talking in low tones. When the last to come had settled themselves, Ross stood by the leather-hinged door and spoke. To be sure that they would understand him exactly, he spoke in English and had an interpreter put his words into Cherokee— better Cherokee, he believed, than he himself could use though he had known the language all his life.

Article by article, he explained the proposed treaty. "Perhaps," he said, "we shall be forced to yield in the end, for the white men are strong and determined. But if we are forced to go, we must have better terms. As it stands, this treaty must be rejected, and we must continue patiently to seek a fuller measure of justice . . . If the President should cease to protect us . . . I say to you, as Job said, 'My mother brought me naked into the world, and I must quit it naked'; such is the bidding of the Great Creator. 'The Lord giveth, and the Lord taketh away; blessed be the name of the Lord.' That also is what Job said, when he was robbed. Bear like Job. Like Job, may you be rewarded!"

When he ceased speaking, the old men, observing an ancient custom, circled slowly around him with nods and short ejaculations of approval. He was Guisgui, the chief, their trusted leader, the white bird whose plumes had never been soiled by lies and deceit! They took up their packs and pushed on to the council ground.

At Red Clay the treaty was rejected unanimously, even Major Ridge, his son, and Boudinot repudiating it now that they were at home, where "the whole tide of national feeling set, in one unbroken current, against removal to the west." Furthermore, at the council, a formal pact of harmony was drawn up and signed by the Ross followers, called Nationalists, and the Ridge Treaty Party.

Ross had suffered banishment from Georgia. Along with many other Cherokees, he had been reviled, threatened with death, arrested; his home had finally been taken from him by strangers; the story of that and similar outrages is picturesquely told in the words of a Cherokee memorial to Congress:

"The Legislature of Georgia passed laws interfering with the Cherokees' working of their own mines; Cherokees were arrested, tried, and imprisoned—some even shot in attempting to avoid arrest. The Cherokees used no violence, but petitioned, in vain, for the protection of the United States. Georgia passed an Act directing the Indian country to be surveyed into districts; another Act was shortly passed to lay off the country into lots and authorizing a lottery for the lands—Indians to be secured in possession of all lots touched by their improvements, and the balance of the country allowed to be possessed by white men. This Act was a direct violation of the treaty of 1819.

"Yet the Cherokees made no resistance, could make none, but petitioned the Government for relief. The answer was, the President could not interpose. After the country was parceled out by lottery, a horde of speculators made their appearance and purchased of the 'fortunate drawers' the lots touched by Indian improvements at reduced prices because it was uncertain when the Cherokees would surrender their rights and the lots would be unencumbered by their claims.

"At the next session of the Georgia Legislature, a further Act was passed limiting the Indian's right of occupancy to the lot on which he actually resided . . . Many Cherokees filed bills and obtained injunctions against dispossession of their improved lands, and would have found relief in the courts if the State's judiciary had not been prostrated at the feet of the Legislature; for the favorable opinion of a judge on the subject, there was an attempt made to impeach him, then to limit his circuit, and when all this failed equity jurisdiction was, by other Acts, taken from the courts in Cherokee cases.

"The Cherokees were then left at the mercy of an interested agent
. . . William N. Bishop,[7] captain of the Georgia guard, aide to the
Governor, etc., and his method of denying Indian rights is here sub-
mitted in his own words:[8]

> Jan. 20, 1835. Mr John Martin. Sir, the legal representative of [five]
> lots of land has called on me, as State's agent, to give him posses-
> sion [of the above described lots of land,] and informs me that
> you are the occupant upon them. Under the laws of the State [of
> Georgia], passed in the years 1833 and [18]34, it is made my duty
> to comply with his request. You will, therefore, prepare yourself
> to give entire possession of said premises, on or before the 20th
> day of February next; fail not under penalty of the law.

"Mr. Martin, a Cherokee, was a man of wealth, had an extensive
farm; large fields of [wheat] growing, ~~wheat. He~~ [and] was turned
out of ~~fields~~ [house] and home and compelled, in the month of
February, to seek a new residence within the limits of the State of
Tennessee. [. . .]

"The same summary process was used towards Mr. John Ross, the
principal chief . . . He was at Washington [city] on the business of ~~the~~
[his] Nation. When he returned, he traveled till about ten o'clock at
night, to reach his family; rode up the gate; saw a servant, believed to
be his own; dismounted and ordered his horse ~~to be~~ taken; went in
and, to his utter astonishment, found himself a stranger in his own
house, his family having been, some days before, driven out to seek
a new home!

"A thought then flitted across his mind, that he could not under
[all] the circumstances [of his situation,] reconcile [it to] himself
to tarry all night under the roof of his own house as a stranger, the
new host of that house being the tenant of that mercenary band of
Georgia speculators, at whose instance his helpless family had been
turned out and made homeless. Upon reflecting, however, that 'man is
born unto trouble,' Mr. Ross [at once] concluded to take up lodgings

there for the night, and to console himself ~~with~~ [under] the conviction of having met his afflictions [and trials] in a manner consistent with every moral obligation towards himself and family, his country, and his God.

"On the next morning, he ~~woke~~ [arose] early and went out into the yard, and saw some straggling herds of his cattle and sheep browsing about the place. His crop of corn ~~was~~ undisposed of. In casting a look up into the widespread branches of a majestic oak, standing within the enclosure of the garden, and ~~overshadowing~~ [which overshadows] the spot where lies the ~~dust~~ [remains] of his dear babe, and ~~his~~ most beloved and affectionate father, he [there] saw, perched upon ~~the~~ [its] boughs, that flock of beautiful pea-fowls, once the matron's care and delight, [but] now left to destruction and never more to be seen ~~by her~~.

"He ordered his horse, paid his bill (!) and departed in search of his family; after traveling amid heavy rains, ~~he~~ had the happiness of overtaking them on the road, bound for ~~a~~ [some] place of refuge ~~in~~ [within the limits of] Tennessee."[9]

Among other moving stories related in the memorial was that of the rich Cherokee, Joseph Vann, for whose eight hundred acres of cultivated fields and fine brick dwelling the governor's agent, Bishop, and a rival white claimant named Riley staged a pitched battle. Vann's possessions were declared forfeited on the pretext that he had violated Georgia law by hiring a white man as overseer without authority from the state, although as a matter of fact Vann had refused to engage the man when it was pointed out that to do so might cause trouble.

Bishop, ignoring the facts, secured an ouster order on Vann, intending to place his own brother in possession. Riley, however, got there first, and when the Bishops arrived, was installed with an armed force in the upper story of the house. The Bishop crew attacked; there were more than twenty guns engaged; while Vann and his wife and children were "gathered tremblingly" for safety in the lower rooms. Riley was not driven out until the house was set on fire; he then surrendered; the fire was put out; and "in the dead of winter, Vann and his family were driven off," to find shelter in a draughty dirt-floored log cabin in Tennessee.[10]

This Vann had volunteered in 1813 as a soldier with Jackson's Cherokee auxiliaries.

Although Georgia law exempted Cherokee land on which improvements stood from confiscation, "nearly all the Cherokees in Georgia, who had improvements of [any] value, except the favorites of the United States agents, under one pretext or another, have been driven from their homes. and [A]mid the process of expulsion, the Rev. John F. Schermerhorn, [the] United States Commissioner, visited the Legislatures of Tennessee and Alabama and importuned those bodies to pass laws, prohibiting the Cherokees who might be turned out of their possessions in [from within the] Georgia [limits,] from taking up [a] residence in the limits of those States!"[11]

In order to support claims for spoliation, Ross secured the appointment of Cherokee appraisers to value Indian property thus taken. The council chose five educated men for the work. After they had begun upon it, Schermerhorn and Currey sent the Georgia guard to arrest them. Four of the five were taken, their records confiscated and never returned, and they were held for ten days in a filthy little guard house without a hearing. Ross then obtained their release on a writ of *habeas corpus*; but, in accordance with the state's policy of harassing the Cherokees by arrest while avoiding the issue of trial, where the tribe's attorneys would be able to put the affair on record, they were never brought before a judge.

CHAPTER 14

Schermerhorn was greatly annoyed by the emphatic rejection of his benevolent treaty proposals. He was further depressed because even the Ridges and Boudinot had turned against him. It was obvious that the Indians distrusted and disliked him. There was only Currey to offer him understanding and sympathy.

It was becoming necessary for him to do something to justify his reputation. Therefore, before leaving the Red Clay Council, which had appointed yet another delegation to Washington, headed by Ross, he sent Currey to President Jackson with "private dispatches of a confidential nature" and attempted to delay the Cherokee delegation's departure by having Ross arrested. As a final gesture, he posted on the wall of the council house a notice of a general meeting to be held in the third week in December at New Echota, the former capital of the Nation in Georgia, "for the purpose of agreeing to the terms of a treaty." The notice promised to all who would attend blankets and rations; furthermore, it declared that all who failed to attend would be counted as assenting to the terms of any treaty there proposed!

Meanwhile, United States agents steadily pursued their task of trying to persuade obstinately opposed Cherokees to remove *voluntarily* to the west. As revealed to Congress by Ross, their methods were brutally forthright; for example:

Openly asserting that the government's policy was to render the situation of the Cherokees so miserable that they would be forced to remove, they induced the wife of an Indian named Wacha to enroll for emigration against the protests of her husband. Soon thereafter she changed her mind, but she and her children were forcibly put on board a river steamboat and transported to the west. Wacha, still refusing to go, was thrown out of his home.

Atlak Anosta was made drunk and persuaded to enroll in spite of the pleading of his family. Sober, he repented and when the time came to go ran away from home. Currey's police were sent after him; he was not found, but his wife and children were brought to the agency "almost dead, in a cold rain, shivering and hungry," and kept under guard until Anosta came in to save them from starvation. Then all were sent off. In the west, their three children died, and the parents returned over the long trail on foot.

Iconatachee also signed up for emigration while drunk and changed his mind when sober. Currey and an aide went after him with drawn pistols and attempted to drive him to the agency, but the Indian managed to escape. Currey then sent a strong detail, with a wagon and team, to capture him and his family; they drove back in triumph, with the man on foot tied to the tail of the wagon in which his wife and children were packed—that is, all but the two youngest children, who had fled into the woods and been left behind.

Richard Chech was away from home, working on the Tuscumbia railroad in Alabama, when his family was taken and put aboard a boat; and all their pleadings could not move Currey to delay their banishment, or even to allow them to stop on the way to see Chech; he was left behind, and never saw his wife again—she died on the voyage to the west.[1]

The final words of Ross's memorial to Congress were these: "We

[The Cherokees] cannot, ~~of course,~~ resist the power of the United States; ~~but~~ [and] should ~~we~~ [they] be driven from ~~our~~ [their] native land then will ~~we~~ [they] look in melancholy sadness upon the golden chains presented by President Washington to the Cherokee people as emblematical of the brightness and purity of the friendship between the United States and the Cherokee Nation!"[2]

By the third week in December Currey had returned from Washington with new credentials for Schermerhorn. He and the ex-preacher traveled to New Echota, where as a result of all their threats, "gentle persuasion," and promise of free beef and blankets fewer than three hundred Indian men, women, and children appeared, a large proportion of whom had already been induced to enroll for emigration. Ross was in Washington, and no other official of the Nation was present.

Even to Schermerhorn the travesty of regarding this handful as a Great Council of the tribe was obvious. He proposed, in order to camouflage the real situation, that the people choose twenty from amongst them as a committee to carry on treaty negotiations and sign for the Nation. Put to a vote, his proposal carried, seventy-nine to seven—a total voting strength of eighty-six!

Whereupon, working swiftly with his own picked representatives, Schermerhorn resubmitted the rejected treaty, changed only in minor details. It was approved by the committee of twenty; and Schermerhorn selected from among them a delegation to accompany him to Washington with authority to sanction whatever changes were required before ratification by the Senate.

So farcical was the New Echota action that a government agent, Major Davis of the army, sent to aid Currey, wrote indignantly to the secretary of war:

"Sir, that paper . . . called a treaty is no treaty at all because not sanctioned by the great body of the Cherokees and made without their participation or assent. I solemnly declare to you that upon its reference to the Cherokee people it would be instantly rejected by nine-tenths of them, and I believe by nineteen-twentieths of them . . .

The delegation taken to Washington by Mr. Schermerhorn had no more authority to make a treaty than any other dozen Cherokees accidentally picked up for the purpose."[3]

Other bitter protests were raised against the New Echota tragic burlesque; and Schermerhorn's background and methods were exposed. He flared up heatedly in reply; referring to the Red Clay Council of October and the rejection of the treaty he had there submitted, he said:

"It was soon manifest to me that Mr. Ross and his partisans meant to play the same game with me that they had played with all the commissioners that had been sent to treat with them for some years past . . . viz, to deceive me with their fair speeches, misrepresentations, double-dealings, and false pretenses; or else to denounce me as everything that was vile, bad, and odious, and as an enemy to the Indians. And because I would not permit them to deceive me and defeat my mission, I am now denounced by them, and not by them only but by such white men and officers of the Government among them as they have deceived and drawn into their course of policy in opposition to all views, policy and interest of the Government.

"In this I have no reason to complain, for I find they have pursued the same course of denunciation towards the President, Secretary of War, Hon. John McLean, Theodore Freylinghausen, Edward Everett, and all their best friends they ever had, because they have advised them to make a treaty and remove west of the Mississippi, the only land of rest and peace for the Indians."[4]

Ross, presenting the signatures of sixteen thousand Cherokees to a denunciation of the New Echota "treaty," showed the falsity of Schermerhorn's statements. Accused by Schermerhorn of holding his position of chief without authority from the tribe, Ross said "the reverend gentleman ought to have observed more closely what he writes upon this subject"; and then, elaborately and with abundant proof, nailed the lie.

Everett's eloquent plea in Congress against the Schermerhorn treaty of removal was on the record:

"Let any gentleman think how he would stand, were he to go home and tell his constituents that they were to be removed, whole counties of them—they must fly before the wrath of insupportable laws—they must go to the distant desert beyond Arkansas . . . That this was the policy of the Government—that the bill ~~was~~ [had] passed . . . ~~that~~ you had voted for it, and ~~so~~ [go] they must ~~go~~! . . .[5]

"Gentlemen who favor the project cannot have viewed it as it is. They think of a march of Indian warriors, penetrating with their accustomed vigor, the forests or the canebrakes . . . Sir, it is no such thing . . . They are to go in families, the old and the young, wives and children, the feeble and the sick. And how are they to go? Not in luxurious carriages; they are poor. Not in stage coaches; they go to a region where there are none. Not even in wagons, nor on horseback, [for] [t]hey are to go in the least expensive manner possible. They are to go on foot; nay, they are to be driven by contract. The price . . . is to be screwed down to the least farthing, to eight dollars per head!" Which does not sound as though Everett thought himself an object of denunciation by the Cherokees, nor yet as though he advised them to go west to "the only land of rest and peace"!

"The imagination sickens," Everett went on, "at the thought of what will happen to a company of these emigrants, ~~who~~ [which] may prove less strong, less able to pursue the journey, than was anticipated. Will the contractor stop for the old men to rest, for the fainting women and children to revive? He will not; he cannot afford to . . . This is what we call the removal of the Indians!"

Like Everett, Ross insisted upon the horrors of forced emigration; and more resolutely than ever strove to defeat ratification of the Schermerhorn treaty. He tried in vain to see Jackson, who sent word that he had ceased to regard Ross as chief of the Cherokees or to recognize the existence of any Cherokee government in the east. Ross was in the Senate day after day pleading with senators, patiently displaying the evidence of his people's overwhelming opposition to removal.

Before the vote on ratification was taken, Ross had assurance that it would fail. Yet it carried by one vote more than the required two-thirds;

two southern senators broke their pledges and turned the balance against the Cherokees.

After all, this final treachery was consistent with the whole long record of white dealings with the Cherokees. Everett had cited the list of broken treaties, unkept promises. One more betrayal could no further blacken the page. The average member of Congress had no fear that his deception towards a small Nation of Indians, however enlightened and however befriended, would ever be punished by his constituents.

Ross, however, uttered this bitter prophecy:

"That possessions acquired, and objects attained by unjust and unrighteous means will, sooner or later, prove a curse to those who have [thus] sought them, is a truth we have been taught by that holy religion which was brought to us by our white brethren. Years, nay, centuries may elapse before the punishment may follow the offense, but the volumes of history and the sacred Bible assure us that the ~~time~~ [period] will certainly arrive."[6] Perhaps some Georgians, twenty-eight years later, under the scourge of Sherman's 100,000 marching to the sea, remembered Ross's words?[7] It is possible; both Gilmer and Lumpkin pictured the Georgians as faithful readers of the Bible; they should have been reconciled to the giving of an eye for an eye and a tooth for a tooth.

CHAPTER 15

Georgia had won. On May 23, 1836, the parchment which the United States chose to consider a valid treaty of removal with the Cherokees was signed by Jackson. The only concession from Schermerhorn's harsh terms was a provision allowing the Indians two years in which to remove voluntarily.

Ross, however, did not confess defeat, but resolved to fight removal more sternly than ever. In him was a great underflow of passion, of resolution that would carry him to the very end of resistance. As deeply as any of the full-blood hillmen, as romantically as any Cherokee woman whose heart leaped to watch the flaming glory of a summer sunset lift over her fruitful garden patch to the broad blue shoulder of the mountain, he loved the land. He was called stubborn by the Ridges and Boudinot, who had once more been won over by the arguments for removal and had signed the Schermerhorn treaty. Stubborn he was, but better than they he knew the futility of flight; better than they he could understand the power and reach of the white man's arm. When they would put up their hands in surrender, Ross was ready once more to mount his horse and lead another delegation to Congress.

When even the stout missionaries Worcester and Butler could so far yield as to apply to the governor of Georgia for release from prison, so acknowledging defeat, Ross continued the fight.

It was not in the flesh and bones of Mother Molly's son to give up his land. If battling to the end meant breaking with Major Ridge, his oldest and dearest friend, with John Ridge and Boudinot of the new generation, and even with his brother Andrew, also a signer of the Schermerhorn treaty, so be it!

He sent a letter from Washington to be read to all the people, advising them to ignore the spurious treaty but to make no active resistance; any show of force within their power would be useless.

His letter, of course, was seen by Currey and the other removal agents, who spread the report that while seeming to counsel non-resistance Ross was secretly preparing for armed insurrection. An alarmist published a warning that the Cherokees meant to go on the warpath and drive all white men from their country. "Horror and indignation" were thereupon registered amongst the borderers; and Ross was bitterly denounced by federal and Georgia officials.

In the tradition of civilized man, the highest reach of patriotism is the willingness to fight and die for home and country; for the Indians, however, this virtue is merely another evidence of savagery!

Ross had reason to fear an outbreak from the hillmen, and his letter was sent as a precaution. He followed it up by having meetings called at which resolutions were drawn showing the futility of armed protest. The mountain men of the Hiwassee region expressed the Nation's view when they admitted that even if they should consider fighting it would be foolish because they no longer had any war organization or equipment.

However, it suited the whites who waited impatiently for possession of the Cherokee lands and gold claims to foster the alarmist view; and the War Department sent General Wool with seven thousand soldiers to overawe the reputedly hostile element and "frown down opposition to the treaty."[1]

Despite Wool's presence, the North Carolina Cherokees met and resolved to fight, but not with physical weapons. The general, angered by their defiance, appeared and demanded an answer to the question, "Will you remove to the west voluntarily?" Before replying, they wished to consult Ross, but Wool would not permit that, saying that Ross had led them astray too long by his "pernicious" counsel; "hereafter, I am the proper person to advise you!" He said a great deal more which amounted to this: You must go or fight my soldiers. The council ended without answering Wool's question, and the Indians started home; he detailed soldiers to overtake and bring back the head men, holding them as prisoners until they promised to observe the terms of the treaty and send the young men in to surrender whatever arms they possessed.

To the secretary of war General Wool reported that not one in a hundred would remove until compelled by military force; and he asked for additional troops.

As civil persuaders, the United States named two ex-governors, Lumpkin of Georgia and Carroll of Tennessee; they were to supervise the execution of the treaty, while Currey acted as superintendent of removal. A large staff of assistants was collected, and "official records prove that the removal provided many a fat job for place-hunters and friends of influential politicians on good terms with the Administration."[2] Printed bills, in Cherokee and English, were posted throughout the Nation describing the "beautiful and luxurious" steamboat provided to carry the people to the west; other bills alluringly pictured the Elysian fields beyond the Mississippi to which they were commanded to go; and reports based on distorted documents were circulated that Ross himself had, while in Washington, agreed to removal.

But the people waited for Ross to speak; with him, they saw a flicker of hope in the fact that before the two years of grace should expire Jackson would be out of office and his successor might listen to their plea for justice. In a private letter, Ross wrote that he hoped Clay would become president, for Clay had protested to Congress. "It is said that annihilation is the destiny of the Indian race. Perhaps it is, judging from the past, but shall we therefore hasten it? Death is the irreversible decree pronounced against the human race, but shall we accelerate its approach because it is inevitable?"[3]

Heeding their chief's advice, the Cherokees refused to enroll for emigration; all the pressure Lumpkin, Carroll, and Currey, backed by General Wool and his soldiers, put upon them could not force them to "come in."

The council of 1836 adopted Ross's resolution denouncing the motives and methods of Schermerhorn, declaring the so-called treaty null, and insisting that it could never be enforced. A memorial to Congress, another of the long series of desperate, eloquent pleas, was also prepared by Ross and signed by the 1,245 present at Red Clay.

"By the stipulations of this ~~treaty~~ [instrument]," Ross wrote, "we are despoiled of our private possessions, the indefeasible property of individuals. We are stripped of every attribute of freedom and eligibility for legal self-defense. Our property may be plundered before our eyes. Violence may be committed on our persons; even our lives may be taken away, and there is none to regard our complaints. We are ~~demoralized~~ [denationalized]! We are disfranchised! We are deprived of membership in the human family! We have neither land nor home, nor resting place that can be called our own. And all this is effected by the provisions of a compact ~~that is not the act of our Nation~~ [which assumes the venerated, the sacred appellation of treaty] . . . The makers of it sustain no office nor appointment in our Nation, under the designation of chiefs, head men, or any other title, by which they hold, or could acquire, authority . . ."[4]

"We [. . .] appeal [with confidence] to the justice[, the magnanimity, the compassion,] of your honorable bodies . . . Our ~~appeal~~ [cause] [. . .] is based on your own principles, which we have learned from ~~you~~ [yourselves], ~~of which~~ [for] we have gloried to count your Washington and [your] Jefferson our great teachers . . . We have practiced their precepts with success. [And] [t]he result is manifest.

The wilderness of [the] forest has given place to comfortable dwellings and cultivated fields, stocked with the various domestic animals. Mental culture, industrious habits, and domestic enjoyments have succeeded [the rudeness of] the savage state. We have learned your religion also. We have read your sacred books. Hundreds of our people have embraced their doctrines, practiced the virtues they teach, cherished the hopes they awaken, and rejoiced in the consolations which they afford . . .

"Spare our people! Spare the wreck of our prosperity! Let not our deserted homes become the monuments of our desolation!"

To President Jackson, Ross addressed an earnest request for a searching investigation of the means by which the Schermerhorn treaty was obtained; he prayed "the God of truth to tear away every disguise and concealment . . . the God of justice to guide the President's determination, and the God of mercy to stay the hands of their brothers uplifted for their destruction."[5]

For forwarding this appeal General Wool was hotly rebuked by Jackson; how dared an officer of the army receive and transmit a document "so disrespectful to the Chief Executive, the Senate, and the American people!" Nevertheless, Jackson answered it. The terms of the Schermerhorn treaty, he said, would be carried out literally and with all possible speed! He directed that when his answer should be handed to Ross, the government make no further communication to him on the subject of the treaty. Furthermore, no councils of the Cherokee people would be permitted to meet for discussion of the treaty.

Wool complied with this last command by publishing an order declaring that a repetition of the Red Clay Council would be regarded as "indicative of a design to prevent the execution of the treaty, even at the hazard of actual hostilities, and will be promptly repressed."[6]

CHAPTER 16

A desperate situation faced Ross in November 1836. He still had eighteen months in which to fight for the abrogation of the treaty, but he was constantly watched by United States and Georgia agents eager to read into his acts a significance which would justify his arrest. They dared not, because of the powerful friends he had in the east and north, order his summary imprisonment, for such an act might result in pressure that would force even Jackson's Congress to repudiate the Schermerhorn trickery.

At the last Red Clay Council, Ross's proposal to send a delegation to the western Cherokees in order to secure their support was adopted, and he was chosen to lead it. He explained to the people the necessity for silence concerning this mission; and so tight-lipped were they all that he and his companions had slipped away and were near their goal before Currey knew they had gone. Then Currey immediately reported the fact to Washington, and an order was sent to the military commander at Fort Gibson, in the western Cherokee territory, to arrest Ross if he appeared and attempted to incite the Indians there to oppose the treaty.[1]

Before that order arrived, however, Ross had finished his conferences, had gained the liking and support of the agent to the western band, had won over their chief, John Jolly, and secured the appointment of an official delegation of Westerners to accompany him to Washington.

Severe winter storms and ice-obstructed rivers delayed the arrival of the delegation at the capital until within a month of Van Buren's inauguration. Once there, they could not get access to President Jackson. Then Ross wrote, begging for a hearing, asking, "How have we offended? In what manner have we stirred your resentment against us?"[2] There was no answer; no official notice whatever was taken of the delegation. A petition for relief from the terms of the treaty was received by the Senate but not acted upon; it could not be brought before the House because of the press of business in the closing days of the session.

Jackson's term ended, and he set off for the Hermitage, a grim, tired old man, but still full of fight, as yet unready to acknowledge the validity of Christ's command to do unto others as ye would they should do unto you, though later in life he became a diligent church-goer.

In Van Buren, Jackson had a hand-picked successor pledged to carry out his policy; to the Ross delegation's plea for the appointment of a commission to investigate the manner in which the spurious Schermerhorn treaty had been obtained, the new president said he regretted that he could do nothing to alter its terms or delay its execution. He was probably sympathetic, but did not care to rouse Georgia to renewed defiance of federal authority. The sacrifice of some seventeen thousand Indians of no national importance politically in order to soothe the Georgians was, for a man of his mind, in the nature of a necessity, however painful.

Lumpkin was sent by the Georgia legislature to the United States Senate as a fit man to combat in Washington the continuing efforts to prevent Cherokee removal. Ross still had as stalwart allies Clay, Everett, Webster, Wise of Virginia, and others, though the valiant Davy Crockett, who had once lost his seat as congressman from Tennessee because of his stout opposition to Jackson's Indian 'policy, had been killed at the Alamo. Lumpkin remained a senator "till the whole of the Indians were removed," and claimed credit for driving the tribe out of the land of their fathers "without the shedding of human blood," although Cherokees were killed in the process. But Lumpkin confessedly shared Gilmer's opinion that an Indian was not really a human being.

Finding it useless to remain at Washington, Ross returned to his people, where the situation grew more and more tragic. Even General Wool, as his stay in the Nation was extended, became indignant at the actions of the borderers; he drew a picture of the whites "hovering like vultures, eager to pounce upon the prey and strip them of everything they have," wrote that "I am surprised that the Cherokees have not risen and destroyed every white man in the country!" and predicted that ninety-nine out of every hundred of the Indians would be destitute before they were started west.[3]

Wool had come to understand and to sympathize with the passionate love for their homeland which held the unhappy Cherokees bitterly opposed to its surrender, though he did his best, facing the inevitable, to persuade them to emigrate. "It is, however, vain to talk to a people almost universally opposed to the treaty and who maintain that they never made such a treaty. So determined are they in their opposition that not one of all those present at the Council, however poor and destitute, would receive either rations or clothing from the United States lest they might compromise themselves in regard to the treaty. These same people, as well as those in the mountains of North Carolina, during the summer past, preferred living upon roots and the sap of trees rather than receive provisions from the United States, and thousands . . . had no other food for weeks. Many have said they will die before they will leave the country."[4]

Another military man, General Dunlap, ordered to lead his east Tennessee troops into the Cherokee country in 1836 when a manufactured "scare" was alarming the borderers, reported that the Indians, rather than the whites, needed protection. Proceeding to give them such protection as seemed proper, Dunlap roused the wrath of the Georgia spoilers. His position became so difficult that, calling his soldiers together, he resigned his command, telling the men that he would no longer dishonor Tennessee arms by helping to execute at the point of the bayonet a treaty made by a tiny unauthorized minority against the will of the people.[5]

In the summer of 1837, John M. Mason of the War Department was sent as a confidential agent to the Cherokees. He found every one against the treaty: "The whole Nation of 18,000 persons is with John Ross, the few—about 300—who made the treaty having left the country, with the exception of a small number of prominent individuals, as Ridge, Boudinot, and others, who remain to assist in carrying it into execution."[6]

Ross and his supporters were doomed to persecution, of course, as they continued the battle against the intruding hordes of whites. But even the treaty signers had to walk through that same hell of hate and greed. Here is the evidence of Major Ridge, wealthiest and most influential of that consenting handful; his letter, dictated to his son John, informed President Jackson, while still in office:

"We [now] come ~~now~~ to address you on the subject of our griefs and afflictions from the acts of the white people. They have got our lands and now they are preparing to fleece us of the money accruing from the treaty. We found our plantations taken either in whole or in part by the Georgians~~, and~~—suits instituted against us for back rents for our own farms~~!~~. These suits are commenced in the inferior courts, with the evident design [that], when we are ready to remove, to arrest our people and, on these vile claims [to] induce us to compromise for our [own] release, ~~in order~~ to travel with our families. Thus our funds will be filched from our people, and we shall be compelled to leave our country as beggars and in want.

"Even the Georgia laws, which deny us our oaths, are thrown aside, and notwithstanding the cries of our people, and protestation of our innocence and peace, the lowest class[es] of the white people are flogging the Cherokees with cowhides, hickories and clubs. We are not safe in our homes—our people are assailed by day and night by the rabble. Even justices of the peace and constables are concerned in this business. This barbarous treatment is not confined to men, but the women are stripped also and whipped without [law or] mercy [. . .]

"Send regular troops to protect us from these lawless assaults, and to protect our people as they depart for the west. If it is not done, we shall carry off nothing but the scars of the lash on our backs!"[7]

Jackson's only answer was, Go west! What Ridge described was exactly what Schermerhorn had predicted: "If you do not remove, the bordering States will forthwith turn the screw tighter . . . And look not for mercy, for the mind of the present ruler of America will not change."

CHAPTER 17

G. W. Featherstonhaugh, an English geologist, in the course of extended explorations in America, traveled across the Cherokee country in the late summer of 1837 and attended the Tribal Council at Red Clay. In vivid descriptive notes, he made pictures of the people and scenes at the council.[1]

Along with much talk of outrages upon the tribe and of Ross's desperate efforts to save the country for his people, Featherstonhaugh had heard rumors of Indian insurrection. He thought it wise, therefore, before undertaking the journey to seek advice from the military commander, Colonel Powell, at Camp Wool. He found the colonel about to march with a body of soldiers to Red Clay where, he was told, Ross had called the Indians to meet in defiance of orders. Believing himself in need of protection, the Englishman joined Powell's march.

Six miles from camp, he came to Brainerd Mission and stopped to visit Mr. Butrick, in charge, "a pious elderly person, apparently out of health." Butrick and the others at the station, "zealous in the cause of the Cherokees" and suspecting that the stranger might be a removal agent, refused at first to talk with him. Reassured on that point, Butrick declared with passion that the people were in the mood to die rather than emigrate; "yet I know that the whites are all powerful and must prevail if the issue is forced. Nevertheless, God has his eye upon all that is passing, and in his own time the Cherokees will be avenged!"[2]

At the moment, Featherstonhaugh heard Butrick rather with amazement than sympathy; the missionary seemed to be just a bitter and disappointed old man; but his view was changed later. He learned that he had nothing to fear from the Indians, and pushed on from Brainerd alone, crossing Chickamauga Creek into a country of "a truly Indian character, short trees sparsely growing amidst tall luxuriant wild grass, and occasional remains of Indian habitations,"[3] deserted and ruined homesteads from which Cherokees had been driven.

Farther on, at a chalybeate spring, he found some mixed-blood Cherokee families occupying log cabins. This was their long-used watering place; "in one of the huts was a tolerable bath, the water being led by wooden spouts from the foot of the hill whence it issues." The Indians spoke English, were educated and intelligent; the women were "well dressed and good looking."[4]

Before going to Red Clay, the Englishman pushed down through the Georgia Indian lands to Gainsville. As he went south, he met many parties of Cherokees traveling on foot to the Great Council, numerous women carrying babies on their backs. He saw more evidences of pillage, "log huts [. . .] with clearings around them, surrounded by broken-down fences," now in possession of whites whom he described as "a tall, sallow, gawky-looking set, with manners of the coarsest kind; their children were all pale and unhealthy looking, suffering, as their mothers told me, from bowel complaint, occasioned evidently by unwholesome food and filth."[5]

Scattered amongst these Georgia usurpers were some holdings still in the hands of Indians, who had fields of corn, sweet potatoes and "pulse of various kinds."[6]

At Spring Place, with the Georgians in full occupation, he found "every store a dram shop."[7] Two men staggered in who, while drunk, had fallen from their horses and been trampled. At Coosawattee, he stopped at a filthy tavern where the only food offered was bad corn bread; "too much trouble," said the landlord, "to keep cows for milk and butter."[8]

Going on, he met still other parties of Cherokees bound for Red Clay, mostly on foot, the few being mounted on horses. With these swarthy, athletic tribesmen he contrasted the group of Georgians he found at Fields's place near Gainsville, "tall, thin, cadaverous animals, as melancholy and lazy as boiled codfish . . . parsnip-looking fellows," depraved by their wretched diet and habits. He heard them talk, bitterly and ignorantly, of "Union and States' rights, execration and vociferation their only equipment for argument."[9]

Returning towards Red Clay from Gainsville, he fell in with a contingent of the Georgia guard on the way to the council. They shocked him by their tatterdemalion appearance: "All had their coats off, with their muskets and cartouche-boxes strung across their shoulders. Some [of the men] had straw hats, some [of them] white felt hats, others [had] old black hats [on] with the rims torn off, and all [of them] were as unshaven and dirty as they could well be. The officers were only distinguished by having Cherokee [fringed] hunting shirts on . . . They rode on talking and cursing and swearing without any kind of discipline," reminding the traveler of condottieri of old.[10]

They rode through a country "pleasingly wooded yet sufficiently open to admit the growth of various beautiful flowers;" after crossing the lovely mountain stream called the Connesauga, Featherstonhaugh saw many quail, and fat deer in numbers. At Young's, a Cherokee supplied for his horse "huge, heavy ears of maize." It was the once friendly, abundant old Cherokee land he was riding through, the land so well loved by the people.[11]

Arriving at Red Clay, the visitor was invited by Charles Hicks, a mixed-blood, to stay in his cabin—an unchinked log shelter carpeted with pine needles and furnished only with two crude bedsteads. Curious Indians came to peep between the logs and speculate upon the stranger's mission. Across the little Coosaholla stream was an "irregular street of cabins, booths and stores, hastily built of logs for families and for public kitchens."[12] For feeding the multitude, Ross was allowing the commissary $300 a day; each morning of the council sessions, fifteen beeves were killed.[13]

Above the encampment, near the great limestone spring at the head of the stream, was the council house, "a simple parallelogram [formed] of logs, with open sides and benches [inside] for the councilors."[14]

The vast camp was impressive in its sylvan setting, and the Englishman's eye was taken by the colorful, orderly flow of men, women, and children in all directions. Though the mixed-bloods seemed like so many whites in dress and speech, he found them "less vicious and more sober." Amongst the fullbloods he saw men with large red and blue handkerchiefs bound about their heads turbanwise. Some of the North Carolina mountain men wore deerskin leggings and embroidered woolen hunting shirts, suggesting the Arabs of Barbary. The younger women were trim of figure and beautiful of face, though the older ones had lost much of their attractiveness.[15]

On his first evening in camp, Featherstonhaugh was drawn to the council house by the sound of hymns "pealing through the forest;" the Rev. Evan Jones was conducting a religious service for the hundreds that crowded the benches. Beside Jones as he read from the New Testament and expounded his text stood Jesse Bushyhead, a Native preacher, to interpret the words into Cherokee, "emitting a deep grunting sound at the end of every verse of Scripture that resembled [resembling] the hard breathing of a man chopping down trees [down]." It was the characteristic punctuation of Indian speeches. The congregation sang from printed Cherokee hymn books.[16]

Featherstonhaugh noted that Jones wore a "peculiar sinister, furtive look," which he learned later was due to the persecutions he had suffered from the Georgians; at the time, Jones was the only missionary who had contrived to remain with the Georgia Cherokees.[17]

Prominent Indians came to welcome the Englishman: Whitepath, seventy-six years of age, and Goingsnake, seventy-nine, with an arm that had been crippled at the Battle of the Horseshoe. He was taken to dine with Mrs. Walker, "a fine old Cherokee lady, where I [and] met John Ross, the principal chief [...]. The dinner was good, [we had] boiled beef, chicken and bacon, [with excellent vegetables]. [C]offee was served with the dinner." He was delighted with the Indian "conahaney," corn boiled almost to a purée; mixed with beef broth, "it makes a capital soup."[18]

Interested and eager, Featherstonhaugh walked much through the camp; in the chill dusk, as he passed their group fires, he saw the people sitting blanket-draped and huddled under lean-to shelters made of sticks and other blankets; their eyes followed him curiously. The days began at dawn, with the sound of singing and preaching, in both English and Cherokee. At noon one day he went to dine at Ross's cabin—a "plentiful dinner," served to a long tableful of visitors at which neither the chief nor his wife sat because they were busied serving the food and attending to the comfort of their guests. He had only a word or two with Ross who, he thought, was under a severe strain, immersed in the endless details of the council proceedings.[19]

There were, however, many other well-informed Cherokees to talk with the Englishman. Hicks, whose father had been described once by Ross as "our beloved antiquarian," told him of the traditions and customs, the history of the Cherokees; told of his father's visit to Philadelphia in 1794, his meeting with a delegation of Chinese, and his conviction that the Cherokees must have come from the same racial stock. To this, Featherstonhaugh answered that he had been struck by the likeness between Cherokees and Tartars in formation of face and set of eye.[20]

The Englishman heard Mason, the government agent, urge, though halfheartedly, removal to the west; it had become evident that "the people have no wish to leave their own land." He heard from Stephen Foreman, an educated Cherokee,[21] "amusing anecdotes of the Rev. Mr. Schermerhorn, a sort of loose minister of the gospel who had taken up the calling of a political demagogue and been rewarded with appointment as special agent ... The reverend agent, [...] being of an amorous turn, had been detected tampering with some of the young Cherokee women, so that he became [to be] an object of detestation to the Indians, who took every opportunity to affront him. Not more than a half dozen in the whole Nation would speak to him at all; [and] whenever the ~~others~~ [rest of them] met him, they made a point of turning [round and presenting] their backs to him." They had given him a derisive Indian name, Skaynooyaunah, Devil's Horn! . . .[22]

As the council sessions continued, Featherstonhaugh was struck by the unflagging interest of the people in the proceedings. They stood for hours in the rain, one day, outside the unwalled council house, two thousand Indian men listening attentively to the discussions. Ross held them firmly to the business in hand, allowed no disorder; the United States troops and the Georgia guard, hovering near and hoping for a sign of insurrection that would justify them in arresting the leaders, especially Ross, found no excuse for acting. They vindicated Ross's contention that they were peaceful, law-abiding people fit to live as any white man's neighbors . . .

Featherstonhaugh left before the sessions ended, riding away one crisp evening with a backward glance at the multitude sitting by their fires with their blankets over their shoulders, waiting—for what?

It was not long before they knew.

Midnight of May 23, 1838, was the moment fixed for the beginning of the forcible removal; not much time left for fighting, but Ross continued his struggle to the end.

Now, within the Nation, he must placate angry leaders who demanded the death of Major Ridge, his son, Boudinot, and others who had signed the Schermerhorn treaty. They were condemned by the council, but Ross succeeded in reducing the decree to the dismissal of Major Ridge from the council; from that time forward the Ridges, Boudinot, and the Treaty Party leaders became implacable enemies of Ross. Often, mercy is more difficult to endure than enmity.

Once again Ross made the weary pilgrimage to Washington with the findings of the council at which Featherstonhaugh had been an interested spectator. Once again he failed to get a hearing. In the Senate, Lumpkin saw to it that the memorial was tabled, crying out against Ross, "He ought to be put in strings and banished from the country!"

Lumpkin further complimented the chief: "Although a large slave-holder, he is well qualified to fill a prominent place among the New England Abolitionists!" and "He is the soul and spirit of the whole opposition . . . a subtle and sagacious man who, under the guise of an unassuming deportment, conceals an unsurpassed arrogance . . . By his dignified, reserved manner he has acquired credit for talents and wisdom which he never possessed."[23]

Shorn of its animus, Lumpkin's portrait of Ross is not bad. He was soft spoken, reticent by nature, a Christian gentleman, but also an indomitable fighter. His was a real power, deriving from a blending of will, intelligence, passionate devotion to justice, self-control and imaginative insight. He was sustained by a genuine belief in God—a faith which men like Lumpkin found difficulty in comprehending. And to back his strength of spirit he had developed a firm-knit body capable of amazing endurance.

The year 1837 drew to its close without any sign from the Cherokees that they intended to comply with the order of removal. Notices were posted throughout the Nation reminding them that less than five months remained before force would be used to uproot them, and warning the tribe that Ross would no longer be recognized by the government.

But to the Cherokees such words were senseless; Ross was in fact their chief and trusted leader, and they refused to admit that he could be disregarded by the United States. Under his direction, they prepared a final appeal to Washington; out of their empty-bellied misery, they demanded: "For adhering to the principles on which your great empire is founded . . . are we to be despoiled of all we hold dear on earth? Are we to be hunted through the mountains like wild beasts, and our women, and [our] children, our aged, and [our] sick, [to be] dragged from their homes like culprits and packed on board loath-some boats for transportation to a sickly clime?"[24]

To this memorial was joined a huge petition from the citizens of Pennsylvania, New Jersey, New York, and Massachusetts for an inquiry into the validity of the Schermerhorn treaty. It was read to the House of Representatives; and speaking on it, Wise paid an eloquent tribute to Ross, "the man who swam the river at the Battle of the Horseshoe and at the risk of his life brought away the canoes which enabled Jackson's force to defeat the Creek warriors, and who is now turned out of his dwelling by the Georgia guard and all his property given to others . . . John Ross is known by many members of this House to be an honest, intelligent man, worthy to sit in the councils of the American Nation, let alone the councils of an Indian tribe." Compar-ing Ross in intellect and moral honesty with Forsyth of Georgia, who had been made a member of Van Buren's cabinet, Wise preferred the Cherokee chief.[25]

In a last effort, as the May 23 deadline was approached, Ross pro-posed to negotiate a new treaty which would, if removal was absolutely inevitable, at least give the tribe a fair price for their land and then allow another two years in which to emigrate. He argued that it would cost the United States less to do justice in that manner than to pay the price of forcible removal.

In response to Ross's plea and to the vehement protest from many sections of the country, Van Buren proposed to Congress to so extend the time for voluntary emigration. But Lumpkin, in the Senate, and Governor Gilmer of Georgia, threatening to expel the Cherokees with state troops if the United States delayed action one minute beyond midnight of May 23, were too strong for the president; Van Buren withdrew his request, and the last hope of the tribe was gone.

CHAPTER 18

Georgia had waited thirty-[four] years, from 1802 to 1836, for the extinguishment of Indian titles to lands within her borders. In the last ten years, since the discovery of gold on Ward's Creek, the struggle to oust the Cherokees had become exceedingly bitter. Ultimate victory was sweet; it must not be delayed by any show of faint-heartedness! The Indians must go on the stroke of the clock.

Lumpkin and Gilmer had reinforcements sent to the military units already in the Cherokee country: General Winfield Scott, the new commander, had under him a concentration of infantry, cavalry, and artillery that could oppose seven soldiers to every five adult male Cherokees, who had already been disarmed; and he was authorized to call on the governors of Georgia, Alabama, Tennessee, and North Carolina for additional militiamen and volunteers to the number of four thousand.

A careful census of the Nation which Ross caused to be made in 1835 showed 16,542 blood citizens of the eastern Cherokee tribe; 201 whites married to Cherokees; and 1,592 slaves. Since that time, accepting the claims of removal agents, 2,000 had been persuaded to go west. General Scott had, therefore, to gather up about 16,500 Indians, whites, and slaves, transport them eight hundred miles over a sparsely settled and difficult region, and set them down in a wilderness unprepared to receive them.

The general arrived in the Cherokee Nation only two weeks in advance of the date for beginning the round-up, and immediately issued a proclamation:

"Before another moon has passed, every Cherokee man, woman, and child must be in motion to join his brethren in the far west, according to the determination of the President which I have come to enforce . . . My troops already occupy many positions . . . and thousands are approaching from every quarter to render resistance and escape alike hopeless . . . Will you, then, by resistance compel us to resort to arms? . . . Will you by flight seek to hide yourselves in mountains and forests, and thus oblige us to hunt you down?"[1]

In his first report, Scott informed the government that Colonel Lindsay, preceding him, had already established twenty-three military posts in the Cherokee Nation, seventeen being stockades suitable for the confinement of Indians. These became "forts," and some were named in honor of those concerned in the removal; Gilmer, Lindsay, Scott, and so on.

Before the hour struck, Ross called the Tribal Council to prepare and adopt a formal protest against what they termed the capture of the Cherokees. No suggestion of resistance was made, however; it was presented to General Scott merely as a matter of record.

It was Ross's acknowledgement that he had been beaten in the long fight. Now he was but one of the sixteen odd thousand who must move, at Scott's orders, with Quatie and his five children. He could only watch while the round-up was accomplished by the soldiers—watch, note with grim diligence for the record the outrages practiced by the undisciplined detachments of troops, and hold the people steady in the attitude of non-resistance.

Few came voluntarily into the stockades, and to gather the others squads of soldiers were sent out. They stole upon the Indian homes, surrounded them, invaded them with fixed bayonets and peremptory orders to get out at once. Families at meals were compelled to leave their food uneaten and take the trail, driven by curses and blows when the sick and aged slowed the pace. Cherokee men were seized in the fields or on the road and sent away without being allowed to rejoin their families; women were taken from their spinning wheels, and children from their playgrounds.

Stubborn? Yes, and sometimes surprising: one squad of soldiers coming upon an old full-blood in his house were temporarily paralyzed when he quietly called his household about him and knelt with them to pray. But before the prayer was ended, the soldiers ordered them out, hurrying them off with only such possessions as they could snatch up—the small children "hugging to their hearts some [childish] treasure, a bow and arrows, a ~~tiny cane~~ blow-gun, a string of beads or [perhaps] a tattered rag-baby."[2]

Close behind the soldiers came the Georgians who had waited so long for the last spoils. "In many cases, on turning for a [one] last look as they crossed a [the] ridge, ~~the captive Indians~~ [they] saw their homes in flames, fired by the lawless rabble," who had no use for the houses. "So keen were these outlaws on the scent that in some instances they were driving off the cattle and other stock of the Indians almost before the soldiers had fairly started the[ir] owners in the other direction. Systematic hunts were made by ~~these~~ same men for Indian graves, to rob them of the silver pendants and other valuables deposited with the dead."[3]

Such abandoned possessions were supposed to be paid for by the United States, but as a last ironic jest it may be noted that the fiscal agent sent to make these payments reported that the banks of Alabama, Tennessee, and Georgia in which government funds had been deposited could supply only a small amount of specie and he must pay in state bank notes at a discount of eight per cent even in the states of issue!

Years later, a Georgia volunteer who served with Scott's force said: "I fought through the Civil War and have seen men shot to pieces and slaughtered by thousands, but the Cherokee Removal was the cruelest work I ever knew."[4]

Under the circumstances, it was bound to be cruel; it must involve the very old, the crippled, the blind, and the feeble, women heavy with child, women in labor, those ill with measles, chicken pox, diphtheria. It was a round-up conducted by exasperated men in squads directed by non-commissioned officers by whom General Scott's order to observe all possible humanity towards the captives was treated as a joke. The soldiers were often tired and hungry on the job; and in their own rage and misery found a sadistic joy in mistreating the Indians. After all, an Indian was of no importance politically!

Here and there, Ross's pacific counsel failed, and in a sudden blaze of resentment against brutalities there was bloodshed, as in the case of old Tsali:

He was surprised and seized in his home with his wife, his brother, his three sons, and their families. Tsali's wife, aged and ill, found it hard to keep up on the march, and the soldiers began to prod her with bayonets. Infuriated at this, the Indian men made a concerted rush upon the soldiers and disarmed them, killing one. The other soldiers fled, and the Indians joined a band of two hundred or more refugees in the mountains under the leadership of a full-blood named Euchela.

Scott ordered the fugitives taken, and so persistently were they hunted, and so severe were the hardships Euchela's band endured, that many died of exposure and starvation during the year and more they managed to evade their pursuers. At last, finding it impossible to take them, Scott sent word that if they would come in and make a pact to observe the peace he would allow them to remain in their old homes until their case could be adjusted by the government. But Euchela answered: "I cannot be at peace now; for a whole year your soldiers have hunted me like a wild deer. I have suffered almost more than I can bear. I had a wife and a little child, and because I would not be your slave they have starved on the mountains and I have buried them with my own hands at midnight!"

On hearing of Scott's offer, however, Tsali came in with his brother and sons, offering himself and them as sacrifices for the rest, who must die in the mountains if they remained out. Euchela and his band then surrendered. In order to impress upon the Cherokees his absolute power, Scott ordered Tsali, his brother, and the two elder sons to be shot. A detachment of Cherokee prisoners was compelled to do the shooting—as a further demonstration that all resistance was futile and would be punished with death.

A few moments before the volley that was to batter his life out was fired, old Tsali spoke, saying: "I am not afraid to die; oh no, I want to die, for my heart is very heavy!" He turned to Euchela, brought as a prisoner to witness the execution: "Euchela, there is a favor I want to ask of you. You know I have a little boy lost somewhere in the mountains. I want you to find him and, if he is not dead, tell him that my last words were that he must never go to the west but stay in the land of his birth. It is best for a man to die in his native land and be buried there beside a stream he knows!" Whereupon, the bandage was tied across Tsali's eyes, and he crumpled down upon the soil he loved, shattered by bullets from guns tremblingly aimed by men of his own tribe, themselves crushed by the horror of the ordeal.

Euchela's desperate defiance and Tsali's sacrifice, however, forced an agreement from the government to permit the mountain Indians of North Carolina to remain in their hill homes; and there some 1,500 of their descendants still live prosperously.[5]

Numbers of men escaped from the stockades, some to go in search of lost members of their families, little boys and girls who had run off into the woods before they could be seized, and the aged and sick left behind when the captors had no means of transporting them to the concentration camps. To the Georgia guard was assigned the not uncongenial task of recovering the fugitives in that state; when they were caught, the routine punishment was a hundred lashes on the bare back.

Slowly the round-up went forward and the stockades filled. The necessity for feeding the prisoners seemed not to have been anticipated, and musty corn meal and fat salt pork was the only ration supplied. To people who had lived largely on green vegetables, fruit, and fresh meat and had spent their days in active outdoor pursuits, the ration was poison and the confinement deadly. There was no milk for even the smallest children. Vainly, women begged to be allowed to go out from the stockades to gather wild onions, greens, and early berries for their families. Army doctors were on duty—even one dentist, though he never touched a Cherokee tooth—but after a number of sudden and inexplicable deaths had occurred the belief that they were being poisoned by the doctors took hold of the Indians. Thereafter, most of the prisoners refused the white man's medicines, even though they were unable to procure their own familiar and tried herb remedies.

The camps had practically no sanitary arrangements, and soon became pest holes, swarming with flies, infested with vermin. Fevers and dysentery drove through the prisoned people, killing many. As the hot weather came on, the number of babies that died was appalling.

"Add to these conditions," said a Cherokee writer, "the facts that whiskey was allowed to be brought into the camps and sold freely to the military, and that drunken soldiers had no regard for the sanctity of Cherokee womanhood when it was at their mercy, and the picture of the last extremity to which the captives could be reduced is complete."[6]

By the end of June, five thousand of the sixteen thousand unfortunates had been collected. They were then marched to steamboats on the Hiwassee and Tennessee Rivers—not the luxurious craft promised by Currey and Schermerhorn, but boats that were incredibly filthy, and leaky—into which they were packed like pigs in a crate. One boat was so overburdened that it almost sank at the landing; it was lightened in a hurry, people being put ashore haphazardly, children separated from parents and wives from husbands, to be reunited, if ever, only after wearisome months, in the new home in the west.

The boats wheezed down the twisting Tennessee, down the Ohio, down the Mississippi to the mouth of the Arkansas, labored up that river to Little Rock, there discharging their wretched cargoes—what was left of them. In the frightful heat of midsummer the survivors were then driven on foot the remaining two hundred miles to the western Cherokee agency.

Over that "Trail of Tears," the marching Cherokees were harried by men bearing the American flag, the symbol of freedom Betsy Ross had made for General Washington. "Wherever," once cried a great American orator, "the flag comes, and men behold it, they see in its sacred emblazonry no rampant lion and fierce eagle, but only *light*, and every fold significant of liberty!"[7]

Conceived in injustice and greed, carried out in anger and resentment, this phase of the removal was inevitably bungled, hopelessly and cruelly bungled. Contractors pledged to establish provision depots along the way and wagons for the final stage of the journey failed to do so. Water in the rivers fell so low that steamboat transportation soon became impracticable. The drought was so protracted that the overland route was a trail of burning thirst, to which hunger was added, for the game the emigrants must have to supplement the contractors' starvation rations had drifted far away from the designated road in search of water.

But for all this dolorous and deadly experience, the pressure for removal did not relax. Georgia attended to that.

With breaking hearts, Ross and the other disregarded officials of the Cherokee Nation saw the tragedy unroll before their eyes. But they raised so desperate a protest that Scott was finally moved to listen. "We speak as prisoners begging for mercy!" they cried; they asked only that the movement should be halted until the cooler months of fall, and that the people should be sent off under their own management in detachments small enough to be conveniently fed on the way and sheltered on arrival in the west. Of one party about to be embarked, they said to Scott, "We feel for them as friends condemned to die."

Scott answered that the people must go, and that the business of collecting them into the stockades must continue. He would, however, suspend removal until September if Ross and the other head men would "discountenance all expectations of any delay beyond that time, prevent any Cherokees from escaping from the camps—or leaving at all except with a written order from the officers in command—prevent drinking and disorder, and assist in getting exact lists of names, families, ages, and sex of the emigrants." He would also allow them to organize, provision, and conduct the emigrant parties, under military supervision.[8]

This concession was welcome; within a few hours, the acceptance (with thanks) of Scott's offer by Ross and the council was in the general's hands. Two days later, at one of the concentration camps, the council prefaced deliberations on ways and means by the formal declaration that the Cherokee government could not recognize as valid the treaty which forced them to emigrate; they were, they asserted for the record, acting under protest, as captives of the United States government.

Stubborn to the last! Consistent, too; for twenty years Ross had striven to the limit of his official and personal influence to lead his people into paths that should merge with the white man's road because he saw that amalgamation of the races was inevitable; he had fought the old lulling, fatalistic belief of the Indians, "What is, is, and what must be, will be!" The people had recognized his wisdom and had responded to his call. Now the ruined Cherokees on the road of exile were miserable, God knows, but they were not broken.

Ross had been unable to keep his promise to save for the people the land of their birth. He was a chief who had failed, and according to tradition he should have been cast aside. Instead, the thousands who remained in the east awaiting removal, suffering the purgatory of confinement, cruelty, pestilence and death, facing the long road of Calvary, continued to look with confidence on his love and intelligence to bring them somehow to better things.

CHAPTER 19

Conferences between Ross and General Scott developed into a battle of wits. The chief chose as associates on the committee to plan and carry out the removal the ablest Cherokees remaining in the east, Whitepath, Sitewakee, Brown, Taylor, Elijah Hicks, and two Gunter brothers. They fought for a sufficient allowance of funds to move the people in reasonable comfort and feed them adequately on the way. Scott, forced to maintain a niggardly attitude by a government incapable of making a generous, or even a fair, gesture towards Indians, haggled over each item of the committee's estimates.

Ross proposed to choose as conductors of detachments leading men of the various districts, who would organize the trains from amongst their own relations and friends; he would pay them five dollars a day each. With each train he would send a physician, an interpreter, a commissary officer, wagon master and assistant, who would also be paid. He proposed to hire for nine dollars a day each, enough four-horse wagon outfits to carry the people. He asked for a ration allowance of sixteen cents a day for each person, and the issue of three pounds of soap with every hundred rations.

Scott roared his protest at such "extravagant" demands. At least half of the people, he argued, could go on foot and cover from twelve to fifteen miles a day—in fact, the marching would be good for them! Another ten per cent could easily walk half the time. Why, then, provide so many wagons? Besides, the ration allowance was absurdly high and must be cut down.

Ross retorted that he did not intend to continue the wholesale tragedy of starvation, sickness, and death being enacted under military oversight! The fight was on; and as usual ended in a compromise. Ross took what he could get, and the general yielded whatever he had to yield, glad to be relieved of the details of removal.

In the month remaining before Ross was to move the first contingent, he sent runners to all fugitive Indians asking them to come into the camps and join their clan groups in preparations to start. His chosen party conductors organized their people. Other aides collected wagons, forage, and equipment. Men were sent forward to establish supply depots along the way. There were a multitude of details to be settled.

As a matter of fact, Ross had the first of the thirteen trains that moved under Cherokee direction under way three days before the first of September, the date fixed by Scott for the start.

Shorey Coodey, an educated Cherokee, described vividly the beginning of that overland exodus:[1]

"I left the agency on the 27th of August, after night, and reached the encampment [. . .] early the following morning, for the purpose of aiding in the ~~necessary~~ arrangements [necessary to get a portion in motion on that day] . . .

"At noon all was in readiness [for moving.] [T]he ~~teams~~ [trains were] stretched out in a line [. . .] through a heavy forest, groups [. . .] formed about each wagon, ~~some~~ [others] shaking the hand of [some] sick [friend or] relative ~~s or friends~~ who would be left behind. The temporary camps [covered with] ~~of~~ boards ~~or~~ [and some of] bark, that for three summer months had been their only shelter and *home* were crackling and falling under blazing flame. The day was bright and beautiful, but a gloomy thoughtfulness was strongly depicted [. . .] [on] every face. In all the bustle of preparation there was a silence and stillness of the voice that betrayed the sadness of the heart.

"At length the word was given to *move on!* ~~As~~ I glanced along the line [and] the form of Goingsnake, an aged and respected chief whose head eighty winters had whitened, [. . .] passed [before] me and led the way [. . .], followed by a number of young men on horseback.

"At this very moment a low sound of distant thunder fell on my ears. In almost an exact western direction, a dark spiral cloud was rising above the horizon~~; it~~ [and] sent forth a murmur~~;~~ I almost fancied ~~it~~ a voice of divine indignation ~~against~~ [for] the wrongs ~~suffered by~~ [of] my [poor and] unhappy countrymen, driven by *brutal* power from all they loved and cherished in the land of their fathers, to ~~satisfy~~ [gratify] the cravings of avarice. ~~But~~ [T]he sun ~~remained~~ [was] unclouded—no rain fell—the thunder rolled away and ~~was~~ [seemed] hushed in the distance. The scene around and before me, and [in] the elements above, were peculiarly impressive [. . .]~~, and remarked upon~~ [It was at once spoken of] by several persons near me, [and looked upon] as ominous of some future event in the west."

Goingsnake, chosen to lead this first detachment out of respect for his age and wisdom, was strikingly dressed in an ancient blue frock coat edged with red, a turban about his long gray hair, and a wide woolen scarf across his shoulders half concealing the United States government's medal, given for bravery in the Creek campaign. Behind him the Cherokee teamsters sent their horses over the stump-encumbered road with shrill "ee-yahs!" of command and encouragement; and in the wagons crouched the softly weeping women in dresses and bonnets so old and patched that, as an observer said, they might have come from some Jew's rag shop.

A long trek lay ahead; 143 days were to be required to accomplish it. Of the 729 well and able-bodied persons who started, supplied with 36 wagons and 288 saddle horses, properly provisioned and cared for, 54 were to die before the train arrived on January 17, 1839, at the western

Cherokee agency. It was of necessity a difficult journey, leading over the broken, forested ridges to the Hiwassee, thence to the crossing of the Tennessee River near Jolly's Island; two hundred miles across the Cumberland plateau of middle Tennessee, by McMinnville and Murfreesboro, to a ford of the Cumberland River at Nashville; on to Clarksville; another hundred and fifty miles of hard going through southwestern Kentucky and the southern extremity of Illinois, crossing the Ohio near the Cumberland's mouth; by ferry over the Mississippi at Cape Girardeau; and a final four hundred miles of tortuous mountain and valley trails across Missouri and Arkansas, with the hunters ranging far on the flanks in search of game.

Succeeding detachments left at intervals from three to six days. Elijah Hicks led 858 on the road; Jesse Bushyhead moved with 950; Sitewakee with 1,250; George Hicks with 1,118; James Brown with 850; Choowalooka[2] with 1,150; and so on. Last to leave were the 231 under Captain John Drew who had been delayed until early in December by sickness and the business of removal.

In that brief time, more than thirteen thousand Indians had taken the road; and while the toll of suffering and death was heavy in the bitter weeks of the journey, it was far lighter than that paid by the fewer than four thousand who had been transported by the United States.

To Ross and his lieutenants goes the credit for organizing and leading this tremendous exodus, but without the courage and resourcefulness of the people themselves it must have been infinitely more terrible than it was. In the people Ross found inspiration for the task; though he had been defeated in the long struggle to save their Nation in the land of their fathers, had been flouted and ignored at Washington, the people knew he had given in their service the last breath of effort that was in him. Like them, he had lost his home, the fruits of years of work, with everything that had made life sweet and flavorous. But he had neither been crushed nor dishonored. He was still fit, in the eyes of the people, to lead them, recover for them in the new and difficult land their prosperity. They could trust him still as the keeper of their spirit and dignity.

Though through proper organization Ross and his helpers could mitigate the rigors of the enforced exile, nothing could have saved it from being, after all, a heartbreaking migration. The long and weary way was signposted with the graves of the weak and the sorrowful. Strange, poignant tales were told by survivors of these tragedies of the route:

Delilah McNair, daughter of the David Vann[3] who years before had opened his home to the first Moravian missionaries on condition that they set up a school there, died as the wagon in which she rode neared the grave of her husband who, driven out of Georgia two years before, had been buried in Tennessee. She was buried beside him, and her children halted to carve and set up over the double grave a stone bearing this inscription:

> Their children, being members of the Cherokee Nation and having to go with their people to the west, do leave this monument, not only to show their regard for their parents but to guard their sacred ashes against the unhallowed intrusions of the white man.

Another grave was that of old Whitepath, who reached the end of his endurance in Kentucky. There, near Hopkinsville, he was buried and over him was placed as a tomb a box weighted with stones, at the ends of which were nailed poles bearing black streamers; and as the slow procession passed, men and women paused to pray for the repose of a beloved chief.

The later detachments reached the Mississippi River after severe winter freezes had filled it with masses of broken ice. Ferry boats could not operate, and for weeks the accumulating multitude waited to cross. The sick filled the wagons, and many were forded to lie on the frozen ground with only canvas sheets or blankets stretched to shelter them from wind, sleet, and snow. Hundreds died. Of many of these—homesick women and old men—it was said that they had no wish to live!

Ross left Georgia with the last small detachment. He rode a horse, swinging back and forth along the line to encourage the people; Quatie and the smaller children, Jane, Silas, and George, were driven by a slave in the shabby old family carriage.

Beyond the Mississippi, Ross and his family diverged from the route in order to visit the former western Cherokee reservation in Arkansas. At Little Rock, in the raw late winter weather, Quatie suddenly finished her fight. Dying in Tsan-Usdi's comforting arms, sighing, she whispered, "I am sorry I can go no further, can do no more." The chief left her there under a gravestone as upright as her life had been, marked with her English name *Elizabeth*. She had been for twenty-five years his love, his valiant partner, the warmhearted mistress of his home.

More silent now than ever, Ross pushed on with the children to rejoin the other exiles.

CHAPTER 20

The price of that exile, in human lives, is told in the stark figures: Nearly seventeen thousand were rounded up for removal, and fewer than thirteen thousand reached the western Cherokee country. Four thousand victims, one out of every four! Nearly 3,500 of the 4,000 died in the concentration camps and during removal under army supervision.

Had a buyer and shipper of beasts shown such a percentage of loss he would have been branded a monster of stupid cruelty.

One in four, a stiff charge for the attainment of Lumpkin's fabled land flowing with milk and honey! And, tragically, the promised milk and honey turned, in the hands of government contractors appointed to feed the survivors for a year after their arrival in the west, to niggardly rations of tough old beef unfit to eat and moldy flour. However, said the contractors, if the Indians didn't care for what was offered they could have instead the sum of one dollar a month each with which to provide their own food!

Ross begged in vain to be allowed to take over the business of feeding the outcasts.

The government had also promised to provide farming tools, axes, saws, and other house-building necessities, but that obligation was as insufficiently fulfilled as was the engagement to supply food.

As a consequence of the government's evasion of its obligations, the fewer than six thousand western Cherokees were obliged to assist twice that number of newcomers, many of them ill and destitute. Thousands, in the pinching days from early January to the middle of March, during which the thirteen detachments arrived at the wooded camp rendezvous where the Illinois River joins the Arkansas, came to envy those who had perished on the way.

Heart-stricken by his wife's death, Ross had no time to brood over his loss; he must plunge at once into the work of sheltering, feeding, and fitting the emigrants into a new framework of tribal organization.

The six thousand already settled in Indian Territory also had their troubles, were still sore from their bruises. First sent to the Arkansas country with the government's assurance that they should be left there undisturbed forever, they had cleared land, built homes, accumulated herds, and begun to prosper when again, in 1828, white pressure forced them to leave their farms and push on. In the newly created Indian Territory, they were compelled once more to broach the wilderness; and at their western border were hostile tribes, not only the resentful Osages who had harried them in Arkansas, but nomadic Indians like the Pawnees, horse thieves and raiders, as willing to plunder the Cherokees as the whites.

But the new land was a good land, its forested flint-rock hills swelling softly and offering wild harvests of nuts, grapes, persimmons, and plums, its grass-covered prairies rich in fine pasturage. It extended west from the state boundaries of Arkansas and Missouri some fifty miles, and north from the Arkansas River to Kansas, comprising roughly seven million acres. The western Cherokees were just becoming well rooted in the eastern section of this reservation when the Easterners were sent out.

These Old Settlers, as the western Cherokees called themselves, were naturally sympathetic towards their newly arrived brethren, but felt themselves, as first comers, entitled to control of tribal affairs. Their attitude was encouraged by certain representatives of the United States, the agent to the Westerners, the superintendent for the western tribes, and the commandant at Fort Gibson who was the voice of the War Department in the new Cherokee Nation. These men took their cues from Washington, where Ross was detested because of his last-ditch opposition to removal and where his deposition from power in the tribe was heartily desired.

Ross was no broken leader, however; he would beg favors neither from the government nor the western brothers. No more were his people beggared in spirit. As they lingered in the wide-flung camp, waiting for the promised tools and ploughs, half starving on the unfit contractors' rations or living on the charity of Old Settlers, Ross persistently pressed for fulfillment of government promises. He was in frequent consultation with officials and prominent men of the western Nation, Brown, Looney, Rodgers, Candy, Tobacco Will, and Sequoyah. To them he made it plain that the 12,500 or more recent arrivals must have full representation in the Cherokee government.[1]

Against Ross, the most active of all who sought to eliminate him from leadership, was General Arbuckle at Fort Gibson. He began by peppering the chief with messages concerning rumors of impending outbreaks among the new arrivals. One alarming message followed close on the heels of another, now reporting that an attack was planned on Lieutenant Hammond's detachment of soldiers on duty at the camp, now that a gang of wild immigrant Cherokees who had been prevented from buying whiskey had threatened to kill the lieutenant because he had been responsible for the death of three tribesmen in North Carolina before the removal.

No outbreak occurred; Ross pointed out, in courteous answers to Arbuckle's messages, that miserable and restless as his people were, without sufficient food or materials with which to work, without decent shelter, they nevertheless remained peaceable and law-abiding. They asked only to be allowed to settle. His words were confirmed by Captain McCall, whom Arbuckle sent to investigate rumors of insurrection.

Ross built his own first western cabin home in a wide "V" of valley land near a place called Park Hill, the pleasant site selected for his mission by his old friend Samuel Worcester who, after his release from the Georgia penitentiary, had joined the Old Settler Cherokees. There, Ross took up the task of checking the accounts for removal and preparing them for presentation to the United States Treasury for payment.

Early in June, he issued an address to the Cherokees, Old Settlers as well as newcomers, proposing a General Council to establish a closer unity between the two sections of the tribe; for "a house divided against itself cannot stand!"

His action was hastened by a growing hostility, stimulated not only by Arbuckle but by the Ridges, Boudinot, Boudinot's brother, Stand Watie, Bell, West, Starr, and others of the signers of the Schermerhorn treaty who had come to believe Ross responsible for their troubles. They called him arrogant, selfish, and ruthless in his attempts to retain his power. His appearance of self-effacement, his attitude of listening to the opinions of others, his demeanor as the people's true servant, they said, concealed the designs of a dangerous, self-seeking man.[2]

Friends turned enemies are the bitterest foes a man can have, and Ross knew that against these vindictive tribesmen the struggle to secure for the newcomers proper representation in the tribal government would be severe. It could not long be delayed, and his call to a council was his challenge of their strength.

Ross faced real opposition, fostered by able and aggressive men who for nearly two years had spread among the Old Settlers their own feeling of hostility. His firm friend John Jolly, who had been Principal Chief of the Westerners for many years, had died six months before. John Brown, chosen at a snap meeting of the Legislative Council at which only eight members were present, had succeeded Jolly; John Rodgers was first assistant chief, and John Looney—nearly every other Cherokee child was named John!—was third in rank. Sequoyah, though not an official, was influential in the ranks of the Old Settlers.

Brown and Rodgers were strongly anti-Ross, but Looney and

Sequoyah were friendly to him and agreed that the newcomers ought to share in the tribal government. Most powerful of the four was Brown, by nature and instinct a reactionary, a lover of the old Indian life who had actively agitated for the flight of the Cherokees out of the United States to Mexico. One of his followers had made a strange allegorical appeal to the people:

> A bird shrieks in the air. Its cries are for its young. Lo! a huge snake outstretched. This is the Troubler. It would crush us . . . The bird shrieking towards the setting sun is ours . . . The snake can be cut asunder . . . You are hemmed in by multitudes, but must give no heed. Perhaps the bird may pluck us out, though your way had been choked.

The "bird" was Mexico, its "young" the Cherokees, the "snake" the United States; at the moment, the feeble new Republic of Texas was struggling, under Sam Houston's presidency, against a Mexico still unconvinced that she had permanently lost that great empire to a handful of American colonists; and it was probable that Mexican agents were working on the western Cherokees in Indian Territory, as well as on a small band that, under Chief Boles, had removed to Texas long before Houston's triumph at San Jacinto.[3]

In his summons to the council Ross reminded the Old Settlers of his visit to them in 1837 and their approval of Chief Jolly's action in appointing delegates to assist in the attempt to nullify the Schermerhorn treaty, and emphasized the present vital necessity for harmonious action if the Nation was to prosper.

In a brief note, Chief Brown answered, "You must speak plainly, say just what your people think we must do to secure unity."

Ross complied: a formal Act of Union, a new constitution, and a code of laws acceptable to the reunited Nation were required.

He secured from a council of the new immigrants the appointment of a committee to arrange for the general meeting and prepare an agenda. George Lowrey and Edward Gunter were named to act with him on that committee; and they invited Chief Brown, Rodgers, and Looney to meet with them.

Brown declined, declaring that the council was unnecessary since there already existed in the Indian Territory an organized Cherokee government. The exiles had been taken in as brothers by the Westerners, therefore they should be willing to live under the western Nation's constitution and laws. The opinion of the Ridges and Boudinot was implicit in this reply.

The weakness of the contention was obvious. Fewer than 6,000 Old Settlers, living under a constitution and code decidedly more primitive than the Easterners had adopted in 1827, were asking 12,500 blood brothers with equal right in the Indian Territory to submit to their government. This would amount to vassalage—a brotherly, benevolent vassalage, perhaps, but intolerable to the Ross men.

Important communal business affecting the new immigrants such as the payment of removal accounts and the distribution of millions of dollars due to be paid for abandoned improvements in the east, and the organization of a much extended school system, must be conducted by the tribal government. It was absurd to attempt to deny the 12,500 a voice in the settlement of such matters.

Ross submitted Brown's answer to the Legislative Council of the Easterners, which denied by formal resolution that the two sections had in fact reunited. Despite their capture and forcible removal, said the Ross council, the Easterners retained unimpaired their tribal sovereignty and authority. They reiterated that they were not broken-spirited supplicants for political charity, but equals demanding their rights.

The controversy grew sharper. Brown and his supporters submitted to the United States agent a report that in spite of their "generous" attitude, and the support of General Arbuckle, they were unable to satisfy the Ross faction. The introduction of Arbuckle's name was surprising; the only possible explanation of his meddling in tribal politics being that he was following instructions from Washington to discredit Ross.

Through old Sequoyah's influence, the Westerners at length agreed to meet the Ross men. But they came reluctantly, and in no mood for compromise. The Ridges and Boudinot upheld, in passion-stirring talks, the contention that an adequate and satisfactory government already existed, and that the recent immigrants would at the next election have their opportunity to share in it. Ross was firm in maintaining that immediate participation was necessary since grave matters affecting the more than two-thirds of the tribe who had been exiled must be dealt with before the next election. To deny them a voice in the discussions and a hand in the settlement could not but "disturb the peace of the community, and operate injuriously to the best interests of the Nation."[4]

A deadlock resulted.

The Easterners then sent a formal request to the United States agent charged with the duty of distributing tribal funds due from the government not to make any further payments to the western Cherokees.

To relieve the tension, Ross and Sequoyah agreed to a ten-day adjournment; the joint session to reconvene on July 1 when, it was hoped, hot heads would be cool.

CHAPTER 21

Almost immediately upon the adjournment of the council, a tragedy occurred that involved Ross dangerously and inflamed the passions of both parties in the Nation. To what extent, if at all, Ross was personally concerned was never established. Here are the fact:

At practically the same hour in the morning of June 22, in widely separated districts of the Cherokee country, Major Ridge, his son John, and Boudinot were set upon by armed Cherokees and done to death. Boudinot's brother, Stand Watie, who was also attacked, managed to escape; and he at once rallied a force of anti-Ross men with the declared purpose of killing Ross and his close advisers.

Ross's enemies based their charge that he was responsible for the killings on this rather slender thread of evidence: Boudinot was slain within two miles of Ross's home; one of the killers was seen in the woods near the chief's cabin an hour or so before Boudinot was attacked; and on the preceding day a considerable number of his full-blood followers visited Ross, who "seemed to be in a bad humor." Moreover, they contended that he must have had knowledge of the killers' intentions, in view of the fact that he had always had their confidence.

It was later discovered that the execution of the Ridges and Boudinot had been decreed at a secret council of three hundred full-bloods, where they were condemned as traitors under the tribal law of 1820. Certain members of this council were told off as executioners, sworn to secrecy and given assurance of protection. Ross denied curtly and categorically that he was privy to the meeting and its decision. His supporters argued that the charge against him was both foolish and baseless, considering his long career as a steadfast disciple of peace; that it was incredible he should turn bloodthirsty when the killings must jeopardize his dearest hope, the union of the two factions. He would have been reckless indeed thus to intensify bitterness and dissention, besides putting himself and those closest to him in grave personal danger! And it must also be remembered that he had in the east, once saved the three men from the vengeance of the hotheaded full-bloods.

News of the killings spread amongst the Indians with characteristic rapidity, as did news of Stand Watie's activities. Within a few hours, Ross sent a message to General Arbuckle reporting Boudinot's death and asking that soldiers be sent to protect him and his friends from Watie's band. In the meantime, five hundred of the chief's friends armed themselves and gathered at his home. They probably saved his life, for Arbuckle waited until the following day before replying to his message, and then suggested that if he believed himself in peril he might come to Fort Gibson and place himself under the general's protection.

Ross knew that Brown and others of the bitter Old Settler faction were at the fort, and he declined to walk into what looked like a trap.

Whereupon an endless chain of messengers began riding between Ross and the fort, the fort and the agency, and the agency and Ross. The chief proposed a meeting at his home of leaders of both parties to make plans for checking further hostile demonstrations. Arbuckle's answer was to demand of Ross the surrender of the killers, whom he described as "murderers." Ross replied that he did not know who they were. Agent Stokes upheld Ross in this, reporting to Washington that he had known the chief for years as a man of peace; and also sent word to Ross that he would withhold all tribal funds pending further instructions from the government.

Arbuckle's letter to the War Department was of an entirely different tenor. He summarized sympathetically the case of the western Cherokees, told of their offer to the newcomers to permit them to vote in the next election for candidates of their own choice, and attempted to justify their rejection of Ross's demand for a new constitution and laws. He said, however, that he hoped to persuade the western leaders who were at the fort under his protection to make satisfactory concessions to the recent immigrants.

Arbuckle declared that unless Ross abandoned his position there would be other killings, followed by reprisals, until finally the whole tribe became involved in civil warfare. But those who knew the general best discounted his alarming words; it was said that when in his cups he could forecast an Indian uprising from the flutter of a single old tribesman's shirt tail.

There were no further killings, and Stand Watie's punitive force evaporated; at the expiration of the ten-day adjournment, Ross calmly called the re-assembled council to order. More than two thousand returned to the meeting, among them many western men. Sequoyah and Tobacco Will, for the western faction, joined Ross and Lowrey in an invitation to Brown, Rodgers, and Looney to attend. Only Looney accepted, the other two sending word that they meant to call a council of their own later.

Ross faced the matter of the killings squarely. His first move was to ask the council to grant a general amnesty to all signers of the Schermerhorn treaty who, under the law of 1820, had rendered themselves liable to punishment by death for treason. This was done, with the provision that such men were to be barred from office in the tribe for five years; also, they were commanded to report to the present council within eight days of the issue of the amnesty order and sign a declaration of peaceful intentions. Next, a strong auxiliary police force was organized to maintain order throughout the Nation and enforce the council's decrees, consisting of eight companies of light horse under Bushyhead's command.

In General Arbuckle's opinion, this action was an arrogant defiance of his own powers. He sent Ross an indignant reprimand; asked why the newcomers refused his good offices as mediator; pictured the whites along the western border of Arkansas fleeing from their homes in fear of warlike bands of Cherokees; and demanded to know if it was true that the council had condemned to death a large number of treaty signers. Either the general was unusually befuddled or chose deliberately to misrepresent the facts, for Ross had already succeeded in demonstrating the peaceful mind of the people assembled in council.

The amnesty order particularly outraged Arbuckle. Holding the Washington theory that the Schermerhorn treaty was a valid document expressing the will of the tribe, he denied that its signers were traitors, subject to an amnesty. He once more demanded the surrender of the men who had killed the Ridges and Boudinot.

In his answer, Ross asserted that the United States had no legitimate concern in the matter, which involved only the tribe and must be handled by the Indians themselves.

After which, to make this attitude clearer, the council formally pardoned the killers on the ground that they had acted under Cherokee law and were not, therefore, punishable.

Within the following two weeks, carrying out Ross's program, the assembled Cherokees passed an Act of Union and formulated a new constitution. Both were signed by Sequoyah as president of the western delegation and approved by Looney as "Acting Chief" of the western Nation.[1]

Before the council ended, the time given the treaty signers to come in and take advantage of the offer of amnesty was extended.

While Ross thus worked diligently for harmony, Arbuckle continued to pursue the phantom of war, notifying the chief that the frontier settlers of Arkansas had become so alarmed over the situation that he had issued arms and ammunition to the state militia!

By now the issue was clearly defined: Could Ross continue as head of the Cherokee Nation against the determination of the United States government to smash him? At Washington it was contended that he had in fact been a usurper for a long time, that the Cherokees had not voted for him as chief since 1830, that he and his cabal had held office in defiance of the tribal constitution.

But these critics neglected to explain that the Cherokee people in the east had not been permitted to hold an election after Georgia extended her laws over the Nation. Or that, in spite of this, the Cherokee Committee and Council had confirmed Ross and the other officials in their positions, thereby as fully as possible carrying out the will of the people.

Unmoved by these attacks, with the knowledge that his people would uphold him, Ross pursued his purpose to bring about a true union of the factions. He ignored Arbuckle's thrust when the general ceased addressing him as chief and substituted "Mr." In sober words, almost invariably wrought into elaborately courteous sentences, he steadily reiterated his position and intentions. He sent a delegation to the council called by Brown and Rodgers on July 22; it was received with such hostility the members were compelled to fly for their lives; reporting this to Arbuckle, Ross recalled the government's promise to lead the immigrant Cherokees not only to a rich land but to a land where they would live in peace under their own laws; and he challenged the general's right to advise Brown and Rodgers to stand firm for the rule of the western faction and thus encourage strife.

Ross's letters, his calmness, his whole attitude roused Arbuckle to a pitch of intemperate partisanship that resulted in a weakening of his influence with many of the Westerners. They listened with disgust to his bitter denunciation of two among them who had opposed Stand Watie's efforts to gather a band to kill Ross: "You, too!" Arbuckle had cried furiously. "You shouldered rifles and went to guard John Ross! But for that, John Ross would have been killed."

Arbuckle's belief that all the western Cherokees would be as pleased as he to see the last of Ross was far from the truth. His definite alignment, on July 29, with Brown and Rodgers and the rule or ruin Westerners not only consolidated the immigrants behind Ross, but caused an increasing number of the Old Settlers to support him as the only Cherokee who could establish and maintain order.

Keeping his mind on the objective of tribal harmony, Ross had the Act of Union and the proposed new constitution published to the people. He called a General Council to meet at Tahlequah, the newly established capital, where both were approved; and amongst the 1,800 signers appeared the names of 115 Old Settlers. A new Cherokee government was thereupon set up, with Ross as Principal Chief and Joseph Vann as Assistant, or Second, Chief, and a proportionate representation of Western men in the National Legislature.

General Arbuckle continued to demand the surrender of the "murderers," went on addressing Ross as "Mr." and professed to see such signs of a Cherokee uprising that he notified the governors of Arkansas and Missouri to be prepared to supply military aid in putting it down. He told the War Department that a band of warlike Seminoles, under a leader called Alligator, lurked in the Cherokee Hills ready to out tomahawks and fall upon the whites!

Arbuckle was the type of trouble-making, panic-breeding military commander that has so often embroiled our frontiers.

In order to secure government recognition of the new Cherokee administration, it was necessary to go to Washington, and in October— Ross was moving swiftly—he notified agent Stokes that he and eight others, included among whom were three Old Settlers, had made their preparations to start. His brother, Lewis Ross, had been made national treasurer, and would accompany the delegation with authority to receive tribal monies.

Not a word to Arbuckle, and the general was furious at Ross's cool ignoring of him. He debated seriously whether or not he ought to have Ross arrested as the instigator of the Ridge and Boudinot "murders" and locked up at Fort Smith. His decision not to do so, but to recommend that he be taken and detained on arrival at Washington as an usurper, was perhaps influenced by the knowledge that all the

12,500 new immigrants and an increasing number of western men were solidly behind Ross. He realized, too, that in the east and north Ross had powerful friends among the whites who would raise a strong wind of protest at such high handed action.[2]

Ross's delegation established itself at Fuller's Hotel in Washington and according to usage reported its presence to the secretary of war, Mr. Poinsett, who replied that he would not receive John Ross but would confer with the rest of the delegates. Whereupon these signed a statement that they would not confer without John Ross. Meanwhile, Secretary Poinsett privately sent for Lewis Ross, rehashing to him the charges against John that Arbuckle had supplied. He branded the chief as instigator of the "murders," charged him with shielding the guilty men, and declared that he had evidence to support his statements. But as the days passed, with the Cherokee delegation maintaining its stand and pressing for recognition, Poinsett was compelled to admit that he not only did not have the evidence of Ross's complicity but that the department had not made any serious investigation of the killings.

The delegation, with Ross at its head, finally got a hearing before a committee of the Senate. There the whole situation was at last made clear. The demand of the Brown and Rodgers delegates, also in Washington, for a division of the Nation was denied on Ross's proof that it was supported only by a small and decreasing minority of the people and his presentation of the repeal of the treason law of 1820, thus assuring the safety of all implicated under that old measure.

Recognition of the Ross government should logically have followed; but when, at Ross's instigation, the Senate committee formally asked Secretary Poinsett what steps he was taking to insure harmony in the Cherokee Nation, it was told that General Arbuckle had been authorized to call a convention of Cherokees to write a new constitution "that will insure entire security in person and property and rights to each individual, the abolition of all such cruel and savage edicts as that under which the unfortunate Ridges and Boudinot were brutally murdered; conformity to the laws and constitution of the United

States; and the election of officers from each party, in reference to their numbers, *excluding John Ross and William Shorey Coodey*."[3]

Coodey was an educated Cherokee known for his loyal support of Ross.

Poinsett had merely authorized Arbuckle to do what Ross had already achieved, except that he insisted on the exclusion of Ross and Coodey from the tribal government.

Acting on his instructions, Arbuckle declared the Tahlequah constitution void, equally with that of the old Western Nation, and summoned a pre-convention conference of leaders of both factions at Fort Gibson for July 25, 1840. Ross and Coodey, however, would not be received.

Ross faced the issue with characteristic confidence. Returning from Washington, he called a session of the government he had established at the capital, Tahlequah. A delegation of its ablest men was chosen to carry to the Fort Gibson conference copies of the Act of Union and the constitution adopted in September 1839, and proof that more than two thirds of the whole Cherokee people had approved them.

The conference was a fiasco. Brown had already left the Nation, to seek in Mexico an asylum for those who persistently held out against Ross. With Brown's flight went the heart of the opposition. Rodgers and a few Old Settler irreconcilables did appear at Fort Gibson, but they had no plan of offense against the Tahlequah government. Arbuckle saw that it would be hopeless to bring about an issue between the respective delegations, and advised the western men to accept the inevitable, make peace with the Ross party and adopt the Tahlequah régime.

This was done, and on yielding for the western faction Rodgers gracefully and generously proposed the toast: "What has been done this day, may it never be undone!"

Thus the year-long struggle was ended, and the reunited Cherokees proceeded to the building of their homes and the reconstruction of life in the new land under the Tahlequah constitution, with Ross as Principal Chief and Coodey as his close adviser.

All as Ross had planned!

CHAPTER 22

About Ross strangely contradictory impressions were current. Despite his force of character and his strong gift for leadership, he had also a baffling, intangible, shadowy quality. His personality was veiled from all but his intimates behind a reserve that was itself concealed by a manner courteous and formal. Many of those opposing him in the tribe denied his force, declaring that his brother Lewis was the real power and that John was a puppet in Lewis's hands.

That legend he did not trouble to destroy; why waste thought on unimportant chatter? In the same spirit, he had submitted to arrest when dragged off to prison with John Howard Payne in Georgia. He had seen his home and the fruits of years of work taken from him without a personal complaint; that outrage was cited in his long memorial to Congress merely as one of a great number. Through all the persecutions directed against him, he remained composed, almost inattentive. His thought was to get free of those who hindered him as quickly as possible, use no energy in idle regrets and useless reproaches, but take up once more his labor for the tribe.

Enemies could not trouble him personally; he dealt with them rather as abstractions, or else ignored them. Save a few of his closest relatives and advisers, he kept even friends at a distance; Payne, who spent months in near contact with him and greatly admired him, left no vital portrait of the man. It is the same with other writers who visited the Cherokees and talked with the chief. They described his house and fields, the aristocratic establishment that was his frame, but gave no clear impression of the human being at its center. They felt him rather than saw him, carried away impressions of his courtesy, gentleness, and a certain velvet-handed force, but the individual escaped them.

The sole approach to the man himself was through his family. The few who gained intimate footing in that circle saw, in the Georgia days of prosperity, a household rich in affection. Between himself and his wife Quatie endured a close and fine understanding. His children adored him, and with him were completely at ease; to them he was tender, expansive, mischievous, a funmaker fond of burlesque; in their company he was not the chief but another child.

There was a feudal flavor about his establishment; it was a sure refuge for anyone of the tribe who had a problem, where no matter was too unimportant to be heard.

These contradictions, reserves, and warmly human qualities are suggested in his portraits. But the living face was far more sensitive than the pictures show; the eyes particularly, deep-set, shining, and inviting, created a sense of grace and power despite the homely features. His shy withholding of himself from close contacts could not keep men from loving and trusting him. They found themselves persuaded to his views without knowing exactly how they had been won. Soft of voice, a little man, a veritable miser in speech and gesture, they could not say from whence came the persuasiveness to which they succumbed. To most of those who fought him, Ross was bewildering, as a man is bewildered by shadows in a forest at night, confusing stripes of airy blackness with actual obstacles.

The long period of violent opposition was now ended. Ross was fifty, at the peak in mind and body, free to begin the rebuilding of tribal institutions and his own fortune. Arbuckle's active interference ceased with the government's tacit acceptance of the tribal union accomplished at Tahlequah. Stand Watie alone remained of Ross's powerful enemies, a long-haired, hawk-like full-blood, nursing his hatred, but without sufficient following either to make war upon Ross or to thwart him politically.

Five miles north of his home, Ross watched the new capital of the Nation, Tahlequah, turn from camp ground to town. It was a pleasant site, where the Plains Utes were said to have pitched their teepees years before. Deep-rooted oaks provided shelter from winter winds and summer shade; springs and a clear creek running over a flat-rock bed supplied plenty of good water; nearby, to the north and west, was abundant pasturage; and east and south, to and beyond the picturesque Illinois River, the country broke into rocky and timbered ridges where ranged deer and wild turkeys.

On a level shelf of land Ross superintended the clearing and fencing of an ample government square. Inside, as a temporary council house, was built an open shed with a rostrum at the side. For executive office, a log cabin was laid up, another for the offices of the legislature, and a third for the Supreme Court. Outside the square rose cabins for the "public cooks," followed by the first store buildings: Murrell's, Meigs's, Ware and Delano's. One Susan Taylor opened a tavern; Johnson Foreman and Tom Wolf set up as her rivals. The place developed rapidly as the people settled to the task of re-creating prosperity.

To the council sessions, each day, Ross rode a sedate gray horse, sometimes accompanied by his eldest son, James, more often alone and using the hour in meditation on the day's problems. Poor as he was, he managed to dress well, in fresh linen, good coat and breeches, fine boots, a new beaver hat which he had bought in Washington. Immaculate, he presided over the prolonged discussions of ragged full-bloods and variously appareled mixed-bloods, with a feminine tolerance of detail, a far-seeing purpose behind every decision.

The big strain was over, but he had use in those years of slow rehabilitation for all the moral stamina he could command. From the visit to Washington in 1839–40, he brought little tangible comfort to a hungry people and a bankrupt government. The United States, refusing formally to recognize the Tahlequah government, though it had been tacitly accepted, withheld all payments of money due—the regular annuity as well as the sums promised under the Schermerhorn treaty; it developed that the treaty, enthusiastically described by Lumpkin as the best ever made with an Indian tribe, was hopelessly vague and contradictory. For example, one section made the United States liable for the cost of removal, while another provided that removal expenses should be deducted from the sum due for the seized eastern land.

It was necessary to return to Washington in the winter of 1840–41, to plead for a settlement of the terms of the treaty. Money was urgently needed in the new land for building homes, breaking out and fencing fields, for horses and milch cows, for school buildings and the hiring of teachers, a thousand pressing individual and community needs.

As ever at Washington, progress toward the final determination of just what was due the Cherokees was glacial. Van Buren's term expired, and the brief administration of William Henry Harrison had been succeeded by Tyler's before the weary delegation even got a hearing from the president. At last, however, after ten months of waiting, they were received by Tyler with a great show of cordiality. He deplored the delay, the injustice the tribe had suffered; explained that he had fully informed himself on their situation, had read all the treaties, as well as President Washington's address inscribed in the silver-bound book presented to the Cherokee Nation at Philadelphia in 1794, and Jefferson's talk preserved on parchment and surrounded by a symbolic golden chain ("Let us keep that chain bright and unbroken; in its preservation consists our mutual happiness!") Tyler promised a new treaty. It should amply indemnify the Cherokees for their losses, establish on a permanently friendly basis the political relations between them and the United States, and include a fee simple title to the western lands. "And," he said finally, "I shall rejoice to have been the President under whose auspices these great and happy results shall have been produced!"[1]

That was something worth taking home! So the delegation thought; and even Ross, with twenty years' experience of the eel-like character of government officials and Congress, believed that a settlement was near. He reported to the October session of the National Council, and turned with a lighter heart to the development of his farm near Park Hill.

However, Tyler's term had ended, Polk had served four years, Zachary Taylor one, and Fillmore was in the second year of his term before, in 1851, the final interpretation of the Schermerhorn treaty was approved and the money due the exiled Cherokees paid. Nearly sixteen years after the ex-preacher had wrought his trickery of December 1835, and thirteen years after the removal!

In those thirteen years much of Ross's energies were required to combat the hostile efforts of government agents, inspired by the disappointed Arbuckle, to keep alive the feud between the small faction led by Stand Watie and the Ross party. The governor of Arkansas also took a hand, abetting the plan of Brown's irreconcilables to move the tribe to Texas—where it was not wanted, and where, in fact, a small band of Cherokees already settled there was being persecuted and harassed—or else to divide the Nation. As late as 1846 the commissioner of Indian Affairs declared that the Act of Union and the new constitution, in force for more than five years, were not binding on the Old Settlers!

As excuse for this protracted interference, Arbuckle and his like dangled the old bugaboo of peril to the whites living near the borders of the Cherokee country through clashes of the rival factions. The fact that no such outbreak occurred convinced neither the general nor the governor of Arkansas that Ross was better able to handle the Cherokees than they.

The people did not sit with idle hands through this long time of waiting. In whatever ways they could, borrowing money or buying on credit tools and materials, they completed their cabins, got land under cultivation, acquired horses and other live stock. From the eleven schools established in 1839, the number grew to more than a score by 1851. The chief's nephew, W. P. Ross, graduated from Princeton College and came home to teach for a year in the combined school and church log structure that had been built on Fourteen-Mile Creek by a Cherokee preacher named Boots. In 1844, W. P. Ross became editor of the re-established tribal weekly newspaper, renamed the *Cherokee Advocate*. A national press was inaugurated along with the paper, and there the missionaries Worcester and Evan Jones began to print in Cherokee the *Cherokee Messenger* and the *Cherokee Almanac*, combining, as had always been their practice, useful notes on house building, farming, gardening, and domestic economy with temperance maxims and godly counsel. Missionary stations flourished at the settlements of Park Hill, Dwight, and Fairfield; Methodists, Congregationalists, Baptists, and Moravians were all hard at work.

The Indians had their own ideas about religious instruction which they did not hesitate to express. For instance, at a meeting where a visiting minister preached, with an educated Cherokee beside him to interpret his words to those who knew no English, the interpreter looked troubled by something the preacher said, hesitated, then told the people: "Mr. B—— asks me to say to you that in the sight of God there are only two kinds of people, the good people and the bad people. But I do not believe him. I believe there are three kinds, the good, the bad, and a middle kind that are neither good nor bad, just like me!"

At another meeting, a Baptist mission worker boasted that he had won Indian converts from a Methodist congregation: "I got them to come to my lick-log, and I put my mark on them." Whereupon an indignant Cherokee cried: "If any man puts his mark on my cattle when they go to his lick-log, I call him a thief!"

To maintain the tribal government, money was borrowed from syndicates of white capitalists who, for a stiff rate of interest, were willing to wait for repayment until the government should settle with the Cherokees. As for officials and teachers, Cherokee national scrip, or promises to pay when funds came in from Washington, was their currency. The national debt steadily mounted.

Ross, however, found the problems of those thirteen years far less vexing than those he had faced in Georgia. Arbuckle and the succession of gad-fly agents and commissioners from Washington were far less formidable than the Georgia guard, or Lumpkin, Gilmer, Currey, and Schermerhorn. His people were meeting the challenge of the new land with increasing courage and competence, and his own position as chief ceased to be seriously disputed.

Thus comparatively unhampered, he led the Cherokees forward on the road of material improvement, often checked but never daunted. He rebuilt amongst them tribal pride. Along with scores of others, he grew wealthy in finely productive fields, cattle, horses, sheep, and slaves. Markets were opened for surplus products, overland to St. Louis and by river to New Orleans. He replaced his first log house with a big simply designed brick mansion in the midst of his thousand-acre plantation, calling it Rose Cottage and furnishing it with the best from eastern cabinetmakers, rosewood and mahogany. He had fine silver for his table service.

A visitor to Ross in the fifties wrote: "The chief and his family attended all the public services [at the Park Hill mission]. It was something strange, that shining coach, that would do for Broadway or Chestnut Street, with driver and footman, glistening here and there as it passed the openings in the thickets, then rolling over the greensward up to the log meeting house."[2]

When at last the accumulated tribal funds were received from the United States, Ross carried out a long matured plan for establishing Cherokee academies. Near the edge of the little town of Tahlequah an ample brick building was erected and called the Male Seminary; at the border of his own plantation another for girls, the Female Seminary. To get able principals and teachers, Ross visited colleges and seminaries in the states, making addresses to their students as an honored guest.

He was creating—re-creating, rather—in the Indian Territory a civilization, like the one which had been crushed out in Georgia, based on material prosperity, racial pride, honest independence of spirit, and a genuine faith in an overseeing Divinity—in a God who, though He might lead the people through the valley of the shadow, would bring them in the end to a fair land of rest.

Set away from the flower-bordered mansion were Ross's blacksmith shop, kiln, laundry, dairy, smokehouse, and the cabins for his seventy slaves. There were always guests to be entertained, and a ceaseless flow of Indians to be welcomed, advised, and fed. The chief surrounded himself with a rich, generous atmosphere; and the Cherokees, poor hill men or prosperous aristocrats, were proud of him.

CHAPTER 23

At the age of fifty-four, five years after the death of Quatie, Ross wrote from Boston, where he had gone after putting a number of Cherokee boys in a Pennsylvania school, to Mr. Stapler of Wilmington, Delaware:

"I am deeply interested in and most fervently attached to your beloved daughter Mary . . . With your consent, I should be happy to be united with her in marriage. Did I not believe it will be in my power to confer upon her the ordinary comforts and happiness of this life, I should never wantonly be instrumental in bringing about any change in her situation calculated to render her situation less happy than it is at present . . . I shall await your response at Howard's Hotel in the City of New York."[1]

Mr. Stapler hesitated to give his consent. Mary was only nineteen, a brilliant girl who had just begun to teach in the young ladies' seminary from which she had graduated. Ross had fallen in love with her on a visit to Willow Cottage, the Stapler home, only a month before.

Mary's elder sister, Sarah, had also been strongly attracted to the Cherokee-Scotch chief, a fact Ross learned when his niece, who corresponded with Sarah, sent him a letter she had received from her

168

friend. His answer, somewhat ponderous in style, was quite clear on the point that it was Mary he sought:

"That such a flow of poetic effusion from the pen of the dame inhabitant of that drooping domicile [a heavily playful Ross joke!] should ever be sung with the soft notes of love for me as has been communicated to you, is a thing that never once entered into my thoughts. [But t]his is a strange world . . . while the thoughts of some are upon us, our own minds are turned toward others . . . Were I to seek a heart that is congenial with my own, in view of uniting both into one, I think I should be inclined to search for it among the teachers of some of the seminarys [sic] for young ladies."[2]

Not Sarah, but Mary!

Mary responded to his wooing with shy fervor. To her, he was not only a great man, a true Christian, and an enthusiast for education, which interested her deeply, but a stirring lover. She responded to the virility of the solid body, the masculine strength of features, the almost feminine qualities of emotion and fastidiousness, the romantic history that made up the man. More experienced in life and thought, he brought her a true sympathy and tender love.

The father's doubts were quickly overcome, and within three weeks of the date of Ross's letter from Boston, Mary Stapler became his wife. They were married September 2, 1844.

In the happy, prosperous years that followed, a fine second blooming came to the man whose youth and earlier period of maturity had of necessity been concentrated upon the problem of actual survival for his people, leaving little time for personal satisfactions.

As it was, he could not at once bring his bride home; he was forced to remain in the east, mostly in Washington, for a whole year after his marriage, struggling doggedly to obtain the definitive interpretation of the treaty of removal or a new and more liberal agreement. Mary's first child was born in her father's home. Ross wrote to her, later, from Washington:

"My beloved wife[!] I am [. . .] much gratified to hear that our dear *little bud* is well and growing finely—but as Mama has so modestly declined to portray her beauty to Papa, and has sent him the bewitching invitation to come and see for himself the charming flower, I will not forego the pleasure of making [her] that [the] delightful visit soon."[3]

Mary had been brought up a Quaker, and because she had married outside the faith she was in trouble with the Society of Friends. This information she had also conveyed in her letter to her husband; and he commented:

"So the 'Friends' have called, and gave thee thy dismissal! And thee can no longer consider thyself a member [number] of this [their] Godly Society! Well, my love, thee has one Friend on earth, for whose sake thou art disciplined [dismissed], who will with all his heart and strength cling to thee as [so] long as life shall last. And in Heaven there is One whose Fatherly eyes rest upon thee and me [I] as well as upon the 'Friends.' [And who,] [p]erchance, thee and I as good and faithful servants [. . .], will never be dismissed [us] from *His fold* though we may seek admittance through a different path from the one blazed out by the 'Friends' for their members to walk in."

Mary agreed that the church of her fathers was well lost for love; and five years later, as recorded in a testamentary diary she kept, she became a member of the Methodist church in Indian Territory.

She was at length able to bring baby Annie to Rose Cottage, which she found more luxurious and far more interesting than the home she had left. Her mother had died when she was a small child, and the much older sister Sarah had since mothered her. Not long after the marriage, her father died; and now Sarah came out to stay with her, as well as a brother, who set up as a merchant at Tahlequah. The two sisters impressed a visitor to Rose Cottage as "pleasant and entertaining in conversation"; the chief seemed "not so sociable but none the less attentive to his guests."[4]

A delightful companionship developed between Sarah and John Ross, drawn to one another by their mutual love of Mary, and strengthened by Sarah's intelligent interest in the problems of the tribe. Ross, remembering his niece's words, might have hesitated to establish the *ménage à trois.* To judge from the letters preserved by his descendants, however, there were no complications or heartburnings. Sarah had yielded him wholeheartedly to Mary. Once he wrote to his wife: "Like the Siamese Twin, the dear sisters cannot be separated. I must therefore on this occasion address them as a unit."[5]

He rejoiced in their love, flourished under Mary's pious care and Sarah's unfailing support. They helped him immensely in the work of clearing and widening the road to the new civilization for the people.

It is a relief to come upon these years in Ross's life! The man had fought so much, been so sternly self-controlled, had abjured so much of personal warmth and comfort that he had become scarcely more than a symbol of patriotism. It was good, in the presence of the "dear sisters," to give rein to tongue and pen, to write sentimentally on one of Annie's birthdays: "I will remember the first words uttered by our *darling child* . . . [W]hen looking up with eyes of celestial blue [into my face], ~~she~~ [and] sweetly said, 'Papa's baby!'"[6]

Mary wrote an essay, "The Poetry and Romance of Indian Character," and sent it to her husband unsigned; he was not deceived by her pretense that she had received it from a friend; he wrote that he knew not only who was author but who had inspired it! While away from home, he summarized the Sabbath sermons he heard and sent them to Mary. He seemed to brood over her, both loverlike and paternal; for years, in his letters to her, he continued to use the Quaker thee, thy, and thou which Mary used all her life.

With Sarah he was hardly less expansive, playful in an elderly brother fashion. Once he wrote to her: "I return unto you my warmest thanks for your very welcome and kind letter . . . But why do you ask an apology for it, when I can see nothing in it but what is *good, kind, gentle,* and *beautiful.* Yes! in quality it is good, in words kind, and in language it is gentle as the placid stream that flows from the fountain of a sister's love." Another letter to Sarah was signed, evidently recalling a shared mood of burlesque, "Koo,we,skoo,wee"—as certain persons pronounced his Indian name, Ghuisgui.

Some words written by John Howard Payne, after attending with Ross the Tribal Council of 1840 at Tahlequah, give an interesting picture of the people's attitude toward the chief and the new government. Payne described the ceremony of reading and explaining in Cherokee Ross's message, Ross and the interpreter standing together on the council platform, the chief repeating sentences in Cherokee "whenever his translator's rendering appeared inadequate to him."

The people listened with the strictest attention, and when the reading was finished and there was a stir of movement, "a voice called out that there was something further for the public ear. A speaker then arose and with much emphasis expatiated on the mischievous reports which had got about of a division in the country, reports that the people had discarded or were disposed to discard their principal chief and to substitute some one more in favor with the United States Government."

The result of that speech was the passage of a resolution quoting with approval, and a certain ironic satisfaction no doubt, a recent statement of the Commissioner of Indian Affairs:

"That the majority shall rule is an axiom in politics now substantially admitted everywhere; and one that must prevail universally. It is as applicable, and its adoption as necessary, to the Cherokees as to other communities."

The Cherokee government, said the council's resolution, had been founded on that very principle! Its officials had been chosen in strict accordance with it; and "in faithful observance of this rule we adhere to the principal chief elected by our majority, whose place we have never pronounced vacant, and whose authority we will respect so long as he shall remain at the Nation's head under the regular constitutional election of our majority."

During the reading of the resolution that in its many "whereases" summarized tribal history leading up to the removal, the people listened "intensely and with deep emotion. On one side was heard whispered in Cherokee, 'That's the plain truth!' On another, 'Right, right!' When the reading was over, the chairman expressed a wish for the assembly to remain seated and in silence, so that if anyone had objections to offer they might be heard. At length someone exclaimed, 'No objection, no remark is offered; let the people's vote be taken!'

"An old man, one of the strongest adherents of John Ross, now arose and, addressing the interpreter, said in Cherokee, 'The resolution seems to embrace two subjects. I would be glad to say something upon one of them.'

"'You must address yourself to the Chair and not to me if you desire to speak to the people,' was answered. Some lowly spoken Cherokee conversation followed amongst two or three who clustered around the old man, who . . . wished to move for the omission of that part of the resolution which approved the Fort Gibson meeting"—where certain Old Settlers were admitted to the tribal government. "When it was explained to the old man that the Fort Gibson action was taken in the interests of peace, he withdrew his opposition . . .

"The Chairman now called aloud in Cherokee, 'Is it the will of the people that this preamble and resolution do pass?' 'It is!' they cried with one voice. 'They are passed,' instantly rejoined the Chairman, and an exultant cry arose on every side, 'Oh-zay-oo! Oh-zay-oo!' (Good! Good!), and the assembly came away all smiles and satisfaction."

Thus Payne's testimony was added to that which showed Ross always careful to submit his motives and actions fully to the people, whom he had taught to listen intelligently and to grasp the fundamentals of his policy. A man of clear vision and of firm purpose, but certainly not the autocratic ruler depicted by his enemies![7]

During the protracted negotiations with the federal government, Ross was often in the east; with Mary, he shared the pleasant social contacts of Washington, Philadelphia, New York, and Boston. In 1848, he had his portrait painted by John Neagle, a popular artist of Philadelphia; also one of Mary, flanked by little Annie and baby John, by the equally well known Benjamin Waugh. The canvases hang today in the home of a grandson at Tahlequah. Mary, a shade buxom, full-breasted, dark, grave, and lovely at the age of twenty-three, faces across a sunny room the picture of John, at the age of fifty-eight a man of mature power, scarred by the years of hard battling yet retaining the faint trace of a charming boyish smile. A recovered smile, perhaps! All four were

painted in the fine raiment he loved; two receipted bills from mer-
chants of Chestnut Street showed that his wife had spent $847 for silk
foulards, poplin, *plaid de beige, poil de chèvre, chène ducals*, a French
Merino wrapper, a black silk-and-lace mantilla, parasols, et cetera.

Later, Mary Ross inherited a Philadelphia home, and there the
family lived like the aristocrats they were. Among their friends was
the woman who, more than a half century before, had delighted
and shocked Washington as the bride of President Madison; in the
Tahlequah home of Ross's grandson is still cherished a crumbling
bit of heather, tied with a narrow time-yellowed ribbon which Dolly
Madison, grown old but retaining her adorable charm, gave as a token
of remembrance to her dear young friend, Mary Ross.

John Mix Stanley, gentleman-explorer and artist, in that period when
pushing over the frontier had come to be applauded in the polite circles
of the east as an adventure rather than just a pioneer's chore, visited
Tahlequah in 1843, during the sessions of an Inter-Tribal Council. He
painted the scene: the open shed, its roof supported by stout posts;
a multi-colored group of squatting Indians in its shade, Cherokees,
Creeks, Chickasaws, Choctaws, Seminoles, Osages, Pawnees, Kiowas,
Comanches, Cheyennes—delegates from twenty-one tribes in all; on
the platform, shaping the course of the proceedings which were to
unite the restless plains Indians with the Cherokees in a vast confederation of peace, the vaguely indicated, modishly clad figure of Ross.[8]

With Stanley and other visitors, along with the Indians who were
tribal guests, Ross smoked the symbolic pipe of peace, helping, in
his own words, to mark out the "white paths from tribe to tribe as
emblematical of [the] attachment [and free] intercourse, and [in]
brotherhood."[9] With them for ten days he shared the bountiful feasts
of barbecued beef, *conutche*, a gruel richened by pounded nutmeats,
the delicious lye-treated boiled corn kernels called *conahany*, and the
equally appetizing "dog's ears," grated corn wrapped in husks and
roasted in campfire ashes. He had one of the "beloved antiquarians"—
the only one, it was said, who still remembered the ancient Cherokee
lore—interpret for them the meaning of the tribal wampum.

Through such contacts, east and west, varying conceptions of Ross permeated far beyond the limits of the Cherokee Nation. Arbuckle represented him as the potential inciter of a dreaded Indian uprising, while the Indians themselves thought of him as a peacemaker. To the missionaries he was a true servant of the Lord, and a staunch supporter of their work. To the cultured and sophisticated he appeared a patron of education and art. To everyone, he was a man of undoubted power.

Two decades of tribal growth, under Ross's guidance, followed the removal. With increasing prosperity, the population grew until, in 1859, there were twenty-one thousand native Cherokees, one thousand whites, and four thousand negro slaves in the Nation. Even the pessimistic Commissioner of Indian Affairs admitted that "from their general mode of living the Cherokees will compare favorably with their neighbors in any of the States."

Before the Civil War broke, and ended for a time the era of progress, more than sixty Cherokee girls graduated from the Female Seminary to become teachers; the Male Seminary also turned out its young men to teach, take up the law, medicine, theology, to become officials of the tribal government, or go back to the stores, farms, and ranches of their fathers trained and fit for intelligent citizenship. Other girls and boys went east to college, to Mount Holyoke, Princeton, Dartmouth, to seminaries for young ladies, music schools, and military academies. For his sons Silas and George, Ross planned college educations, writing to his niece in 1844 that he hoped they would demonstrate the capacity of the Cherokees for leadership in modern civilization. Of his son John he wrote: "I would have him remember and keep constantly before him that it is the 'long pull and the steady pull' that achieves in life the most . . . Uniform effort, day in and day out, makes the man."[10]

Ross was approaching the age of seventy, a happy and a mellowed man. He loved to visit the two seminaries in his shining coach, drawn by a pair of fine black horses, bringing excited and flashing-eyed students to the windows; to enter with his unfailing, natural dignity, and confer, if it was the Female Seminary he honored, with Miss Worcester,

Miss Whitmire, and his niece Jane Ross, teachers and graduates of Mount Holyoke; or to lead his wife, in her silks and fine laces, into the assembly room where he was to speak. Groups of boys from the Male Seminary returned his visits, crowding into Rose Cottage for the privilege of shaking his hand and hearing his few words of counsel, mingling proudly with men of authority in the tribe who waited to consult the chief.[11]

Among a small faction, followers of Stand Watie who kept alive the feud resulting from the Boudinot and Ridge killings, enmity to Ross persisted. This group charged that he permitted tribal offices to be filled only with relatives and friends who, like himself, grew rich through the use of tribal funds. It was certainly true that many of the Ross kin held offices, and prospered; Ross preferred that his friends rather than his opponents should be in power, and he was humanly loyal to those who had shown loyalty to him and his ideals. No proof exists, however, that he permitted the misuse of Cherokee tribal funds.

He gathered about him the ablest of the tribe, mixed-bloods like Coodey, the Vanns, and Reece, whom he made superintendent of schools, and full-bloods like Bushyhead, Benge, and Tekechulaskee, strong and clever men who expressed the minds of the hill people.[12]

There is a legend, which certain investigators have insisted is history, that one of Ross's closest advisers, who became secretary to Ross's successor as chief, was an errant Scottish nobleman, a Highland Gordon who had taken the name of Miller during his wanderings. Miller was unquestionably a man not alone of fine education and background, but of mystery and strength. Perhaps Ross knew his secret. Ross's own line is said to have led back to Ferquard, Earl of Ross, named in a charter granted by King Alexander II of Scotland in 1220 as Macaw-t Sagirt, son of Gills Anrias, founder of the Highland Clan of Aindreas. The Ross coat of arms, adopted according to this legend in 1681, bore the motto, "Floret Qui Laborat," he prospers who labors—surely a fitting Ross maxim. It was not John Ross, however, who speculated on such doubtful genealogical possibilities; the brief family notes he left behind him have to do only with his boyhood in Georgia, with memories of his father, Daniel Ross the trader, and his mother, Daniel's faithful Cherokee wife.

Every two years from 1839 to 1861, on the first Monday in August, the Cherokees voted for chief; during all that time, no other candidate besides Ross was ever seriously considered by them.

CHAPTER 24

As the fishes that are taken in an evil net, and as the birds that are caught in the snare, so are the sons of men snared in an evil time, when it falleth suddenly upon them.

—ECCLESIASTES 9:12

Past the age of seventy, Ross was pitched into the turmoil of the Civil War; caught up, first, by the boiling rush of secession, then wrenched back to the Union cause, while all the time his heart was set only on saving his people from participation in a struggle that did not concern them.[1]

He had watched with apprehension the widening of the rift in the Democratic Party preceding the election of 1860. From Washington, he wrote to his wife predicting the nomination of both Douglas and Dickinson by the opposing factions of the party, and the consequent triumph of the Republicans. He did not, however, foresee the violent repercussions Lincoln's election would cause in the Cherokee Nation.

The Cherokees were Southern, and slaveholders; most of the inter-married whites among them were Southerners; and the government officials in Indian Territory were practically all strongly Southern in sympathy. As the crisis approached, these agents of the United States declared their sympathies by driving from among the Indians certain missionaries and white teachers who were known abolitionists; others left before being expelled. Thus, even before war became inevitable, a state of tension was created.

Indian leaders of the Old Settlers and signers of the Schermerhorn treaty took advantage of the situation to fan the ancient feud against the Ross party, organizing a pro-slavery secret society, the *Knights of the Golden Circle*. Their move was countered by the full-blood Ross men, few of whom were slave-owners, who formed the *Ketoowah Society*, reviving a brotherhood that had anciently centered about the eastern town of Ketoowah and which expressed the pride of race felt by Cherokees of unmixed blood. "Ketoowah, the real people," was their phrase.

Reborn in the congregation of the little Baptist church at Peavine, in the district named for old Goingsnake, the Ketoowah Society spread rapidly. At the outbreak of the war, it had three thousand members, and its emissaries were effectively at work among the Creeks. It adopted as emblem a common pin stuck into the coat lapel in a special way, and as a greeting sign a particular mode of touching the hat. In the darkness, when two Ketoowah met, one would ask, "Who are you?," and the other would answer, "Tahlequah—who are you?," and then the first, "I am Ketoowah's son."

The Ketoowah loyalists tried to enlist Ross, spreading the report that, although the owner of more slaves perhaps than any other Cherokee, he was Unionist in sympathy. But Ross at once made his position clear. Invited to represent the tribe at a joint council of all Indian Territory Indians, met to consider their attitude, he protested that the impending conflict was purely a white man's quarrel, "a family misunderstanding,"[2] in which the Indians ought not to become involved. At the urging of the white agents of the South, however, the council was nevertheless called; even before it convened, the Choctaws and Chickasaws had committed themselves to the secessionists.

The Cherokees, Creeks, and Seminoles followed Ross's counsel, agreeing that "it behooves us [. . .] to refrain from adopting any measure liable to be misunderstood or misrepresented." Ross voiced the hope that enough "wisdom, virtue, and moderation" would be discovered among the whites to end the quarrel without fighting. He did not believe the federal union was seriously threatened, and the only concern of the Indians should be to observe strictly their treaty obligations.

Ross spoke to the other tribes as a man of peace, calling himself, "in the language of our fathers, 'Elder Friend and Brother.'"

But neutrality was difficult, particularly for the Cherokees and Creeks, the eastern border of whose Nations touched Arkansas,[3] in which state secession forces were extremely active. Governor Rector of Arkansas wooed Ross in a long ingratiating letter, insisting that the Cherokees and the people of Arkansas, both being slaveholders, were natural allies. He alleged that Lincoln's administration regarded the Nation "as a fruitful field ripe for the harvest of Abolitionists, Free Soilers, and Northern mountebanks," and he promised protection if the tribe would declare for the South.[4]

Ross answered that he could see no reason for breaking with the federal government, even though the Cherokees were slaveholders and sympathetic neighbors.

The next attempt was made by the Confederate Commissioner of Indian Affairs, Hubbard, in a letter that contained both a plea and a threat: Unless the Cherokees went with the South, all their funds invested in Southern securities, the income from which supported their government, would be forfeited.

Ross still held out for neutrality: "We have no cause to doubt the entire good faith with which you would treat the Cherokees [people], but neither have we any cause to make war against the United States, or to believe that our treaties will not be fulfilled and respected [. . .]. At all events, a decent regard to good faith demands that we should not be the first to violate them."[5]

Alluding to a certain passage in Hubbard's letter, he continued: "A comparison of northern and southern philanthropy as illustrated in their dealings towards the Indians within their respective limits would not affect the merits of the question . . . I therefore pass it over, merely remarking that the 'settled policy' of former years was a favorite policy [one with both sections] when extended to the acquisition of Indian lands, and that but few Indians now press their feet upon the banks of either the Ohio or the Tennessee."

Ross was asked by Washington to report on subversive activities of Indian agents among the Cherokees. He named one R. J. Cowart, who was "officially advocating the Secession policy" and "uttering words of denunciation against all the distinguished patriots who are exerting their efforts to devise measures of reconciliation . . . Mr. Cowart brought [out] with him from the State of Georgia a man named Solomon, who is a notorious drunken brawling disunionist. He is strolling about Tahlequah under the permission of the so-called 'U. S. agent,' and is creating strife and getting into difficulties with citizens of the Nation—a perfect nuisance." He asked for the removal of both Cowart and Solomon.[6]

Secessionists of western Arkansas continued to demand of Ross an answer to the question, "Where do you stand?" They told him they preferred him as an open enemy rather than as a doubtful friend. He replied: "I am—the Cherokees are—your friends [. . .], but [we] do not wish to be brought into the feuds . . . Our wish is for peace, ~~with you and at home~~ [peace at home, and peace among you]."[7]

His stand was sensible, his steadfast reiterations the words of a wise man; but "the old chief was crying 'Peace! Peace!' when there was no peace." The war broke, and the Confederacy started to raise regiments of Indian soldiers in Indian Territory. The issue became too big for Ross to determine.

To make his position more difficult, all federal troops were withdrawn, whereupon the Confederacy formed the Military District of Indian Territory, with the Texas Ranger, McCulloch, in command. He was instructed to recruit Indian units to supplement the three regiments assigned him from Texas, Louisiana, and Arkansas. In order to influence the Cherokees, he planned to establish headquarters at Fort Gibson, in their Nation.

This development stirred the Knights of the Golden Circle to action. Though weak in numbers compared with the Ketoowahs, they decided to make a surprise rush upon Tahlequah, capture the tribal government, and raise the Confederate flag over the council house. But news of their intentions leaked, and when they found "the flinty streets of the little town filled with stonier-faced full-bloods, gathered from all parts of the Nation for the purpose of checkmating them," they attempted no hostile action.[8]

A messenger was hurried to Ross, who came at once to the Cherokee capital accompanied by his wife. There in capitol square, it was said, Mary Ross hotly declared her Union sympathies and defied the Knights. With difficulty, Ross induced both factions to disperse quietly. He then issued an emphatic warning to all to observe—in almost the very futile words of President Wilson generations later—"strict neutrality in thought and action."[9]

Aware that Ross's control over his people was still too strong to be broken, McCulloch altered his plans and set up his headquarters at Fort Smith, just over the line in Arkansas, the next most convenient place from which to work on the Cherokees.

Then, in the succession of southern emissaries to the Cherokees, came the picturesque Albert Pike, explorer, former Bostonian and Harvard law student, school teacher with literary pretensions, reputed author of "Dixie," and self-appointed expert on Indians. From the Confederate capital he was sent to Fort Smith; there he received a delegation of Cherokee Knights and assured them that the Confederate government would protect them if they would defy Ross and the Ketoowahs; after which he and McCulloch, attended by a glittering escort, rode the fifty miles to Park Hill.

Ross received them courteously, but was moved neither by their pageantry nor by Pike's plea. War is a barbarous practice, an unsatisfactory method of settling quarrels, and for the Cherokees it would be pure folly; so Ross argued, and at his request McCulloch promised that his soldiers would not enter the Nation unless, he added, it became necessary to expel federal troops from the new military district or to protect southern sympathizers among the Cherokees.

That promise proved worthless. Only a few days later McCulloch wrote to Ross demanding that the Knights be allowed to form companies of home guards to protect themselves from Northern invaders. It was the nose of the camel pushing at the tent-flap. Ross replied that he could not sanction the proposed action. It would not only be a violation of neutrality, but would create in the Nation bands of armed men not authorized by Cherokee law and not amenable to it.

Successive steps in the efforts of McCulloch and Pike to involve the tribe followed swiftly. The general collected a considerable body of troops just over the southern Cherokee border in the Choctaw Nation, and let it be known that they were preparing to intimidate the hesitant Cherokees and drive Ross from his neutral position. Pike went on to the Creeks, who refused to treat with him, then to the Choctaws, Chickasaws, and other smaller bands that signed formal treaties of alliance and appointed delegates to Richmond.

The time came when madness must prevail over wisdom. With Confederate forces menacing them on both the Arkansas and Choctaw borders, with propagandists working on the Knights, and Pike busy amongst the tribes to the west, Ross's stand grew progressively untenable. He tried to strengthen his position by forming a federation of Cherokees, Creeks, Seminoles, and bands in the western reaches of Indian Territory. In response to his call delegates met at Antelope Hills, in the far west. Ross and his old friend Hopothleyohola,[10] chief of the Creeks, by the eloquent presentment of the case for neutrality won over the delegates, and an agreement was signed.

But even as the Antelope Hills Indians were declaring for neutrality, Pike was winning to the Confederacy a faction of the Creeks. On his return home Ross found the Cherokees in a high fever of excitement over exaggerated reports of a victory of Southern arms at the battle of Wilson Creek. The Knights were exultant. McCulloch came back, a victor, to his camp on the border of the Nation. No federal support for the Ketoowah loyalists was anywhere in sight.

Ross realized now that he must abandon neutrality if he would save the Cherokees from a civil war of their own. He called a General Council at Tahlequah on August 21, 1861. To the four thousand who crowded capitol square he said that it was for them to decide; he was their servant, and would abide by their decision. Backed by McCulloch's nearby forces and abetted by the agent, Crawford, who ostensibly represented the Union, while feverishly preaching secession, the armed Knights dominated the council, silencing all talk, either of continued neutrality or of loyalty to the Union.

Ross acted promptly, issuing a declaration that the Cherokee people could no longer maintain neutrality, the Nation having been abandoned by the federal government, the Union having in fact been dissolved, and that the people had chosen to go with the South. At his suggestion the council resolved to sever relations with Washington and, on condition that the Confederacy would assume the federal government's obligations to the Cherokees, form an alliance with Richmond.

Pike was sent for. He came, escorted from Fort Gibson to Park Hill by a newly formed regiment of Ketoowah home guards under the Cherokee, John Drew, and with Ross drew up a treaty of alliance. It was agreed that all able-bodied men of the tribe would enlist in the Confederate forces but would not be required to serve outside the Nation. On behalf of Richmond, Pike promised protection against federal invasion, the immediate payment of $250,000 for equipping Cherokee troops, and indemnity for all losses suffered by the tribe on account of the break with Washington.

Thus was closed the breach between Knights and Ketoowahs, who followed Ross into the Confederate fold as unhesitatingly as they had always followed his leadership. Ross and Stand Watie shook hands publicly. Regiments of Knights under Watie co-operated harmoniously with Drew's Ketoowahs.

Once committed, Ross sent a circular letter to the Creeks and other neutral Indians explaining the circumstances under which the Pike treaty was made and urging a union of all Indian Territory tribes in support of the South. Hopothleyohola, for the Creeks, returned his copy with the laconic notation, "Can this be the writing of Chief John Ross!" The old Creek's trust hurt; Ross sent a delegation to him with further explanations and a request for a pact which would insure peace between Creeks and Cherokees. Hopothleyohola, however, would not receive the delegates; since the Cherokees had violated an existing agreement, they could expect neither sympathy nor support from the Creeks!

Following this, Creek warriors raided the Cherokee country, burning houses, barns, and stacks and driving off stock. Then, painting their faces, they fortified themselves against the retaliatory expedition, made up of Cherokees, Choctaws, Chickasaws, and Seminoles under Colonel Cooper of the Confederate army. They were easily routed in spite of the fact that Colonel Drew's regiment refused to attack, saying that they were willing to shoot Yankees but not their old Creek friends.

The beaten Union Creeks were driven north into Kansas, where they were soon joined by their families and by various harassed small contingents of loyal Indians from other tribes. It was winter and they suffered from exposure. The people among whom they camped were sympathetic, but few in numbers and poor, so the refugees found themselves facing starvation. Washington seemed unaware of their existence and, during the late months of 1861 and the early part of 1862, hundreds died, among them some Cherokees who had refused to follow Ross.

The story of these Kansas exiles, though it seems to lead away from Ross, is essential to an understanding of the backswirl which caught him later and plunged him into the tragic last act of his life.

In the spring of 1862 Senator Lane of Kansas suggested organizing a Union force to recapture Indian Territory and restore the suffering refugees to their homes. Washington approved the plan, but due to local political jealousies this "jayhawking expedition" came to nothing.

In June, however, federal troops marched west from the Mississippi and in two hot engagements at Pea Ridge and Elkhorn Tavern in Arkansas defeated McCulloch and Pike (who had been placed in command of all Confederate Indian soldiers.) This threat cleared the Cherokee country of Southern troops, except for Drew's regiment in camp at the extreme southern edge of the Nation.

It was a propitious hour for the invasion of the reorganized Lane expedition. Under Colonel Weer, a regular, it advanced from the Kansas border towards Tahlequah. Weer opened negotiations, inviting the Cherokees to return to their allegiance. Ross declined, and in his answer rehearsed the story of federal abandonment that had led to the Cherokees joining the Confederacy.

The country was, however, at Weer's mercy unless the South would redeem its treaty promise of protection. Ross hurried a message to General Hindman, who had succeeded to the command of the Trans-Mississippi Military District after McCulloch's death at Pea Ridge. Hindman responded by ordering Pike to march his Indian force north from the Choctaw Nation, pick up Drew's regiment at the Arkansas River, and drive Weer back to Kansas. Pike refused to move; receiving a second peremptory order, he resigned his command, charging that his Indians had been refused equipment and pay, had been despised and reviled by white troops with whom they had fought, and used outside their own country against their will.

Colonel Cooper succeeded Pike, and marched a badly equipped and disaffected force north. Drew joined him, also Stand Watie (whose regiment was recalled for the purpose from a raiding expedition into southwestern Missouri) and a battalion of Missouri infantry. He met Weer thirty miles north of Tahlequah and, outnumbered two to one, was beaten. Whereupon Drew's Ketoowahs went over to the Union side, justifying themselves by the identical arguments Pike had used, and further charging that the Confederate authorities had discriminated against them in favor of Watie's Knights.

It was a frightful mess; the old feud brought to life, the Cherokee Nation a cockpit!

Weer moved on south, sent a battalion to occupy Fort Gibson and a company to Tahlequah. Cooper, drawing back, reminded Ross of the

186

treaty with Richmond and commanded him in the name of President Davis to call to arms all male Cherokees between the ages of eighteen and thirty-five. This demand roused the Ketoowahs, naturally sympathetic with the Union and familiar with the shabby treatment of Drew's men, to action; they gathered in force at Ross's home and insisted that he should again declare the Cherokees neutral.

The Ketoowah ultimatum, delivered by men actually posted in Ross's dooryard with rifles and a rope with which they proposed to hang him in case he refused, carried more weight than the command of a Cooper fleeing south for safety. To the worn chief of seventy-two a bitter draught was offered. There was no hope of succor from the demoralized Confederate forces; Richmond had proved a weak prop, no more faithful in the fulfillment of treaty obligations than Washington.

As Ross hesitated over his decision, the Union captain, Gaino, who had moved with his company from Tahlequah to Park Hill and joined the two hundred and more Ketoowahs surround the chief's house, took action which he believed would release Ross from his dilemma. He placed Ross under arrest; then, paroling him, reported back to Weer, who renewed the effort to win him to the Union.

Inside his home, as Weer's ally, was Mary Ross, staunch Unionist at heart. What effect she had on the chief can only be guessed. But to Weer's second appeal Ross yielded, accepting of necessity the colonel's offer to shelter him from the certain future vengeance of the Knights. Taking only such household goods and valuables as could be loaded into two ox-drawn wagons and the family carriage, Ross and his family set off under Captain Gaino's escort to Fort Gibson. From there they drove to Fort Scott, Kansas, on their way to Philadelphia.

Ross was an exile, a chief in name only.

CHAPTER 25

Quoting De Maistre, Foch said, "a lost battle is a battle that one thinks he has lost." Man lives by imagination. The Indian in Ross might have counseled resignation to fate if the Scotch of him had not demanded resistance. To the old chief flight was not a lost battle, it was merely a temporary reverse. There was marvelous toughness of mind and courage of heart in Ghuisgui! He felt that his usefulness to the Cherokees was not past. He was still their chief, in possession of the small remnant of the tribal funds, and he would do for them whatever lay in his power to do at Washington.

What Ross had foreseen if the Cherokees were drawn into the white man's quarrel had happened. But the situation had passed beyond his control. From that time on, the red tide of war surged back and forth through the Cherokee Nation. At one stage, Watie triumphed, and was made a Confederate Brigadier General; whereupon he called a council of Southern Cherokees, which deposed Ross and made Watie chief. As a consequence, Ross adherents and Union sympathizers suffered at the hands of the victors; homes were burned, plantations devastated, men, women, and children driven out of the Territory to find what asylum they might in Kansas. Among the rest, Ross's home went up in flames. Destitution was the fate of non-combatants and the fighting forces alike, starvation and death marched in step across the land.

In his exile, Ross divided his time between the difficult task of providing for the needs of not alone his immediate family, but a constantly increasing number of relatives driven from home to the shelter of his Philadelphia establishment, and work for the Nation. He saw Lincoln, wrote out for the president full accounts of the situation and needs of the Cherokees. He labored with the War Department. He left no corner unexplored where a possible friend with the power to aid might lurk. At length he induced the government to send into the Territory a force strong enough to retake Fort Gibson from Watie, and drive the Confederates out of the Cherokee Nation.

This was early in 1863. A Ketoowah leader, Thomas Pegg, called a council to undo the work of Watie's Knights. It met at Camp John Ross, formally repudiated the treaty of alliance with Richmond, pledged support to the Union, abolished slavery, and restored Ross to chieftainship. It also took revenge on the foe by authorizing the confiscation of all property belonging to Cherokee enemies of the Union.[1]

Union refugees came drifting back and began to plant crops, but the harvest was lean because the federal force in the Nation was unable to prevent enemy raiders from dashing in and destroying fields and rebuilt cabins. This merciless guerilla warfare continued through 1864. The Cherokee Nation became a famine stricken land, with the people living in a state of savagery. In winter, even parched corn was a luxury and old men died of exhaustion in plodding and ineffective pursuit of game. In summer the fare was better, helped out by berries and other wild fruits and "greens." What horses and cattle survived the raids had been taken for the armies.

The curse of Cain was on the Nation, the fulfillment, so the old men said, of the evil forecast by the dark cloud seen by the followers of Goingsnake on the day they started away from Georgia.

Now the Confederate Cherokees suffered in their refugee camps on Red River, at the Texas border, as their Union brothers had done in Kansas.

Ross was little better off than his people; his purse had flattened alarmingly, and he was distracted by doubts of his wisdom in remaining in the east. What he could say in letters to his supporters in the Nation seemed hollow and unsatisfying: "Though far away, I have watched you with unceasing pride and solicitude, and have not been inactive in the effort to keep our cause fairly represented at Washington, for it is there, after all, that we must look for the redress of our Nation's wrongs and grievances."

What he wrote was true, but it seemed to him stale and vague. He began to think of going back, and to Sarah Stapler he wrote that he meant to "brave the perils" of the journey and of the enemies at home.[2] But he was failing in health, and was persuaded by those dearest to him to give up the project. Added to his load was grief for the death of his son James, eldest of the three who had joined the Union army, who died after fourteen months in a prison camp. Ross wrote the obituary notice, in which he recalled the boy's fine devotion to his mother and younger sister and brothers in the gloomy days in Georgia when Ross himself was away from home.

On his visits to Washington he continued to write summaries of sermons to his wife, and quote reports of Union successes. Letters to relatives in the Cherokee Nation were obviously written under great strain; copies which he preserved show many deletions and changes, confessions of a mind terribly distracted. A written appeal to Lincoln drew a soothing, sympathetic answer, but there was little the president could do at the time to relieve Cherokee distress.

CHAPTER 26

The war ended, only to bring on the turbulent years of Reconstruction. Upon those tribes in Indian Territory that had supported the South either voluntarily or because of inescapable pressure, fell the heavy hand of the government. By their disloyalty, said officials of the régime following Lincoln's assassination, they had forfeited their treaty rights. There must be fresh treaties, treaties that would satisfy the loud clamor for land by the trans-Mississippi whites, cut down the reservations, and throw the sliced-off portions open to settlement.

A commission, headed by Commissioner of Indian Affairs Cooley, met in September 1865, at Fort Smith to consider the fate of the Indians of the Territory. Cooley laid down the terms on which the United States would renew treaty relations: Mutual agreements of amity between the tribes, and pledges of peace to the government; abolition of slavery; the cession of enough land to make homes for various small tribes and fragments of tribes at the moment living in Kansas and nearby western states; and a consolidated Indian government for the whole territory.

The Cherokees made a firm plea of not guilty to Cooley's blanket charge of treason. The tribe's delegates explained the circumstances under which the alliance was made with the Confederacy, and insisted upon the fact that most of the Cherokees had remained loyal to the Union. At length, Cooley admitted this, but claimed that those who, with John Ross and other "bad men," had gone over temporarily to the South rendered the whole tribe liable to punishment.

"Mary B., wife of Hon. John Ross, Principal Chief of the Cherokee Nation, 29th June, 1865, aged 40 years."

Mary was gone, departing as Quatie had done before her at a time when Ross was heavy-laden with the troubles and responsibilities of his position, a broken-hearted man of seventy-five, desperately poor.

Sarah took charge of the Philadelphia home and the children, while Ross left for the west to join the Cherokee delegation that had been chosen to meet Cooley at Fort Smith. He departed in time to visit Park Hill before the conference. He traveled alone, a pathetic, weary little man, whose face had suddenly become deeply channeled and wasted, sitting in the saloon of the rackety Arkansas River steamboat and writing to Sarah:

"I am fast approaching my country and my people, and [. . .] I shall soon meet with my dear children, relatives, and friends, who will greet me with joyous [joyful] hearts. But where is that delightful home, and the matron of the once happy family who so kindly and hospitably entertained our guests? Alas, I shall see them no more on earth! The loved wife and mother is at rest in the Heavenly mansion prepared for the redeemed, and the family homestead ruthlessly reduced to ashes by the hands of rebel incendiaries; and while the surviving members of our family circle are scattered abroad as refugees, I am journeying [. . .] alone to find myself a stranger and homeless in my own country."[1]

Later, the visit over, he wrote to his daughter Annie:

"I [. . .] hastened to our once lovely home and witnessed the ruins and desolation of the premises. The only buildings standing were Johnny's chicken house, the carriage house, and Peggy's cabin. We found the old dun mare and the broken-leg horse in the garden [and r]iding through the orchard, ~~we~~ found a few peaches, other fruit ~~was~~ [being] all gone. From ~~there~~ [thence] we rode up to the graveyard. The railings [. . .] stand as usual, ~~but~~ the grounds were full of weeds. I cannot express the sadness of my feelings in my rambling over the place."[2]

To Cooley, at Fort Smith, this broken, rambling, shabby old man was in no wise formidable. The commissioner announced that he would not be recognized as chief; in the view of the government, Ross was only one of the supplicant delegates in the Cherokee camp across the river from the military barracks. At the first hearing of the commission which Ross attended, Cooley publicly branded him an enemy of the United States, a breeder of discord amongst the Cherokees, and an evil influence on the Creeks, whom Ross was advising not to agree to the terms of the proposed treaty. Furthermore, Cooley insisted that Ross did not now represent any element of his people.

But the tired old chief was not past fighting, as the commission soon discovered. To Cooley's statement purporting to strip him of authority, Ross answered:

"Sir, I deny the charges asserted against me. I deny having used ~~any~~ [my] influence either with the Cherokees, Creeks, or any other persons to resist the interests of the Indians or of the Government of the United States . . . I know that prejudices have existed against me for years past, but, Sir, I have maintained a peaceful course throughout my whole life. I claim to be as loyal a man as any other citizen of the United States . . . I have been ~~for~~ forty-odd years chief of the Cherokees, elected time after time. They re-elected me in my absence, and I came ~~here at~~ [on with] my advanced age, after burying my wife and [. . .] my son, ~~to represent them~~. I had three sons in your army, also three grandsons and three nephews . . .

"I came [on] with the hope that I might be useful to my people, to those of my people who had separated from the Nation, and to the Government of the United States. I came [here] not ~~here to~~ [for the purpose of] resist[ing] the policy of the ~~Government~~ [U.S.]~~, but~~ [I]f we have rights we ought to be permitted to express them. [. . .] I have been three years [. . .] in communication with the Department, Sir, with the President; with Mr. Lincoln. I was constantly in communication [. . .]. Far from a desire [. . .] to prejudice any against the interests of the United States, I resisted to the last moment the policy of disunion . . .

"I have a character, ~~Sir~~, [. . .] a reputation that I have maintained to the present time, [sir], which is worth more to me than [is] my life. I have done nothing that was wrong."[3]

On that statement the Cherokee delegation stood; its members signed a protest against the commission's ruling deposing Ross, affirming their confidence in him and his good faith toward the United States. "We also," they said, "beg leave to assure the Honorable Commissioners that Mr. John Ross is not 'the pretended chief of the Cherokee Nation,' but that he is Principal Chief in law and fact, having been elected to that position without opposition in the first Monday in August by the qualified voters, in accordance with the constitution of the Cherokee Nation."[4]

Ross stiffened the Indians' resistance to the offered treaty, especially to the provision lumping them together under an unworkable consolidated Indian government. Also, as he was able to point out, the tribes had been misinformed of the commission's purpose and the delegates had come without authority to conclude such a treaty as was presented.

All that the Fort Smith conference could accomplish was a preliminary agreement of amity. Ross and the other Cherokee delegates then left, promising to send to Washington men properly authorized to negotiate a definitive treaty.

Though warned that the government would not recognize Ross, the Tribal Council made him head of this delegation; he was still their chief, their leader. Once again he took the long road to the capital. He was never again to see his own land.

Early in the year 1866 the delegation arrived in Washington,[5] and went to stay at Joy's boarding house.[6] Sarah, concerned about her brother-in-law's health, begged Ross for a description of his quarters, knowing that in more prosperous days he had lived at the fashionable Willard's Hotel. He assured her that he was quite comfortable: "It is a Yankee boarding house, conducted systematically, economically, orderly, and quietly. There is no superfluity of eatables on the table, but enough of good plain wholesome food, well cooked." There were fifty boarders; at the head of one of the long tables in the dining room sat Representative Dawes of Massachusetts, and Whitecatcher of the Cherokee delegation was at its foot. Ross had a room to himself, at the price of $60 a month for lodging and meals; the others, doubling up, paid $50 a month each. He told Sarah that he was really faring better that when he had paid $5.50 a day at Willard's![7]

By now his personal resources were exhausted, and it was difficult for the delegation to secure funds due the Cherokees from the government. Sarah was making shift to maintain the Philadelphia home and with his daughter Annie using every scrap of influence she could command to have revoked the government commission's edict deposing Ross as chief. Sarah knew how keenly he felt that senseless, unauthorized action, though he had written to her, "Let not your hearts [not] be troubled by the extraordinary proceedings [of the Hon. Commsrs at Fort Smith] . . . God is just and truth is mighty, and when the facts . . . shall be impartially investigated [. . .] I fear not of the result."[8]

He could valiantly write those words, but did he believe them? The God of Justice had been so often inattentive; and John Ross was old now and the time short for playing the role of patient waiter on Providence.

The Washington winter took savage toll of his strength in the succeeding weeks of his battle for recognition. He was the active, dominating head of the delegation, yet had no admitted status; he had to school his associates in the multitudinous details involved in treaty negotiations, and sit silent while Cooley maintained the fiction that he did not represent his people. Brief spells of stomach trouble and recurrent fever and ague struck him down; recovering, he maintained in letters to the anxious Sarah that the illnesses had been trivial.

At the beginning of April, however, in the first letter he ever wrote showing the least trembling of the hand that had penned so many thousands of pages of bold copper-plate, he told her that he must yield to Dr. Hall's advice to have someone with him. He enclosed twenty dollars for Sarah's fare, and regretted that it was all he could send.[9]

Both felt that the end of his life was near. Both, being God's children, the elderly Sarah and the feeble old John, prayed together that he might not have to go to join Mary (and surely Quatie) in the Heavenly mansion prepared for the redeemed before two things had been accomplished: a just treaty for the Cherokees, and recognition by Washington of his chieftainship. This latter was not merely a fervid, sentimental wish for personal vindication, but involved important political consequences for the Cherokees, including recognition of the validity of many tribal acts passed at his urging and approved by him as chief.

Treaty negotiations dragged on through April and May and well into June. Boudinot's son, who had taken up his dead father's quarrel, and another ex-Confederate member of the Cherokee delegation demanded a division of the Nation—the old cry, echoing that of the reactionary faction in Georgia as far back as 1808.[10] As he had always done, Ross fought the proposal. He said that though the sores caused by the war were deep and angry, time would heal them; that the Cherokees must go on as a united people to the inevitable amalgamation with white America. "A house divided against itself—" he quoted for them again that eternal truth. All of the strength of the tribe pulling together would be required to rebuild their wrecked churches and schools, to bring fields back into production, fill the prairies with new herds.

The government's negotiators finally gave up their demand for a union Indian government in the territory, but held out stoutly for land cessions. One wonders why the donor who takes back what he bestows is called "Indian giver!" Surely it must be due to a confused reading of history, since almost invariably grants to Indians by the United States government have been either wholly or in part revoked. Should the phrase not be, "Uncle Sam giver?"

In June, as an added pressure on Ross, the government concluded a treaty with Boudinot and his former Confederate associates: the Nation was to be divided, one part for the Ross Nationalists, and the other for the ex-Confederates; a portion of the reservation, incidentally, to be given up to the United States. The old tactics, reminiscent of Schermerhorn's double dealing with Boudinot's father and the Ridges in 1835. This time, however, the so-called treaty was not sent to the Senate for ratification, but held as a club over the Ross delegates.

The inevitable compromise followed; another treaty was agreed upon, and signed on July 19. Its main provisions were formal repudiation of the Confederate alliance; a general amnesty and the repeal of tribal confiscation laws; equal rights to land in the Nation for negro freedmen; establishment of a United States court in Indian Territory for whites; and the settlement on unoccupied Cherokee land of certain bands of Indians evicted from neighboring states. It was not a wholly satisfactory settlement, but infinitely better for the Cherokees than the one Cooley had proposed at Fort Smith.

Toward the end of the strenuous negotiations, Ross was too ill to rise from his bed. Lying there, with the devoted Sarah watching over him, he directed the final phases of the battle. When the old friends had gone from the room for the last time, bearing his signature to the completed document, and the only sounds coming in through the windows were the clop-clop of horses' feet, or a snatch of negro song, "'Way down, 'way down yon-der—" Ross's mind turned to the final refuge of the faithful Christian; he asked for pen and paper, and wrote:

> Safe in the arms of Jesus,
> Safe on His gentle breast,
> There by His love o'ershadowed,
> Sweetly my soul shall rest.

His longtime friend and lawyer-ally, Ewing, sent him a bottle of port, stocked in 1815 by Chief Justice Marshall, "a patriot statesman of his day . . . with the hope that your already long and useful career may reach far beyond the arrogances and trials of this turbulent hour."

His daughter Annie came to the Joy house to help Sarah nurse her father. Desperate in the face of the Interior Department's indifference to the chief's pleas for recognition, she secured an audience with President Johnson. He heard her, and passed out the word to the secretary of the interior, who relayed it to Cooley. The decree of deposition was rescinded.

John Ross was again the acknowledged chief of the Cherokees; he had won his last fight. The news was brought to him before, at sunset on August 1, 1866, he died.

CHAPTER 27

And when thy son asketh thee in time to come, saying, what mean the
statutes and the judgments which the Lord our God hath commanded
you? then thou shalt say unto thy son, We were Pharaoh's bondmen
in Egypt, and the Lord brought us out of Egypt with a mighty hand.

—DEUTERONOMY 6:20-21

Three white men joined in producing the song which was sung at
Ross's funeral in Philadelphia.[1] The first, Janvier, wrote the words;
Janvier's friend Jost set them to music; and Trumpler published the
song. In the grandson's home at Tahlequah is a fading, brittle copy;
I listened to his wife sing it, sitting at the piano near a window with a
sunset glow on her graying hair. She had never known John Ross, of
course, for it is a long stretch of years between 1866 and the present.
The old chief had become but a memory, too, before I myself was
born, almost within rifle shot of Park Hill. Yet I shared as I listened to
Mrs. Ross the pride with which she voiced Janvier's lament, singing
with a fine lift of the head:

> Dead! The mighty chief is dead—
> Fallen is the Nation's head!
> Eyes unused to tears today
> Weep in sorrow o'er his clay.

"Let all his people mourn," Janvier cried, "and gaze with sad surprise on this costly sacrifice!"

It was what the Cherokees did. They sent an official embassy to bring his body home; they entombed it ceremoniously at Park Hill; and on the tribal records inscribed their last tribute to him, closing in these words:

"The Cherokees, with John Ross at their head, alone with their treaties achieved recognition of their rights though they were powerless to enforce them. They were compelled to yield, but not until the struggle had developed the highest qualities of patience, fortitude, and tenacity of right and purpose on their part."

Ross's gravestone guards the dust of a chieftain whose life was no less romantic and courageous, no less ruled by a spirit unconquerable than were the lives of those Highland chiefs whose blood ran in his veins. In him was combined the staunchness of the Scot with the subtlety and imagination of the Indian. From both he drew a passionate devotion to his own soil, a reverence for the past, a reserve that held him apart, and a democracy of mind and heart that made him one with every member of the tribe. He made mistakes, but they were not those of a small man. Freely he spent himself in the service of his people.

At the end of his story, I am not sure that I have made a clear picture of the man. But if he must remain a shadowy, evasive human figure, certainly his projection over the troubled and dramatic history of my people is a valid reality. Because John Ross lived and labored for them, the Cherokees preserved an extraordinary race pride and integrity, stepping without fear or difficulty, when the time came to extinguish the tribal organization, into the ranks of American citizenship.

NOTES

CHAPTER 1

1. Daniel Ross emigrated from Scotland to America at the end of the eighteenth century. Molly McDonald was the daughter of John McDonald, who had also emigrated from Scotland to South Carolina in 1766, where he became a trader. Molly's mother was Annie Shorey, whose own mother was a full-blood Cherokee woman known in the records as Ghi-goo-ie (Ruskin 1963, 12–14), although this word was more likely a title, translated as *beloved*, that influential Cherokee individuals could acquire (Timberlake 1765, 71; Hoig 1998, 14).

2. Thomas McKenney (1872, 160), Rachel C. Eaton (1914, 3), and Sara G. Harrell (1979, 5) write Hillstown. Malone writes "Wills Town," "near present-day Fort Payne, Alabama" (1956, 61). Stanley Hoig writes that Willstown used to be a Creek town named after its founder, trader William Webber, and that it is now Fort Payne, Alabama (1998, 81).

3. Twelve years before, in 1785, the Cherokees had signed the Treaty of Hopewell with the United States. It was a treaty to restore peace after some Cherokees had sided with the British during the Revolutionary War. Like many future treaties, it placed the Cherokees "under the protection of the United States of America" (Article 3). The Treaty of Holston was signed in 1791, partly to reinforce the previous one.

4. Fort Prince George was built near the Cherokee town of Keowee in 1756, and was besieged by Oconostota (Oskison writes Oconastata) in his opposition to the British during the French and Indian War of 1754–63 (Mooney [1891] 1992, 40–42, Hoig 1998, 35–38). He was an eighteenth century war chief, when Atakullakulla (or Ada-gal'kala, according to Conley, and also known as the Little Carpenter) was a peace chief. Lieutenant Henry Timberlake adequately summed up, in 1765, the merits of either—along with a third chief, Ostenaco—in obtaining the prestige they enjoyed among their fellow Cherokees and others: "Attakullakulla has done but little in war to recommend him, but has often signalized himself by his policy, and negotiations at home. Ostenaco has a tolerable share of both; but policy and art are the greatest steps to power. Attakullakulla has a large faction with this alone, while Oconnestoto, sir-named the Great Warrior, famous for having, in all his expeditions,

taken such prudent measures as never to have lost a man, has not so much power, and Ostenaco could never have obtained the superiority, if he had not a great reputation in both" (1765, 73). Oconostota died in 1785. As opposed to Oconostota, Atakullakulla always believed in maintaining peaceful and friendly relations with the English. He died in 1778 (Starr 1921, 26).

5. Keanotah (or Kanitta), Little Turkey, and Ocunna (Badger) were Beloved Men in the 1790s (Hoig 1998, 80). They put their X mark down a speech given on behalf of the Cherokees in Tellico, on April 28, 1797, in the presence of Benjamin Hawkins and Silas Dinsmoor, commissioned by the United States to determine the boundary line and the location of military posts which were to be built on Cherokee land, after some misunderstandings ensued from the 1791 Treaty of Holston (Hawkins 1916, 163–64). Little Turkey remained principal chief until his death in 1802, when he was succeeded by Black Fox (Hoig 1998, 90). Badger was among the Chickamauga Cherokees in 1777 (McLoughlin 1986, 20; Conley 2005, 67). Pathkiller (c. 1742–1827), whose name in Cherokee was Nanohetahee (or Nunnahidihi, Nenohuttahe; "He Kills in the Path"), succeeded Black Fox as principal chief of the Cherokees in 1811. He led the Cherokees until 1827, with Charles Hicks to assist him. According to Stanley Hoig, he proved "to be an honorable and capable principal chief. Under his leadership, mission schools were permitted to open inside the nation, and for the first time Cherokee children began learning to read and write" (1998, 115). He signed several treaties. In 1813, he led the Cherokees through the Creek War, alongside General Andrew Jackson (Hoig 1998, 91, 122; Moulton 1985, 2:729; McClinton 2007, 1:559, 647; McLoughlin 1986, 145). Doublehead (Dhuqualutauge) was a Chickamauga leader fighting along Dragging Canoe against the Americans during the Revolutionary War. In 1794, he personally confronted Washington in Philadelphia and successfully argued that the annuity guaranteed by the 1791 Treaty of Holston was too low. He signed the treaty of 1805. Doublehead was executed in 1807 by The Ridge and others because of his illegally ceding Cherokee lands to the federal government in exchange for a personal reserve (McLoughlin 1986, 20, 60–61, 120–21; Hoig 1998, 59, 95–96). Dragging Canoe (Tsiyugunsini), son of Attakullakulla, emerged as a war leader during the Revolutionary period when he led part of the Cherokees into a movement against Euro-American encroachments and settled along the Chickamauga River, in opposition to his father, Oconostota and Nancy Ward (Hoig 1998, 59). He died in 1792, and was succeeded by Doublehead, John Watts, and Bloody Fellow as leaders of the Chickamaugans (McLoughlin 1986, 24). The Ridge (c. 1771–1839), whose Cherokee name was Kahmungdaclageh ("The Man Who Walks on the Mountaintop"), and who became Major Ridge after his participation in the

Creek War of 1813–14, is well known. As a young man, he was a warrior, fighting against Euro-Americans or other traditional enemies of the Cherokees. In 1807, he executed Doublehead, convicted of relinquishing lands to the United States without official authorization. Throughout his life, he endorsed various political and diplomatic roles, lobbied in Washington, and signed treaties. At the beginning of the 1830s, he became a leader of the Treaty Party and signed the Treaty of New Echota in 1835 that imposed removal on the Cherokee Nation. He was assassinated in 1839 by anti-treaty men (Moulton 1976, 2:731).

6. The more common spelling for the name of this Cherokee agent is Dinsmoor, although John Ross, like Oskison, spelled it Dinsmore. Silas Dinsmoor (1766–1847), of Irish stock, came from New Hampshire. According to Cletus F. Fortwendel Jr., "Dinsmoor should be considered important in the era, though, because he helped lay the basis for much of the acculturation which took place among the Cherokees in the late eighteenth and early nineteenth century" (1996, 28). He was appointed Cherokee agent in 1794 and quickly "earned the friendship and trust of most of the Cherokees who had met him" (34). During his service, Dinsmoor focused his energy on making sure the Article 14 of the Treaty of Holston—the one promising that the United States would lead the Cherokees "to a greater degree of civilization"—did not remain unheeded, and on trying to curb the flow of Euro-American intruders who did not respect the Treaty of Holston boundary line. Among his achievements, Fortwendel Jr. counts the National Council's decision to limit the practice of the clan revenge law (39). Dinsmoor's service to the Cherokees ended in 1799, when he was replaced by Thomas Lewis, who proved to be "totally inept" as an Indian agent (43). John Ross expressed respect and admiration for Dinsmoor in different ways. One of his sons was named Silas Dinsmore (Moulton 1985, 1:4). In a letter to Secretary of War John C. Calhoun, dated February 17, 1825, Ross requested that the position of Cherokee agent, made vacant by the death of Agent Joseph McMinn, should be filled by "such a person as may possess the virtues and necessary qualifications for the station," Silas Dinsmoor. He explained that, "It is known to the Department that the Cherokees view Mr. Silas Dinsmore as a Gentleman worthy of that trust and would be gratified to have him appointed their Agent" (Moulton 1985, 1:97).

7. James Vann (1768–1809) is called a "notorious half-breed town chief" and "a peculiar combination of benevolent leader and rip-snorting hoodlum" by Henry T. Malone (1956, 60). Malone also writes that "Vann was outstanding in his aid" to the first Moravian missionaries, notably allowing them to establish themselves on his property, for which the missionaries commended him greatly in their diaries: "Indeed, he was the instrument in His hand for our

acceptance and establishment in this nation, and even in his wildest rages never did us any harm" (McClinton 2007, 303). He owned a large plantation and many slaves. His name appears down the treaties of 1804 and 1806 (Kappler 1904, 74). In 1809, he was assassinated in an inn, probably as a revenge for a punishment he had enacted as a participant in the Cherokee Light Horse Brigade. According to the Moravians' diaries, Vann had never converted, in spite of the help he provided the missionaries: "How sincerely we would like to have seen this man, who had been a longstanding *enemy* before his demise, become *a friend of Christ!*" (McClinton 2007, 1:302–3, 628; 2:475). The Gunters were Edward (1789?–1842) and Samuel (1787?–1838). Edward owned slaves and operated a ferry in Chattooga District. He was wounded during the Creek War of 1813–14. He was an interpreter for the Methodists. He signed the 1839 Constitution. Samuel served in the Cherokee Council and the Cherokee Committee in the 1820s and 1830s (McLoughlin 1984, 176; Moulton 1985, 2:724). By an act of the National Committee passed on October 28, 1821, the Gunter brothers, along with John G. Ross, Captain John Brown, and Jesse Lovett were "authorized and privileged to open [. . .] roads and to establish a turnpike gate thereon for the term of five years" (*Laws* 1852, 20–21). John (Jack) Thompson was James Vann's brother-in-law (Starr 1921, 454). He was an American Board missionary. He protested against Georgia's policies regarding the Cherokees, and was arrested by the Georgia guard in 1831. However, that same year, he eventually refused to support Worcester and Butler in civil disobedience to Georgia's laws, and declared that "it may be part of God's plan in promoting the interests of His church, to destroy the Majority of the Cherokees" (McLoughlin 1984, 256, 259; quoted in McLoughlin 1984, 332). Arthur Coodey is probably Arthur Archibald Coody, a planter and slaveholder who died in 1809 (McClinton 2007, 2:481).

8. Oskison refers particularly to Article 14 of the Treaty of Holston: "That the Cherokee nation may be led to a greater degree of civilization, and to become herdsmen and cultivators, instead of remaining in a state of hunters, the United States will from time to time furnish gratuitously the said nation with useful implements of husbandry, and further to assist the said nation in so desirable a pursuit, and at the same time to establish a certain mode of communication, the United States will send such, and so many persons to reside in said nation as they may judge proper, not exceeding four in number, who shall qualify themselves to act as interpreters. These persons shall have lands assigned by the Cherokees for cultivation for themselves and their successors in office; but they shall be precluded exercising any kind of traffic" (Kappler 1904, 31).

9. Oskison made a mistake or a typo by stating here that Washington had secured an increase of annuities from $1,000 to $8,500. On February 17, 1792, an additional article amended the Treaty of Holston, stipulating that "the sum to be paid annually by the United States to the Cherokee nation of Indians [. . .] shall be one thousand five hundred dollars instead of one thousand dollars, mentioned in the said treaty" (Kappler 1904, 33).

10. Benjamin Hawkins (1754–1816) was appointed by President Washington Superintendent of Indian Affairs in the southwestern territory in 1796. He supported Cherokee Agent Silas Dinsmoor in his efforts to implement the "civilization" policy guaranteed by the federal government in the Article 14 of the Treaty of Holston. White settlers' disregard for the Treaty of Holston boundary line was one major bone of contention between the Euro-Americans and the Cherokees during the 1790s. In 1797, Superintendent Hawkins, along with Generals Andrew Pickens and James Winchester, was appointed to a commission charged with running and marking the boundary, which was done with the collaboration of Cherokee leaders, and which earned him to be accused by white settlers of being a traitor (Fortwendel 1996, 40–41).

11. Zachariah Cox was a trader and land speculator with a long history of tense relations with the Cherokees. He founded the Tennessee Company and attempted to found a colony at Muscle Shoals, on the Tennessee River, in 1791. In 1797, he "laid out Smithland, a small settlement on the Ohio between the mouths of the Tennessee and Cumberland rivers," to which Oskison here probably refers. "Later, he tried to plant a second settlement at Muscle Shoals, but again the Indians, with encouragement from Indian Superintendent Benjamin Hawkins, blocked it" (Haynes 2010, 32). In 1803, Cox filed a petition for redress for having been wrongfully arrested in 1798. He was accused by Brigadier General Wilkinson of violating "the law regulating trade and intercourse with the Indian tribes, in taking a position upon their land." However, the House of Representatives committee in charge of examining Cox's petition found no evidence that his arrest had been justified (United States Congress 1803, 361–62).

12. Walker is probably a reference to Joseph Walker (1798–1876), a famous Tennessee frontiersman who blazed trails towards California. In 1792, he defended a fort near Kingston against a Cherokee war party (Gilbert 1983, 49). Smith could be Jedidiah or James. Jedidiah Strong Smith (1799–1831) was an explorer of the Southwest. Oskison more likely refers to James Smith (1737–1812), a frontiersman and the leader of the group of rebels known as the Black Boys, with whom he fought the British out of Fort Loudoun in 1765. After the Black Boys' rebellion, Smith explored Kentucky before Daniel Boone, and before raiding "Indian trade convoys along the Forbes Road" (Dixon 2005, 323n24).

In the preface to his *Account of the Remarkable Occurrences in the Life and Travels of Col. James Smith*, Smith writes that "the principal advantage that I expect will result to the public, from the publication of the following sheets, is the *observations on the Indian mode of warfare*. Experience has taught the Americans the necessity of adopting their mode, and the more perfect we are in that mode, the better we shall be able to defend ourselves against them, when defence is necessary" (1799, 3–4). Daniel Boone (1734–1820) is a legendary frontiersman. After the French and Indian War, in which he fought along with General Braddock, he explored and settled in Kentucky. Throughout his life, he was involved in various violent skirmishes with Indians. His life and career became the stuff of legend, and even myth, after the publication of *The Adventures of Col. Daniel Boone*, by John Filson, in 1782 (Hine and Faragher 2000, 116, 472–74).

13. William Weatherford (1780–1824), also known as Red Eagle, was a mixed-blood leader of the Red Stick Creeks who fought five hundred Cherokees and Andrew Jackson during the Battle of Horseshoe Bend in March 1814 (Conley 2005, 91–92, 94; Eggleston 1878, 318–39). During the French and Indian War, in 1760, Col. Archibald Montgomery, at the head of twelve hundred High-landers and Royal Scots, Col. James Grant as second in command, marched against the Lower Towns of the Cherokees. Every man was put to death by the bayonet, the crops and towns torched. The following year, Grant, refusing peace offers made by Attakullakulla, marched over the Lower Towns again. Only after a Cherokee defeat did Grant allow Attakullakulla to negotiate peace at Fort Prince George (Hoig 1998, 39, 42–43; Woodward 1963, 74–75). John Sevier (1745–1815) led his first attack against the Cherokees in 1780, during the Revolutionary war. Several towns were destroyed, including Echota, the capital (Mooney [1891] 1992, 57–58). Later, Sevier and his followers attempted to form the state of Franklin, claiming huge Cherokee territories, in defiance of the 1785 Treaty of Hopewell. He was opposed by Cherokee leader Corn Tassel (or Old Tassel). In 1786, Sevier led a militia against several Chero-kee towns, killing many. Corn Tassel was subsequently murdered by Sevier's men (Hoig 1998, 67–72). Sevier would later become governor of Tennessee (McLoughlin 1986, 51). Sevier's son, Joseph, married the granddaughter of Cherokee chief Oconostota (Fortwendel 1996, 38).

14. The anecdote about young Ross's suit can be found in many biographies of Ross—some of which might have more to do with myth-building than history-writing—with the same conclusion relating to his embrace of Cherokee identity. For example, this is how Ruskin concludes this story: "John Ross though actually only one-eighth Cherokee was purely Cherokee in response" (1963, 17). Rachel Caroline Eaton tells the anecdote in very much the same terms

as Oskison (1914, 4). Gary Moulton writes that "as a youth Ross favored the ancient dress and customs of his people. At the annual Green Corn Festival, he was reluctant to appear before his young friends in American clothes and stayed behind until his mother let him change to more familiar Cherokee attire" (1978, 6). The proof that this possible "myth-building" is, as often, anchored in truth, may reside in an 1830 letter by Samuel Worcester which could be the archival origin of this story: "The present principal chief is about forty years of age. When he was a boy, his father procured him a good suit of clothes, in the fashion of the sons of civilized people; but he was so ridiculed by his mates as a *white* boy, that he took off his new suit, and refused to wear it" (Worcester 1830, 42).

CHAPTER 2

1. Ruskin spells his name John Barbour Davis, and writes "it may be said that Daniel Ross established the first school in the Rossville and Chattanooga section" (1963, 15).
2. David Brown (c. 1801–29), son of influential John Brown—co-founder of the Creek Path Mission, co-author and signer of the 1827 Constitution, principal chief of the Old Settlers—and brother of Catherine Brown—Brainerd Mission student, Creek Path teacher (Malone 1956, 104), and "religious leader" (Higginbotham 1976, 73), entered the Brainerd school in 1819, where he was baptized in April 1820 (Phillips and Phillips 1998, 167). He attended the Foreign Mission School in Cornwall, Connecticut, from 1820 to 1823 (Phillips and Phillips 1998, 489n60; McLoughlin 1984, 140). He and George Lowery translated the New Testament from Greek to Cherokee. Both of them also translated the Cherokee laws into the characters invented by Sequoyah (Higginbotham 1976, 77, 82; Malone 1956, 105; *Laws* 1852, 81). According to the editors of the Brainerd Journal, Brown was "the first person to bring the Cherokee syllabary to the attention of government officials in Washington" (Phillips and Phillips 1998, 489n60).
3. This quote is from a letter written at Rossville, dated July 13, 1822. Although Oskison faithfully rendered the meaning of the quotes he chose, he was not exact in transcribing them if one relies on Moulton's authoritative two-volume compilation of the papers of John Ross. Moulton's transcription of this passage is: "To reflect seriously on the condition of the Indian Tribes inhabiting the continent of America, and to review the miserable fate which has befallen and swept into wretchedness and oblivion the numerous Tribes that once inhabited the country bordering on the Atlantic, is enough to make the remnant of those Tribes, who are now encompassed by the white population, shudder. Yet I cannot believe, that the Indians are doomed to perish in wretchedness, from

generation to generation, as they are approached by the white population, until they shall be annihilated from the face of the earth" (Moulton 1985, 1:42). After this passage, Ross shows himself very optimistic and hopeful: "The small experiment made by the exertions of benevolent societies, through their faithful missionaries, has awakened the American people to a sense of what might be done to better the condition of the Indian race. Under such circumstances, when the Indians are themselves seen to manifest a thirst to reach after the blessings and happiness derivable from civilized life, I cannot believe that the United States Government will still continue to pursue the luke-warm system of policy, in her relations with the Indians, as has hitherto been adopted, to effect the purpose of removing nation after nation of them from the lands of their fathers into the remote wilderness, where their encroachments on the hunting grounds of other Tribes has been attended with the unhappy consequences of quarrels, wars, and bloodshed" (1:43).

4. Usually spelled Fort Loudoun (Moulton 1978, Hoig 1998, Conley 2005), or Fort Loudon (Mooney [1891] 1992, Woodward 1963).

5. Ghigooie, meaning Beloved, is a title earned by man or woman either for their courage at war or their diplomatic skills and wisdom.

6. Bloody Fellow, whose Cherokee name was Nenetooyah, was a chief of the Chickamauga Cherokees, who, following Dragging Canoe, had sided with the English during the Revolutionary War and had split with the main tribe after its older chiefs made peace with the Americans. However, his x mark is at the end of the 1791 Treaty of Holston and, as principal chief, he presided over talks for the 1798 treaty. In 1792, he had negotiated better annuities and more goods after the 1791 treaty and adopted new peaceful intentions when he was satisfied. As a consequence, he acquired a new name, Clear Sky (or Eskaqua), from President Washington (Kappler 1904, 33, 54; McLoughlin 1984, 16; Hoig 1998, 63, 76, 90).

7. According to Rowena McClinton Ruff, Charles Hicks "related to the [Moravian] missionaries in 1819 that he had heard only one white man speak the Cherokee language perfectly, John McDonald, the grandfather of John Ross" (1996, 17).

8. The Glass (Tauquatehee), "Not a Friend of White People" (McClinton 2007, 1:148), was a Chickamauga leader who resisted increasing Euro-American settlements during the Revolutionary War. However, he signed the treaties of 1805 and 1817 (Kappler 1904, 84, 144). In 1805, he and others—Black Fox, Doublehead—signed a secret deal with the United States to exchange lands east for lands in the west, including personal reserves, which resulted in the assassination of Doublehead (McClinton 2007, 2:462; Kappler 1904, 54; McLoughlin 1986, 144).

9. These two quotes are from a letter dated September 6, 1801, signed by Wilkinson, Pickins, and Benjamin Hawkins, and addressed to Secretary of War Henry Dearborn (Hawkins 1916, 383–84).

10. Here, Oskison crossed out the following passage: "It was a statement by implication of the persistent claim of later negotiators that the Cherokees were making use of but scanty fractions of their domain ignoring the fact that four fifths of it was mountain and rocky forest land fit only for hunting, trapping, and stock raising and that most of the tribesmen were mountaineers."

11. These quotes and paraphrases by Oskison are from a letter written by Hawkins on the same day as the one previously cited written with his two colleagues, September 6, 1801, also addressed to Dearborn: "I find that the pressure for land exhibited from all quarters had alarmed the chiefs of the nation. The exultation of the frontier citizens on the election of the President produced a belief that the President would favour [sic] the views of those deemed by Indians inimical to their rights. The report circulated through the nation soon after the adjournment of Congress that a treaty was soon to be held to extinguish the Indian claims to the lands on the right side of the Tennessee, and the withdrawing the troops from this frontier. All these circumstances, combined by mischief-makers, produced on the Indian mind a distrust of the President and of every thing proceeding from him. It produced a panic terror in the nation, which the chiefs have endeavoured [sic] to spread throughout the agency South of Ohio. They have consulted me as agent for the department, on the propriety of looking out west of the Mississippi for an eventual residence where this nation has a settlement of near one hundred gun men." A few lines below, Hawkins wrote: "In the Cherokee agency the wheel, the loom and the plough is in pretty general use; farming, manufactures and stock raising the topics of conversation among the men and women, and the accumulation of individual personal property taking strong hold of the men. It is questionable with me whether the division of land among the individuals would tend to their advantage or not. In such an event, the long and well tried skill of land speculators might soon oust a whole tribe, whereas the whole country being a common, each of the community having exclusive property in their own farms only, the combined intelligence of the whole might be sufficient to resist such an evil, and secure at all times land for the cultivation of the indijent [sic] and improvident" (1916, 385).

12. Cherokees started to settle west of the Mississippi as early as the end of the eighteenth century, although James Mooney claimed that Cherokees had always crossed the Mississippi on hunting expeditions (Mooney [1891] 1992, 101). The first Cherokee settlement west of the Big River recorded by history, however, may be the one alluded to by Oskison here. According to missionary

Cephas Washburn, a Cherokee chief named The Bowl and his followers moved west in 1794, after what was termed the Muscle Shoals Massacre, during which traders were killed after swindling the Cherokees out of their money (Washburn 1971, 76–77; Mooney [1891] 1992, 100–101). They first settled in Missouri, before moving to Arkansas in 1811 (Conley 2005, 89). They would eventually move all the way to Texas. More would move, following John Jolly, by virtue of the treaty of 1817 (Conley 2005, 99; McLoughlin 1986, 239).

13. By the 1802 "Georgia Compact," Georgia agreed to turn its western claims (later to become the states of Alabama and Mississippi), some of which was Cherokee territory, over to the federal government. In exchange, President Jefferson agreed "that the federal government would extinguish all Indian claims to land within the limits of Georgia as soon as reasonably possible and return that land to Georgia" (McLoughlin 1986, 22).

14. Molly died on October 5, 1808, at the age of thirty-nine (Ruskin 1963, 17).

15. Glass was one of the Chickamauga leaders. He was deposed as chief in 1808 after he became favorable to removal west of the Mississippi (Hoig 1998, 64; McLoughlin 1986, 144–45). Toochalar (or Toochalee), a Lower Town chief, was second principal chief until he supported removal by signing the treaty of 1817. He was then deposed and replaced by Charles Hicks. He had also signed the treaty of 1805 (McLoughlin 1984, 42; Kappler 1904, 83, 144; McClinton 2007, 2:521n42).

16. The act dated September 11, 1808, in "Brooms Town," signed by Principal Chief Black Fox, Second Principal Chief Pathkiller, Toochalar, and Charles Hicks, Secretary to Council, created the police force referred to by Oskison, and established that any person convicted of horse theft "shall be punished with one hundred stripes on the bare back, and the punishment to be in proportion for stealing property of less value." It also stipulated that "should the accused person or persons raise up with arms in his or their hands, as guns, axes, spears and knives, in opposition to the regulating company, or should they kill him or them, the blood of him or them shall not be required of any of the persons belonging to the regulators from the clan the person so killed belonged to." On April 10, 1810, at Ostanallah, an act was signed by Turtle at Home, Speaker of Council, and approved by Principal Chief Black Fox, Second Principal Chief Pathkiller, Toochalar, and recorded by Charles Hicks, Secretary to Council, which stipulated that "the various clans or tribes [. . .] have [. . .] agreed that if, in future, any life should be lost without malice intended, the innocent aggressor shall not be accounted guilty" (*Laws* 1852, 3–4).

17. Meigs was not Dinsmoor's immediate successor. Thomas Lewis served for a couple of years between them. Coming from Connecticut, Return J. Meigs

(1740–1823) replaced Thomas Lewis as Indian agent to the Cherokees in 1801 and remained at that position until 1823. He is considered by some to have been rather sympathetic for their problems and devoted "to promoting the well-being of the Cherokees" (Malone 1956, 57). However, significant cessions of land were also negotiated during his service among the Cherokees, whom he repeatedly encouraged to move west, and he had several enemies among the Cherokee nationalists. For example, he was accused of being Doublehead's accomplice in the secret land deals that caused the latter to be assassinated in 1807 (McLoughlin 1986, 121; McClinton 2007, 2:489). The Ross and Meigs families seem to have been close. Return's son, Timothy, was Ross's partner in a business venture started in 1813 (Moulton 1978, 8).

18. After the Broomstown council of 1808, a delegation was sent to Washington, formed of delegates from the Upper Towns, who favored adjustment to Euro-American ways, and delegates from the Lower Towns who, supported by Agent Meigs, would rather exchange their part of the territory for new territories in Arkansas. According to McLoughlin, "The Upper Town delegates admitted [to President Jefferson] that at Broomstown there was a general feeling that separation of the two regions might be useful, but the council favored this only because the Upper Towns considered the Lower Towns to be backward, lazy, and opposed to new laws to improve social order" (McLoughlin 1986, 149). Jefferson ended up approving of anyone who wanted to migrate west, but declared that he could not agree to a division of the nation without the consent of all parties (150–51).

19. Rowena McClinton spells the name of the second missionary "Gottlieb Byhan" (2007, 1:22). First-hand information about the Moravians among the Cherokees, and about the Springplace mission in particular, can be found in the Gambold diaries edited and introduced by McClinton (2007) and in the *History of the Moravian Missions Among Southern Indian Tribes of the United States*, by Rev. Edmund Schwarze (1923). The Moravian Church, or the Unity of Brethren, "emerged from German Pietists and remnants of Czech Hussites, followers of fifteenth-century martyr Jan Hus." The Moravians "faced considerable oppression for their pacifism and unorthodox practices in the Lutheran Church" (McClinton 2007, 1:1). They had attempted and failed to establish a mission in Cherokee country as early as the 1770s. When they came back in 1800, Steiner, supported by progressive Cherokees like James Vann and Charles Hicks, managed to convince a wary council, more concerned with the education of the children than with religion. Principal Chief Little Turkey is said to have told the council: "Their desire appears to be good, to instruct us and our children and improve our and their minds and Nation. These gentlemen, I hope will make the experiment; we will be the judge from

their conduct and their attention to us and our children, this will enable us to judge properly. Should they not comply as now stated, the Agent will be the judge for the Red people" (quoted in McClinton 2007, 1:21 and Malone 1956, 93). Sick with malaria, Abraham Steiner did not stay very long. Byhan and his wife served Springplace from 1801 to 1812 and again from 1827 to 1832. John and Anna Rosina Gambold ministered to the Cherokees from 1805 to 1821 (McClinton 2007, 1:22).

20. Gideon Blackburn (1772–1838) arrived in the Cherokee Nation in 1803 and was authorized by the council to open a school on the Hiwassee River, in eastern Tennessee (McLoughlin 1984, 54–55, 58). Blackburn put schooling before the teaching of the Christian doctrine because he believed the latter would naturally follow the former. For instance, he wrote that "the prospects of a future day opening the Gospel fully on this nation are apparent. The attention of the Indians to the exhortations frequently given, their beginning to move out into farms, their adopting civilized customs and habits, &c, but especially the ground to hope that before long their own children will be able (and I hope willing) to preach Jesus, lead to this expectation" (Blackburn 1805, 35–57). According to his own account, the idea that something may "be done with this people to meliorate their condition" first came to him in 1794 as he was settled in Blount County, Tennessee, near Cherokee country. In 1803, after several attempts at opening a mission among them, he finally obtained the support of the Committee of Missions and of a Cherokee council "consisting of upwards of 2000 Indians, assembled, including all the Chiefs of the nation. . . . The school was open in the spring of 1804. In the course of the first week we had twenty-one children, who all gave flattering evidences of promising geniuses" (Blackburn 1807, 191–94).

21. In 1816, Cyrus Kingsbury (1786–1870) purchased the improvements of John McDonald, Ross's grandfather, to establish the Brainerd mission, which opened its doors in March 1817, supported by the American Board of Commissioners for Foreign Missions (Phillips and Phillips 1998, 1, 27, 432n2; McLoughlin 1984, 110). It was named after David Brainerd, a missionary who served in New England and Delaware between 1742 and 1747. The mission was located seven miles east of Lookout Mountain. Kingsbury left the mission in 1818 to open another among the Choctaw Indians (Phillips and Phillips 1998, 431n1; DeRosier 1972, 272–73).

22. Although Mooney calls Priber "the Jesuit" ([1891] 1992, 113), considering all these missionaries the "successors" of Christian Priber is a stretch, if only because Priber's story appears to be mainly the stuff of legend (Larré 2014, 77–82). Mooney seemed to believe that Priber had "familiarized the Cherokee with the forms of civilized government" ([1891] 1992, 113). According to

James Adair, Priber was sent by the French among the Cherokees in 1736, in order to "seduce them from the British to the French interest." He supposedly learned their language, adopted their customs, married into the tribe, and "easily formed them into a nominal republican government—crowned their old Arch-magus, emperor, after a pleasing new savage form, and invented a variety of high-sounding titles for all the members of his imperial majesty's red court, and the great officers of state [. . .] He himself received the honourable title of his imperial majesty's principal secretary of state" (Adair 1775, 240–41). Antoine Bonnefoy, a French traveler who was captured by the Cherokees in 1741, recorded his encounter with Priber, who told him of his project to establish "a republic, for which he had been working for twenty years," and toward which he made significant progress among the Cherokees. Bonnefoy reported that Priber "was adopted into the nation," and that he believed he had found there "the things necessary for laying the first foundations of his republic, under the name of the Kingdom of Paradise" (Bonnefoy 1916, 248–49).

CHAPTER 3

1. This is a quote from "a treaty held between the Officers of the State of Franklin and the Cherokee Indian Chiefs July 31st and August 3rd, 1786" ("Talks" 1786, 655–59; Ramsey 1853, 344–46).
2. Although a treaty was signed in 1804, the secret land deals arranged by Tolluntuskee and Doublehead were attached to the treaties of October 1805 and January 1806. These treaties, signed by a minority of the Cherokee headmen, ceded important tracts of land, granted the right of way for two roads, and set aside reserves for Tolluntuskee and Doublehead (McLoughlin 1986, 104–6).
3. Oskison published a biography of Tecumseh in 1938.
4. John Brown and John Rogers were leaders of the Western Cherokees (Hoig 1998, 156, 192, 194).
5. This man was Samuel Riley, interpreter for the Cherokee agent (Moulton 1976, 47).
6. Ross's letters to Meigs, edited by Moulton, attest that this trip took place at the end of 1812 and the beginning of 1813, not in 1809. Ross tells of his buying Isaac Brownlow's boat in a letter dated December 15, 1812. In the two subsequent letters, he mentions the names of his companions, Peter, Kalsatee, and "Mr. Spears." Moulton writes that Ross travelled with "John Spear, a mixed-blooded Cherokee interpreter, an old full-blood, Kalsatee, and Peter, a Spanish-speaking servant" (1976, 46, 49–50).
7. "Red Sticks" was the name given to the Creek conservatives, after their red-painted war clubs.

8. In 1819, Gideon Morgan, John Ross, and others were sent to Washington by Principal Chief Pathkiller as part of a delegation led by Charles Hicks. They signed the treaty of 1819 (Kappler 1904, 179; Phillips and Phillips 1998, 477). Richard Brown, father of John Brown (previously mentioned), was a respected half-Cherokee war captain, a "personal friend of [Andrew] Jackson" at the time of the 1814 Creek War (Hoig 1998, 89, 120). He signed the treaty of 1817 (Kappler 1904, 144). James Brown (1779?–1863) served first as captain, then as major in the Creek War. He played several political and diplomatic roles throughout his life, in the National Committee and in delegations to Washington. He notably signed the treaties of 1817 and 1819 (144, 179). He headed a removal detachment in 1838 and 1839. He signed the 1839 Constitution (Moulton 1985, 2:717–18). Like the Vanns and the Hicks, the McNairs were a prominent and large family. Oskison undoubtedly refers here to David McNair (1774?–1836), who served as a captain in the Creek War. He was also known as a strong supporter of the Moravians (Moulton 1985, 2:728; McClinton 2007, 2:489). "Saunders" probably refers to one of two Sanders of note who can be found in the archives, George and Alexander, two of eight children by a Cherokee mother and a Revolutionary War deserter who moved to the Cherokee Nation and became a citizen by marriage. George was a wealthy banker. He signed the treaty of 1817 (Phillips and Phillips 1998, 538; Kappler 1904, 144). Alexander was known to be a staunch nationalist. In 1807, Alexander Sanders was one of Doublehead's executioners, and a member of the Constitutional Convention in 1827 (McLoughlin 1986, 120; McClinton 2007, 2:471; Phillips and Phillips 1998, 538). A few pages of the *Payne-Butrick Papers* are dedicated to several anecdotes about Shoe Boots (or Chulioa, or Tah-see-key-yar-key), who was a great Cherokee warrior, and who got his English name from "his great pride in wearing high hessian military boots" (Anderson et al. 2010, 106). Payne confirms that Shoe Boots was the captain of one of the Cherokee companies during the war against the Creeks in 1814 (107). He was also remarked for marrying a young white girl whom he had captured during a raid in Kentucky (106). A few years later, and after three children were born, she left him. He then married one of his slaves and petitioned the National Council to grant free status to his children with his new wife. The council granted his request but "ordered that Shoe Boots cease begetting any more children by his said slave woman" (108–9), presumably to avoid further such legal conundrums.

9. Oskison published a biography of Sam Houston entitled *A Texas Titan* in 1929.

10. Malone (1956), Hoig (1998), and McLoughlin (1984) spell it Junaluska. He was at the head of a Cherokee regiment of both foot and mounted soldiers who joined the Tennessee militia during the war against the Creeks (Hoig

1998, 117; McLoughlin 1986, 192). He distinguished himself in battle, notably at the Horseshoe Bend: "At a crucial point a group of Cherokees under Chief Junaluska silently swam the Tallapoosa River to the enemy's rear and took all hostile canoes" (Malone 1956, 71). In the words of Donald R. Hickey, the Battle of Horseshoe Bend was a "slaughter" which made about eight hundred casualties among the Creeks. Even though part of the Creeks sided with the British, the whole tribe paid the price: "On August 9, 1814, Jackson forced all the tribal leaders to sign the Treaty of Fort Jackson, which stripped the Indians of more than 20,000,000 acres of land—over half of their territory" (Hickey 1989, 151).

CHAPTER 4

1. According to Gary Moulton, nobody is quite sure about who Quatie's father was. Her English name was Elizabeth Brown Henley and, although some sources say she was a full-blood Cherokee, "the best evidence suggests that she was the daughter of a Scottish trader and the sister of Judge James Brown of the Cherokees" (Moulton 1978, 12).
2. Black Fox succeeded to Little Turkey as principal chief in 1802. He signed the treaties of 1805 containing secret land deals to benefit several individuals, Doublehead among others. He remained principal chief until 1811, when he was succeeded by Pathkiller (Hoig 1998, 90; Kappler 1904, 84).
3. James Mooney writes: "In a Washington newspaper notice of the treaty delegation of 1816 the six signers are mentioned as Colonel [John] Lowrey, Major [John] Walker, Major Ridge, Captain [Richard] Taylor, Adjutant [John] Ross, and Kunnesee (Tsi'yu-gûnsi'ni, Cheucunsene) and are described as men of cultivation, nearly all of whom had served as officers of the Cherokee forces with Jackson and distinguished themselves as well by their bravery as by their attachment to the United States" ([1891] 1992, 97). The "Washington newspaper" mentioned by Mooney is the *National Intelligencer* quoted by Oskison in the next paragraph. According to McLoughlin, Kunnesee (whom he calls Cheucunnessee) was Young Dragging Canoe (1986, 199). The delegation's mission was not only to clarify the boundary line between Cherokee and Creek territories. In *The Papers of Chief John Ross*, Gary Moulton included Pathkiller's January 10, 1816, letter of instructions to the delegation: "take our Father the President by the hand & express to him the satisfaction we feel in being successfully carried through the late war in which our nation have had the honor to participate with our white Brothers"; agree on the cession of a tract of land in South Carolina "for a valuable consideration"; bring to the president's attention that "the multiplied intrusions on our lands by disorderly men from all the states or Territories of the United States by

which our country is surrounded has become alarming to us"; bring also to the President's attention "the spoliations committed on the property of our people in that part of our country where the armies marched in carrying on the war against the Creeks" ([1891] 1992, 1: 23–24). Communications with Secretary of War William H. Crawford can also be found in Ross's papers.

CHAPTER 5

1. This commission gathered in June 1817 "at the agency just relocated at Calhoun on the Hiwassee River" (Moulton 1978, 19). I corrected Oskison's spelling of Meriwether, which he consistently spelled "Merriwether."

2. This quote is from Article 6 of the Treaty of 1817 (Kappler 1904, 143).

3. Elijah Hicks (1796–1856), son of former Chief Charles Hicks, married Ross's sister Margaret (1803–62). He was a clerk of the National Council from 1819 to 1825, and played several other political and diplomatic roles as a strong opponent to removal, during which he ended up heading a detachment in 1838–39. In 1832, he was appointed editor of the *Cherokee Phoenix*. He settled near present-day Claremore, Cherokee Nation, signed the 1839 Constitution, and became an associate justice at the Cherokee Nation Supreme Court in the 1840s (Moulton 1985, 2:724–25; Hoig 1998, 153; McClinton 2007, 2:464; Phillips and Phillips 1998, 497).

4. Here and in the next few paragraphs, Oskison seems to be conflating two treaties, both negotiated by Jackson and his fellow commissioners. The first— McLoughlin writes that it was an agreement called "treaty" only by Jackson—was signed on September 14, 1816, by Toochalar (Oskison spells Toochelar), of the Lower Towns and in favor of removal, and fourteen followers, among whom was the name of George Guess, better known as Sequoyah. The signers had been sent by the Cherokee Council as delegates and did not have the authority to negotiate a treaty (Kappler 1904, 133–34; Hoig 1998, 119; McLoughlin 1986, 209–10). A few months later, on July 8, 1817, another treaty was signed by forty-six Cherokee leaders (notably Richard Brown, John Walker, George Lowry, Richard Taylor, Charles Hicks, etc.), including fifteen "Arkansas chiefs" among whom were John D. Chisholm and Toochelar (Kappler 1904, 144; McLoughlin 1986, 216). By virtue of the law of 1817 that disenfranchised any Cherokee who enrolled for emigration, Toochelar was deposed from his position as second principal chief under Pathkiller (McLoughlin 1986, 232).

5. John D. Chisholm had been an accomplice of Doublehead when the latter signed the 1807 treaty with the secret clause guaranteeing him a personal reserve. He escaped assassination when Doublehead was not so lucky (Hoig 1998, 119–20; McLoughlin 1986, 120–21; McClinton 2007, 1:604n87; Hoig 1998, 94–95).

6. Biographical information on Charles Hicks can be found in McClinton Ruff, Rowena, "Notable Persons in Cherokee History: Charles Hicks" (*Journal of Cherokee Studies* 17). Charles Hicks (1767–1827) was the son of a white trader and a Cherokee woman. He served as an interpreter, a diplomat, and a mediator between the Cherokee Nation and the federal government. He was a member of what Indian Agent Meigs called the "patriot party," along with The Ridge and Vann (McClinton Ruff 1996, 21). According to Moulton, he tutored chief John Ross "in the oral traditions of the Cherokees; through Hicks, Ross gained greater understanding of the fullbloods" (1978, 31). According to McClinton Ruff, "Hicks was both a power-broker and a cultural mediator. He surrendered many Cherokee religious traditions when he became a devout Moravian in 1813, but he continually struggled to thwart the designs of white settlers to take over Cherokee lands" (1996, 16). At age forty-six he was baptized Charles Renatus by the Moravians. A history of the Moravians relates the event: "The year 1812 was memorable for the mission by the coming-forward of Assistant Principal Chief Charles Hicks with the request for Baptism. With heartfelt joy he was accepted as a Candidate and taken into special instruction. On Good Friday, April 16, 1813, he was received into the fold of the Brethren's Church by Baptism at a most remarkable service, held again in the barn which the audience filled to overflowing. Hicks answered the questions before Baptism with great conviction. He received the name 'Charles Renatus'" (Schwarze 1923, 118). In 1819 "he headed a delegation to protest against the encroachment on the Cherokee lands by the State of Tennessee" (119). This resulted in additional cessions. However, "Hicks thought the Cherokee Nation had retained most of its homeland" (McClinton Ruff 1996, 22).

7. From the Bible, Exodus 1:8, 1:14, 12:34, and 12:38.

8. In 1824, missionary Elias Cornelius published a small volume telling the story of the two young Osage captives, focusing mainly on Lydia Carter. Versions of the story of the Osage boy rescued by John Ross, and of Lydia Carter, another Osage prisoner who found shelter at Brainerd and who was believed to be the boy's sister, can also be found in Rev. Cephas Washburn's memoirs (1971, 160–65), in the Brainerd Journal (Phillips and Phillips 1998, 186–87, 236), and in Robert Walker in *Torchlights to the Cherokees* (1931, 71–84). Cornelius and Washburn were sources for Oskison, who cites both in his original bibliography. According to Cornelius, however, Lydia Carter was not the boy's sister (1824, 64–65). Cornelius tells of how John Ross rescued the young boy (68–73). John Osage Ross was adopted by Rev. Ard Hoyt as a member of his family (Walker 1931, 78) and was baptized at Brainerd on December 12, 1819 (Phillips and Phillips 1998, 144; Cornelius 1824, 73). In a letter to Hoyt dated August 10, 1820, Agent Meigs required that the two children should be sent

back to the Osages in Arkansas as agreed in peace negotiations between the Western Cherokees and the Osages (Phillips and Phillips 1998, 186). At the beginning of the 1820s, he was taken to New England to pursue his education, where he finally became a saddler (Washburn 1971, 165).

9. On December 14, 1818, Principal Chief Pathkiller addressed his instructions to a delegation composed of Charles Hicks, John Ross, John Walker, John Martin, Gideon Morgan, Lewis Ross, Teeyonoo, George Lowrey, Cabbin Smith, James Brown, Chestoo Culleaugh, and Currohee Dick. They were "authorized to conclude any outstanding provisions of the Treaty of 1817, especially as it regards their relationship with the Arkansas Cherokees and the distribution of annuities between the two groups," and they were given "full power and authority to act in behalf of our common property, and anything else which may appear conducive to the peace and happyness of our people" (Moulton 1985, 31–32). Charles Hicks, not John Ross, actually appears to be the leader of the delegation. His name appears first in letters to Secretary of War John C. Calhoun and President James Monroe, followed by John Ross's (Moulton 1985, 33–35). A treaty was signed on February 27, 1819.

10. Theda Perdue writes Boudinot's Cherokee name Gallegina. Before he changed his name to Elias Boudinot, he was Buck Oo-Watie. Elias Boudinot the older, Buck's "white benefactor," was the first president of the American Bible Society, and president of the Continental Congress, under the Articles of Confederation. In 1816, he published *The Star of the West*, in which he attempted to identify the Native Americans with the descendants of the lost tribes of Israel (Perdue 1983, 5–6; Phillips and Phillips 1998, 456).

11. Oskison probably got this quote and the one in the next paragraph from Eaton (1914, 27–28), who got them from Niles's *Weekly Register*.

12. According to *The Brainerd Journal*, Wicked Jack did not have to be persuaded. On the contrary, in August 1822, "he expresse[d] a great desire to stay some time, for the purpose of further instruction in religion but says it is not right to spend his time in idleness; if we [want?] him to work he shall be very glad to stay." In February 1823, "he expressed a desire to receive baptism." The same journal entry briefly tells his story: "Until within about a year he spent all he could get in whiskey and was often drunk. Being discarded by a near relative, on whom he had partly depended, he came to Br. Mills' neighborhood friendless and disconsolate. When he heard br. Mills talk about the Saviour—the evil of drinking whiskey &c & since that time he had left drinking & been seeking the knowledge of Christ." He was baptized in April 1823, received the name of John (or Jack) Crawfish, and "was admitted to the communion in August of the same year" (Phillips and Phillips 1998, 300, 322, 336, 342, 348).

According to Phillips and Phillips, John Arch (c. 1797–1825), whose Cherokee name was Atsi or Atsee, turned out to be, after his education at Brainerd, "one of the mission's most faithful and trusted interpreters, and the missionaries acknowledged him as one of the finest examples of success in their missionary cause," although their first impression of him, when he first came to Brainerd in January 1819, had been less than enthusiastic indeed: "A Cherokee man who does not know his age, thinks he is about 25, apparently not quite so old, offered himself as a schollar. He spoke english, & his countenance indicated a mind that might admit of improvement; but having the dress & dirty appearance of the most uncultivated part of the tribe, & withal a mind & body for so many years under the influence of these habits, we were sorry to hear him say any thing about entering the school. But after hearing his story, which was somewhat interesting, we thought best to take him on trial. [. . .] He readily agreed to our terms of entering & continuing in the school; but said he had no way to get clothes, except by selling his gun, that being all the property he had in the world. [. . .] His willingness to part with his gun (a piece of property so dear to the Indian) we considered a favorable omen; & agreed to take his gun & pay him for it in clothes as he should want them. [. . .] He says his name is John Arch" (1998, 18, 104, 154). He was baptized in February 1820. When the Creek Patch Mission was established, Daniel Butrick chose Arch as his assistant. He also served as an interpreter, at Brainerd and other missions, notably during a tour with Butrick meant to meet as many Cherokees as possible and tell them about the benefits of Euro-American education and religion (McLoughlin 1984, 136; Walker 1931, 201–13). Oskison got the last quote of the paragraph from Bartlett's *Historical Sketch of the Missions of the American Board among the North American Indians* (1878, 7).

CHAPTER 6

1. The act authorizing schoolmasters, blacksmiths, etc. to reside in the Cherokee Nation was passed in New Town on October 26, 1819, signed by John Ross as president of the National Committee (*Laws* 1852, 6). On October 28, an act was passed to regulate the establishment of stores and to forbid the sale of alcohol. The control of alcohol consumption, as well as gambling, was reinforced by an act of November 8, 1822, observing in its preamble a "great variety of vices emanating from dissipation, particularly from intoxication and gaming at cards," and again on January 27 and November 11, 1824 (6–7, 26–27, 36). On October 30, 1819, The Big Rattling Gourd, William Grimit, Betsey Broom, The Dark, Daniel Griffin, and Mrs. Lesley, "proprietors of a privileged turnpike," were confirmed the "only legal proprietors and privileged company to establish a turnpike on the road leading from widow Fool's, at the forks

of Hightower and Oostenallah river to Wills Creek, by way of Turkey Town," another competing company, established illegally, being "abolished" (7–8). The act regulating marriage was passed on November 2, 1819. It required white men to marry Cherokee women legally, "after procuring license from the National Clerk for that purpose, before he shall be entitled and admitted to the privilege of citizenship," and it guaranteed that the property of the wife should "not be subject to the disposal of her husband." It also deprived the husband of citizenship in case of a "breach of marriage." Finally, it was "also resolved, that it shall not be lawful for any white man to have more than one wife, and it is also recommended that all others should also have but one wife hereafter" (10). The act imposing monogamy to everyone was passed in New Town on November 10, 1825 (57).

2. At the end of the 1820s, George Rockingham Gilmer was representative of Georgia at the U.S. House of Representatives. He became governor of Georgia in 1829 (McLoughlin 1986).

3. The quotes from this and the following paragraphs are from George Gilmer's *Sketches of Some of the First Settlers of Upper Georgia, of the Cherokees, and the Author* (1855, 318–21). I have corrected a few typos by crossing out words and adding others between square brackets. I also indicate elisions not marked in Oskison's manuscript.

4. Young Wolf and The Crawler were brothers. Young Wolf signed the treaties of 1806 and September 1816. His children attended Springplace Mission. His name came up during the so-called Creek Path conspiracy, when Lower Towns chiefs, pressured by Jackson, agreed to sell lands without the authorization of the National Council. He became an itinerant exhorter for the Methodists in the 1830s (McClinton 2007, 2:477; McLoughlin 1986, 260–76; McLoughlin 1984, 176).

5. The act dividing the nation into eight districts and organizing the judicial system was passed in New Town on October 20, 1820, signed by John Ross as president of the National Committee, Pathkiller, and Charles Hicks (*Laws* 1852, 11–12). An act was passed on October 25 to raise a poll tax of fifty cents on each head of a family (12–13). The act prohibiting liquor traffic was passed a year earlier, on October 28, 1819 (6–7).

6. These quotes are from a biography of Sequoyah, entitled "Sequoyah or George Gist," told by Major George Lowrey in 1835 and transcribed by John Howard Payne (Anderson et al. 2010, 136).

7. Turtle Fields fought in the Creek War of 1813–14, and became a Methodist convert and a successful itinerant exhorter in 1826 (McLoughlin 1984, 176).

8. At the end of his life, in 1825, before he died of dropsy, John Arch undertook the translation of the Gospel of St. John in the Cherokee alphabet. McLoughlin

writes that after his death, Arch "became a symbol of Christian martyrdom in the cause to which he dedicated his life" (1984, 136; Walker 1931, 201–13).

9. Boudinot married Harriet Gold (1805–36), whom he met at Cornwall. This marriage, as well as John Ridge's to another young Euro-American woman, Sarah Northrup, inflamed the local community, and divided Harriet's own family, while Boudinot received death threats. A mob burned the young couple in effigy. Harriet shared her impressions in a letter to her brother-in-law dated June 26, 1825: "Yes, it is so, the time has come when your sister Harriet is already 'published' to an Indian. If you have seen Mr. Stone's quarterly report you have seen our names and intentions. Pen cannot describe nor language express the numerous and trying scenes through which I have passed since you left us [. . .] Never before did I so much realize the worth of religion, and so much pity those who in time of trouble were without this inestimable treasure. I have seen the time when I could close my eyes upon every earthly object and look up to God as my only supporter, my only hope—when I could say with emotion I never felt before to my Heavenly Father, 'Other refuge have I none, so I helpless hang to Thee.' [. . .] I know that I appear at present to stand alone, the public, good people and bad, are against me. I cannot say all are against me—there are many who are still my friends, but the excitement at present is such that they dare not have it known that they are on my side. You can have no idea of the scenes we have witnessed the week past. Yes, in this Christian land! The members of the Mission School, many of them, said it was more than they ever knew among the heathen. But it was not done merely by the wicked world, professed Christians attended and gave their approbation. [. . .] A painting had before been prepared representing a beautiful young lady and an Indian, also on the same, a woman as an instigator of Indian marriages—Evening came on—The Church bell began to toll, one would certainly conclude speaking the departure of a soul. Mr. John C. Lewis and Mr. Rufus Payne carried the corpse and Brother Stephen set fire to the barrel of tar, or rather the funeral pile, the flame rose high and the smoke ascended; some said it reminded them of the smoke of their torment which they feared would ascend forever. My heart truly sunk with anguish at the dreadful scene. The bell continued to toll till ten or eleven o'clock" (Boudinot Church 1913, 211–15). Harriet Gold's letters are published in *To Marry an Indian. The Marriage of Harriett Gold and Elias Boudinot in Letters, 1823–1839* (Gaul 2005).

10. Isaac H. Harris, by an 1826 act of the Cherokee government, was "appointed principal Printer for the Cherokee Nation, whose salary shall be four hundred dollars a year, and whose duty shall be to attend to the printing of paper to be printed at New Echota; and it shall further be the duty of said Harris to

employ, and he is hereby authorized to employ a journeyman printer, of sober and studious habits in behalf of the Cherokee Nation, in order that the aforesaid paper may be successfully carried into effect" (*Laws* 1852, 84).

11. The medal to Sequoyah was voted by the National Council in 1824 and was sent to him, along with a letter written by Ross, in 1832. The letter is reproduced in the Payne-Butrick papers (Anderson et al. 2010, 1:141–42).

12. Situwakee is spelled Sitawakee in Moulton (1978), Situagi in McLoughlin (1984), and is also known as Deer in the Water (Oskison later calls him Deer in Water), "an elderly fullblood from Valley Towns who could not read or write English," who was chosen by Ross to lead a detachment during removal, assisted by the missionary Evan Jones (Anderson et al. 2010, 325; McLoughlin 1984, 326; Moulton 1985, 1:670–71; Hoig 1998, 173).

Although traces of a Jim (or James) Martin (1780–1847), grandson of Nancy Ward, can be found (McClinton 2007, 2:466), Oskison probably refers to John Martin, mentioned in note 9 of chapter 5 as a member of a delegation sent to Washington in December 1818. Judge John Martin signed the treaty of 1819 (Kappler 1904, 179). He acted as national treasurer in the 1820s (Starkey 1946, 104). He died in 1840. According to Grant Foreman, "The inscription on the monument over his stone-walled grave recites that he was the chief justice of the first supreme court of the Cherokee Nation" (1932, 238). White Path (1763–1838), whose Cherokee name was Nunnatsunega, fought in the Creek War of 1813–14, and served several years on the council. He became an anti-mission leader of what is known as White Path's Rebellion (1824–27). Although Oskison counts him among the progressives, he was, according to McLoughlin, "one of the first chiefs to oppose publicly the rapid acculturation" (1984, 214). James Mooney, who called him "a noted chief who led the conservative party about 1828," writes that, in 1828, White Path "headed a rebellion against the new code of laws" ([1891] 1992, 113). He was "removed" from the council in November 1825. McLoughlin suggests that the reason for his removal had to do with his opposition to a new oath of office which required officials to swear "by the Holy Evangelists of Almighty God" (McLoughlin 1984, 214). According to Mooney, he died on the Trail of Tears (Mooney [1891] 1992, 113, 132, 528; on White Path, see also *Laws* 67, 68; McClinton 2007, 2:471). Kelechulee (or Kelachula, Kelechulah, Ki li tsu li) was a nationalist chief, opposed to Doublehead. He was a full-blood, "owned no slaves and spoke no English" (McLoughlin 1984, 227), which tend to indicate that he was not a progressive. He may have been a leader in the anti-mission movement of the 1820s. He came to, however, and signed the 1827 Constitution. He died in 1828 (McClinton 2007, 2:465; McLoughlin 1984, 224, 229, 235).

CHAPTER 7

1. Catherine Brown (1800–1823) is the best known, and probably the best documented Brainerd convert. Much information on her life and work can be found in the Brainerd Journal and in a hagiography written by Rufus Anderson, Assistant Secretary of the American Board of Commissioners for Foreign Missions, published in 1825.

   William Wirt (1772–1834) was the Cherokee Nation's lawyer, who defended the Nation and Samuel Worcester at the Supreme Court in 1831 and 1832. Previously, he had been Attorney General of the United States in the Monroe administration. In 1832 he ran for presidency on the Anti-Masonic Party ticket against Andrew Jackson (McLoughlin 1986, 438).

   Francis Scott Key (1779–1843) was the author of the lyrics to "The Star-Spangled Banner."

   Rev. John Haeckwelder (or Heckewelder) (1743–1823) was a Moravian missionary and a student of Indian languages and of the Delaware in particular. He notably published *An Account of the History, Manners, and Customs of the Indian Nations, who Once Inhabited Pennsylvania and the Neighboring States* (Philadelphia, 1819) and *A Narrative of the Mission of the United Brethren Among the Delaware and Mohegan Indians, From its Commencement, in the Year 1740, to the Close of the Year 1808* (Philadelphia, 1820).

2. Joseph McMinn had been governor of Tennessee and an ardent promoter of removal. He replaced Meigs as Cherokee agent in 1823 (McLoughlin 1986, 207, 221, 283).

CHAPTER 8

1. George Lowrey (1770?–1852), whose Cherokee name was Agili ("He is Rising"), was a prominent figure in the Cherokee Nation. He signed the treaties of 1817 and 1819 (Kappler 1904, 144, 179), the Constitution of 1839, was second principal chief in 1828 and from 1843 to 1851. He was also an interpreter and translator of religious scriptures (Moulton 1985, 2:726). By act of the Cherokee government dated November 4, 1826, he and David Brown were "appointed to translate eight copies of the laws of the Cherokee Nation, as early as convenient, into the Cherokee language, written in characters invented by George Guess, and also to translate one copy of the New Testament" (*Laws* 1852, 81).

2. According to Phillips and Phillips, the purpose of the delegation was "to ask the United States government to do away with the Compact of 1802, to ask for the removal of McMinn as Indian agent, to demand payment promised to the Cherokees since 1804 for land known as 'The Wafford Settlement,' to seek relocation of the Cherokee agency, and to seek help in collecting taxes

on white traders" (542). Details of this mission can be found in Moulton (1978, 26–28).

3. Nancy Ward (Nanye-hi) was known for a war feat during the battle at Taliwa against the Creeks in 1755, which earned her the title of *Ghighau*. During the Revolutionary War, she urged neutrality for the best interests of the Cherokee people (Pesantubbee 2014, 177–206), and opposed her cousin Dragging Canoe when he promoted war against the British (Hoig 1998, 26, 59). Cherokee historian Emmet Starr wrote that "she was of queenly and commanding presence and manners and her house was furnished in a style suitable to her high dignity. She was a successful cattle raiser and is said to have been the first to introduce that industry among the Cherokees" (1921, 470). For more on Nancy Ward, and notably on how her decision to help American revolutionaries was informed by Cherokee ideals rather than a conviction that American ways were superior, see Michelene E. Pesantubbee.

4. Joel Chandler Harris (1845–1908) is the famous author of Uncle Remus's Tales, which are part of popular American folklore. Harris grew up in the South and his tales were inspired by stories told by slaves and Indians (Thursby 2003, 126). Many Cherokee animal tales were recorded by James Mooney.

5. Oskison names the "queen" after the town she governed. According to James Mooney, Cofitachiqui was "an important Indian town on the lower Savannah governed by a 'queen'" where De Soto's men found objects of copper that they took for gold ([1891] 1992, 22). The "Indian queen" refused "to furnish guides and carriers, whereupon De Soto made her a prisoner, with the design of compelling her to act as guide herself, and at the same time to sue her as a hostage to command the obedience of her subjects. Instead, however, of conducting the Spaniards by the direct trail toward the west, she led them far out of their course until she finally managed to make her escape." Probably a "queen" of the Uchee Indians, later absorbed by the Creeks, she led De Soto to "a province called Chalaque," that is Cherokee country (23, 193–94).

6. According to Emmet Starr, "Alexander Dougherty, a Virginia trader, was the first white man to marry a Cherokee, the date was 1690" (1921, 24). Mooney, citing John Haywood's 1823 *Natural and Aboriginal History of Tennessee*, writes that "Cornelius Dougherty, an Irishman from Virginia, established himself as the first trader among the Cherokee, with whom he spent the rest of his life" ([1891] 1992, 31). Haywood wrote: "Cornelius Dogherty, a refugee of James the second's party, came to those settlements shortly after the accession of King William, probably about the year 1690. He died in 1788, at a very advanced age. He said that he was 120 years of age. He was a trader, and sent peltry, by the Indians packed to Charleston, who returned also packed with merchandise, which they received in exchange. He afterwards taught

the Indians to steal horses from Virginia, which were the first horses the Cherokees ever had" (1823, 233–34). Cummings is Sir Alexander Cuming, who visited the Cherokees in 1730 and led six Cherokee warriors to London in order to meet the king. He had several accounts of his journey published in London newspapers, in which he had the readers believe that England owed him the Cherokees' allegiance to the Crown. Ludovick Grant's 1756 account, however, qualifies Cuming's story of his deeds, which Robert Conley calls "totally absurd" (2005, 29). For more on the fable of Cuming's diplomatic trip, see my own *Histoire de la nation cherokee* (Larré 2014, 69–77) and "A Mad Narrator as Historian: Sir Alexander Cuming among the Cherokees (1730)" (Larré and Stevens-Larré 2014).

7. Corani, Nellawgitehi (Hoig's [1998] spelling), Caunasaita, and Canacaught were among the signers of the first treaty on record, made with the Cherokees by the colony of South Carolina in 1684. Another signer was "Sinnawa, or Hawk," whom Oskison calls Tlanuwi (18). Kalanu, with Corn Tassel, was a signer of the 1777 Treaty of Long Island with Virginia and North Carolina (62–63).

8. The Timberlake quotes are taken from *The Memoirs of Lieut. Henry Timberlake* (1765, 73).

9. This quote from Ridge could not be located, but it closely echoes accounts found in Adair (1775, 232–34) and Mooney ([1891] 1992, 36).

10. George M. Troup (1770–1856) was governor of Georgia from 1823 to 1827, when he was succeeded by John Forsyth. Troup spoke for his state when he found it impossible to incorporate the Cherokees—or any other Indians—into the Georgian society. In a letter dated February 28, 1824, he wrote to Secretary of War John C. Calhoun, that "the utmost rights and privileges which public opinion would concede to the Indians would fix them in a middle station between the negro and the white man, and that as long as they survived this degradation, without the possibility of attaining the elevation of the latter, they would gradually sink to the condition of the former—a point of degeneracy below which they could not fall." In the same letter, he called the Cherokees' refusal to cede more lands "a boldness bordering on effrontery" (Harden 1859, 203–7).

11. This quote is actually made of two passages taken from two different documents. The first, which ends with "not one word has been put in our mouths by a white man," is a message addressed to the Senate and the House of Representatives dated April 15, 1824 (Moulton 1985, 1:76–78). The second, which starts with "Whilst we profess . . . ," is a letter dated April 20 of the same year, addressed to Joseph Gales and William Seaton, publishers of the *National Intelligencer* (1:78–80). Both documents are signed by the four delegates.

12. For John Forsyth, in a long speech he gave in response to Senator Frelinghuysen's opposition to the Removal Act, the Cherokees were "a race not admitted to be equal to the rest of the community [. . .] and probably never to be entitled to equal civil and political rights" (Forsyth 1830, 7).

CHAPTER 9

1. The exact quote is: "But the excuse of the general government for not complying with her contract, is, that, according to her stipulation, she has never seen the time, in twenty-three long years, when it was in her power to effect it upon 'reasonable and peaceable terms.' What a miserable evasion! whatever people out of this state may think on the subject, there is not an honest man in it who believes it. What! not able to fulfill a contract in twenty-three years! If not in that time, when can it be done? Do they not believe if Georgia had kept her lands and undertaken to extinguish the title herself, she would not have accomplished it in that time?" (Atticus 1827, 19).

2. George Barber Davis had been hired as a tutor by Ross's father when John was a young child (Moulton 1978, 6). Between 1805 and 1809, at the request of Agent Meigs, Davis realized a survey and a census of the Cherokee Nation (McLoughlin 1986, 168–73). Theodore Frelinghuysen, a senator from New Jersey, was strongly opposed to the removal bill. On the congressional debate over the removal bill, and especially on Frelinghuysen's position, see McLoughlin (1986, 434–37).

3. Elizur Butler, Daniel Butrick, and Isaac Proctor were all missionaries sponsored by the American Board of Commissioners for Foreign Missions. Butler started work at the Brainerd mission in 1821, and then worked in several missions in the Cherokee Nation. He was arrested by the Georgia authorities in 1831 along with Samuel Worcester and remained in prison until 1833. After removal, he served at Dwight Mission in Indian Territory in 1839. In 1850, he served at the Cherokee Female Seminary. Butrick served mainly at Brainerd and went with the Cherokees on the Trail of Tears. He started serving at Dwight Mission in 1839. Proctor served as teacher and farmer at Hightower (McClinton 2007, 2:456, 499–500; Phillips and Phillips 1998, 503–4, 528–29). Isaac Harris was a white man employed as the printer of the *Cherokee Phoenix* (Perdue 1983, 36n47, 87).

4. This exact quote was not found in Ross's papers. However, the gist of it is the object of a letter signed by Ross and William Hicks, dated July 19, 1828, addressed to Francis W. Armstrong, who was "instructed by the Secretary of War to visit the Cherokee nation, for the purpose of ascertaining, as far as practicable at this time, the disposition of the nation to cede to the United States a strip of land sufficient to make a canal." The letter expressed in

plain terms the sentiments of the Cherokees, "that is, the Cherokee nation objects making further cession of lands to the United States, for any purposes whatever" (Moulton 1985, 1:139).

5. Richard Taylor (1788–1853) was a captain in Gideon Morgan's regiment during the Creek War of 1813–14, worked occasionally as an interpreter for the agency, was a member of the National Council, signed the treaties of March 1816 and 1817, served as a delegate on numerous occasions, and headed a removal detachment in 1838–39. He signed the 1839 Constitution, and was second principal chief in 1851 (Kappler 1904, 125–26; Moulton 1985, 2:736). John Baldridge signed the treaty of September 1816 (Kappler 1904, 134), and was a member of the delegation led by Ross in 1836 (Moulton 1985, 1:378). Sleeping Rabbit, brother of Goingsnake, signed the treaties of 1817 and 1819 (Kappler 1904, 144, 179), and was a member of the delegation led by Ross in 1836. He was a member of the Cherokee legislature in the 1830s. He died in 1837 (Moulton 1985, 1:34–35, 589; *Cherokee Phoenix* May 1, 1830). John Benge (1796?–1853) signed the treaty of September 1816 (Kappler 1904, 134), fought in the Creek War of 1813–14, served as a delegate on various occasions in the 1830s and 1840s, and headed a removal detachment in 1838–39. He was a member of the National Committee in the 1840s (Moulton 1985, 2:716; Phillips and Phillips 1998, 524). Nat Hicks is probably Nathan Hicks, son of Charles Hicks. He was anti-removal and a strong supporter of John Ross (McClinton 2007, 2:464). Sicketowee was a member of the legislature in the 1830s. He died in 1837 (Moulton 1985, 1:242, 589). James Starr (1796–1845), along with Ross's brother Andrew, lobbied in Washington for removal at least from 1832 to 1834, telling Secretary of War Lewis Cass that many Cherokees were ready to emigrate and even entering a removal agreement with U.S. commissioner John H. Easton without any authority from the Cherokee government and people; he moved west in 1833, and signed the Treaty of New Echota in 1835. He was a member of the Old Settlers' Executive Council in 1839 and a member of the National Committee in the 1840s. He was killed by Anti-Treaty Party individuals (1:241–42, 299, 317, 2:736). Daniel McCoy (1798–1857) was a justice at the Supreme Court at the end of the 1820s and the beginning of the 1830s, served as a delegate to Washington in 1834 lobbying against removal, and signed the 1839 Constitution (1:282, 294, 296, 2:727).

6. Here Oskison crossed out a short list of these polling places: "Hick's Mill, Hunter Langley's in Lookout Valley, and the district court house . . ."

7. Deer in Water is Situwakee (or Sitewakee) (Anderson et al. 1825, 325). Although several Walkers can be found in the archives, Oskison probably refers here to either John (Jack) Walker Jr. (c. 1798–1834) or Major John Walker (c. 1773–1835). It is difficult, though, to assert categorically that it is one or the other.

The confusion is due to the fact that both played political and diplomatic roles, and that various ways are used to refer to them in the papers of John Ross. The name of the older John Walker appears down the treaty of 1806 (Kappler 1904, 91). One "John Walker," as well as John Ross and four other individuals, received in January 1816 a letter from Principal Chief Pathkiller to appoint them delegates to Washington in order to protest intrusions and "spoliations committed on the property" of the people during the previous Creek war (Moulton 1985, 1:22). In March 1816, the same "John Walker" co-signed letters addressed to the federal authorities to express the people's grievances and opinions as far as further cessions of land were concerned (1:24–27). This "John Walker" in Ross's letters becomes "Major John Walker" down the treaty signed at Washington in 1816. "John Walker" appears down the treaties of 1817 and 1819. Presumably the same "John Walker" was appointed a delegate again in December 1818, along with Charles Hicks, Ross, and a few others (1:31). In at least two letters addressed to the federal authorities in early 1824, John Ross refers to a man, first as "John Walker," then as "Major (John) Walker," who filed a claim regarding slaves stolen by U.S. citizens from a Cherokee citizen, Thomas Foreman (1:75). It is difficult to know with certainty whether this Walker and the delegate of previous years are the same person. Things get more confusing when a "John Walker Junior" is mentioned, related to a different subject in May 1824, while Major Walker never reappears in Ross's papers. The same "John Walker Junior" is mentioned in a December 1826 letter as one of two "officers of the Cherokee Nation" who confiscated whiskey from Euro-American peddlers (1:127). It appears clear that at least John Walker Junior became pro-removal since John Ridge wrote in a letter dated April 3, 1832, that he had learned "that John Walker Jr., and James Starr had told Secretary of War Lewis Cass that many Cherokees were despondent and ready to emigrate." In the same letter, Walker is said to "divide the tribe" (1:241). A few days later, referring to the Ridge letter, Ross wrote of "the reprehensible conduct of John Walker Jr. & James Starr" (1:242). In a February 1833 letter, Ridge, still anti-removal at the time, refers to "Jack Walker," undoubtedly the same person as "John Walker Jr." Jack was invited by President Jackson to Washington as a leader of the pro-removal Cherokees (1:259–60). Finally, in a letter to Jackson dated September 15, 1834, Ross evoked the assassination of John Walker Jr., clearly killed by an opponent to removal—James Foreman according to McClinton (2007, 2:476)—because of the leading role he seems to have played in promoting removal.

One Charles Duncan is mentioned in a letter to John Ross dated July 12, 1842, as one of the Cherokees who escaped forced removal in 1838–39. One John Duncan, "a half-blood Cherokee," and one Darcus Duncan are mentioned by Ross in a letter dated November 22, 1843. One Walter Duncan is mentioned by Ross in a letter dated November 22, 1854 (Moulton 1985, 2:140, 189, 390). John Timson was a bilingual Cherokee from Valley Towns who became a Baptist preacher and interpreter in 1823 (McLoughlin 1984, 157, 161). He was a member of a delegation to Washington led by Ross, in 1834 (Moulton 1985, 1:276–99).

One David Downing, "charged with the murder of Frederick Fisher . . . tried and acquitted," is mentioned by Ross in a letter dated March 22, 1842 (Moulton 1985, 2:113–14). One Walter Downing is mentioned as "Lieutenant Walter Downing in the police Company for Goingsnake" district in a letter from William Coodey to Ross dated October 16, 1843 (Moulton 1985, 2:182). One John Downing, according to Hoig (1998), was among the attackers of Treaty Party members in 1839 (198). Oskison more likely refers to Samuel Downing, mentioned by Ross as one of the Old Settlers in a letter dated June 30, 1839, and to whom he addressed several letters after the reunification of the Cherokee Nation and the Old Settlers. He was a member of the National Committee of the Cherokee Nation at the beginning of the 1840s, when David Downing was in the National Council. The latter would become judge in Goingsnake District in 1844. Samuel Downing was the father of Lewis Downing, who would play a prominent role in Cherokee politics in the post-Ross era (Moulton 1985, 1:724; 2:137, 162, 195).

8. The first quote, from Harriet Gold, is slightly altered. Mary Boudinot Church transcribes: "My mother will remember what my opinion was with regard to my dear husband before I left Cornwall. Indeed he is all that I could wish him to be, and my sisters need not think it is saying anything against their husbands to say I have excelled them all. I know they are all good *positively*, but mine *superlatively*. This is no joke I assure you" (Boudinot Church 1913, 216; see also Theresa Strouth Gaul, *To Marry an Indian: The Marriage of Harriet Gold and Elias Boudinot in Letters, 1823–1839*). The other quotes are from a letter written in New Echota by Benjamin Gold, Harriet's father, addressed to his brother Hezekiah, and dated December 8, 1829. It was published by Boudinot's granddaughter in *The Magazine of History* in 1913. In the letter, Gold gave interesting details about the prosperity he witnessed during his stay in the Cherokee country. The quotes and information Oskison put in the following paragraphs—about the *Cherokee Phoenix*, the lay of the land, and the economic situation of the town—are from the same letter. Although he was reconciled with his daughter, and reassured by her conditions of living, one can also sense relief at the fact that his grandchildren did not look too Indian: "We are in good health, and likewise Mr. Boudinot and his family. They have two beautiful and interesting children, (Elinor and Mary) who

would pass in company for full-blooded Yankees. My wife says she thinks they are rather handsomer than any she has seen at the North" (Boudinot Church 1913, 218).

9. Boudinot Church (1913, 216).

CHAPTER 10

1. William Hicks was Charles Hicks's brother and Elijah's father. McLoughlin calls him "not only a Christian but a leading acculturationist" (McLoughlin 1984, 218). He ran against Ross for principal chief in 1827. He became interim principal chief while the Cherokees waited for President John Quincy Adams's reaction to their new constitution. Ross was chosen to be second principal chief (McLoughlin 1986, 401; Hoig 1998, 132; Moulton 1978, 35). In the 1830s, he became a member of the Treaty Party. (McLoughlin 1984, 146; McClinton 2007, 2:464; Hoig 1998, 148, 157; Moulton 1978, 56).

2. According to Ross's letters (Moulton 1985, 1:149–65), the delegation—composed of Ross, Richard Taylor, Edward Gunter, and William S. Coodey—was in Washington from January to May 1829, not 1828. Jackson succeeded John Quincy Adams in office in March 1829. Oskison corrects himself in the next chapter.

3. These quotes, and the ones in the following paragraphs, are from the second volume of Lumpkin's *The Removal of the Cherokee Indians from Georgia* (1907, 2:150–51). The crossed-out words and words between square brackets are my corrections of Oskison's typos.

4. This and the quotes from the next paragraph are from Lumpkin (1907, 1:186–87). A few lines down, Lumpkin qualified his "tribute" to Ross: "John Ross, compared with such men as John Ridge and Elias Boudinot, is a mere *pygmy*" (1:187).

5. Lumpkin (1907, 2:159). Lumpkin also denounced "the corruption and perversity of this vile combination of feed lawyers, who acted as stipendiaries to John Ross, who would have utterly ruined and extinguished from the face of the earth the remnant of the Cherokee Indians but for the interposition of the Government of the State of Georgia" (2:178–79). In April 1838, he declared in the Senate that Ross "writes well, but has had the credit of being the author of many able productions which were written by others, and not himself. Some of the first writers of the age, such as Sergeant, of Philadelphia, Wirt, of Virginia, &c., &c. have long been his *feed* counsel, and have suffered their pens to be brought into requisition in aid of this man Ross" (2:230).

6. The quote is from Lumpkin. I correct and complete here the last part that I put between square brackets: "I think it probable that they would at this day

have been represented in the Congress of the United States, by delegates who would do honor to any State in the Union, and that their present state of prosperity, great as it is, would have been fifty per cent. better than it is at present" (Lumpkin 1907, 1:192).

CHAPTER 11

1. William Carroll, governor of Tennessee (1821–27 and 1829–35) was one of the commissioners, with John F. Schermerhorn, in charge of negotiating a treaty of removal (Moulton 1985, 1:342, 2:740, 362). Previously, as indicated by Oskison, he had been sent by Secretary of War John H. Easton in 1829 to visit the Cherokee Nation "for the purpose of discussing the subject of the Cherokees removing West of the Mississippi" (1:167). According to Easton's instructions, quoted by McLoughlin, Carroll was asked to "'undertake to enlighten the Cherokee and Creeks' on the necessity of emigration. 'In your progress through their Country, it would be well to ascertain, if you can do so without disclosing the purpose of the Executive' in appointing [Carroll], whether or not the Cherokees manifested 'a willingness to negotiate for a cession' of their land." In the same letter, Easton implied that a majority of Cherokees really wanted to emigrate but were under the influence of their chiefs and missionaries and he encouraged Carroll to use means of bribery to convince Cherokee individuals to break free from this influence: "'offers to them of extensive reservations in fee simple and other rewards' should be made that would 'it is hoped, result in obtaining their acquiescence' to a total cession of Cherokee land in the east" (McLoughlin 1986, 426–27).

2. Senator Peleg Sprague of Maine and Representative Henry Storrs of New York were among the supporters of the Cherokees against the removal bill, while Senators Hugh Lawson White of Tennessee and John McKinley of Alabama supported it (Moulton 1978, 42; Anderson et al. 2010, 1:331).

3. This act was passed on November 8, 1828 (*Laws* 1852, 100).

4. Benjamin Franklin Currey (or Curry) was appointed by the War Department to urge the Cherokees to enroll for removal to Arkansas or, in Ross's words, "superintendant of the enrolling and emigration business in our country" (Moulton 1985, 1:274). In a letter dated March 12, 1834, Ross unsuccessfully asked Jackson "to suspend or remove forthwith Mr. Currey from his official station" because of "excitement" he caused in the nation (Moulton/Ross 1985, 1:279–80; McLoughlin 1984, 324; Anderson et al. 2010, 1:145, 305). The quote in which Currey slanders Ross could not be located.

5. Goingsnake (c. 1759–1839) fought at the Battle of the Horseshoe Bend, served in the Cherokee Council several times, as a member or as the speaker, signed the Treaty of 1817 and the Act of Union of 1839. After removal, a district of

the new Cherokee country was named after him (Moulton 1985, 2:62; Hoig 1998, 119, 173; Anderson et al. 2010, 1:309, 2:345–46).

6. This quote is from a letter that Samuel Worcester sent to Cherokee delegate to Washington William Shorey Coodey, at his request to write "a statement respecting the progress of improvement among [Coodey's] people, the Cherokees" (Worcester 1830, 41). The letter was written at New Echota and is dated March 15, 1830. It was published in the appendix (41–44) to the *Speech of Mr. Frelinghuysen, of New Jersey, Delivered in the Senate of the United States. April 5, 1830*. It was also published in the *Cherokee Phoenix* on May 8, 1830.

CHAPTER 12

1. Lumpkin (1907, 1:186).
2. The first quote in the paragraph could not be located. However, it might be Oskison's rephrasing of Chief Justice Marshall's opening statement when he delivered the opinion of the Court in *Cherokee Nation v. Georgia*: "This bill is brought by the Cherokee nation, praying an injunction to restrain the state of Georgia from the execution of certain laws of that state, which, as is alleged, go directly to annihilate the Cherokees as a political society, and to seize, for the use of Georgia, the lands of the nation which have been assured to them by the United States in solemn treaties repeatedly made and still in force" (Peters 1831, 159). Wirt's quote is from his plea to the Supreme Court in the same case (66).
3. For this episode of the rendezvous at Ridge's place, and the results of the vote, see Anderson et al. (1:177–83).
4. The quote is from a speech delivered by Congressman Everett of Massachusetts in the House of Representatives in February 1831 (1831, 22–23). I indicate a few alterations from the speech as recorded in the archives. I do not indicate differences in punctuation as these often vary from one record of a speech to another.
5. The quotes in these two paragraphs are from different places of another speech by Everett, delivered in 1830. Oskison condensed three pages of the speech as it is recorded in *Speeches on the Passage of the Bill for the Removal of the Indians* (1830, 261–63). For the sake of exactitude, I indicate in the text some elisions not marked in Oskison's manuscript. The quote in the first of these two paragraphs is mainly from page 263 of *Speeches*. The quote in the second paragraph is from two distinct passages on pages 261 and 262. The last part is Oskison's rephrasing of "I had supposed the general idea of the nature of law was settled in the common agreement of mankind. Sages, when they attempted to describe it in its highest conception, had told us, that its seat was the bosom of God, and its voice the harmony of the world" (262).

6. This is from a letter that Governor Troup addressed to Secretary of War James Barbour on February 17, 1827. Reproduced in *The Examiner, and Journal of Political Economy* (Troup 1827, 212).

7. Gilmer (1855, 424–25).

8. This quote can be found page 274 of *Acts of the General Assembly of the State of Georgia, Passed in Milledgeville at an Annual Session in November and December, 1831*, which reproduces the whole report (1832, 266–74), which was agreed to by the assembly.

9. Ross and Payne were arrested by the Georgia guards on November 7, 1835 (Moulton 1978, 69; Anderson et al. 2010, 1:xvii). On November 13, 1835, from Camp Benton, Ross wrote to Governor George Gilmer to protest against his and Payne's arrest and to ask for justice: "It is with deep regret, I have to complain to your Excellency that on the night of the 7th inst. at my present residence within the chartered limits of Tennessee, I and a Gentleman from New York named Jno [*sic*] Howard Payne was arrested and made prisoners and our papers seized & brought here by the Georgia Guard where we are now prisoners of the State. For what offence or crime committed we are altogether ignorant. What motive could have dictated this policy I am equally unaware—as nothing having been alledged [*sic*] against us. I now apply to your Excy. as the Commander in Chief of the State for a speedy trial should there be any charges against us & if not that we may be liberated and our papers restored. It is due to myself and justice to Mr. Payne that I should say this Gentleman came highly recommended to me by Gentlemen of high standing of your state as a literary Gentleman and a man whose object was to collect matter for a periodical work. At the time of our arrest he was engaged in taking minutes from the public documents of the Nation in my possession" (Moulton 1985, 1:7, 373).

CHAPTER 13

1. This quote is from an address to the Cherokees dated April 14, 1831 (Moulton 1985, 1:218).

2. These quotes are from a speech Ross addressed to the General Council at New Echota in July 1830 (Moulton 1985, 1:190–93). The last quote is recorded by Moulton as: "Yet, he says, that such power as the laws give him for our protection, shall be executed for our benefit, and this will not fail to be executed in keeping out intruders; beyond this he cannot go" (1:191).

3. This is from the April 14, 1831, speech to the Cherokees quoted previously (Moulton 1985, 1:217). Corrections are mine.

4. John Freeman Schermerhorn (1786–1851) was Jackson's appointee as Indian Commissioner from 1832 to 1837. He headed the negotiations that would lead

some Cherokees to sign the Treaty of New Echota. Many letters exchanged between Ross and Schermerhorn can be found in Moulton (1985).

5.   These quotes are more or less the same as recorded in the Payne-Butrick papers as being from the three hour and twenty minute speech Schermerhorn gave in July 1835 (not 1834 as indicated by Oskison) on the election grounds where close to three thousand Cherokees had gathered to vote on how the annuities should be paid to the tribe (Anderson et al. 2010, 1:181–82; see chapter 12).

6.   Here again, Oskison took bits and pieces from a long address in order to reconstruct a coherent quote. Here are the different passages, in the order they appear in Jackson's address, from which Oskison took his quotes: "What have you gained by adhering to the pernicious counsels which have led you to reject the liberal offers made for your removal?" In the next paragraph: "I have no motive, my friends, to deceive you. I am sincerely desirous to promote your welfare. Listen to me, therefore, while I tell you that you cannot remain where you now are. Circumstances that cannot be controlled, and which are beyond the reach of human laws, render it impossible that you can flourish in the midst of a civilized community." A dozen paragraphs later, at the conclusion of his address, Jackson wrote: "The choice is now before you. May the Great Spirit teach you how to choose. The fate of your women and children, the fate of your people, to the remotest generation, depend upon the issue." This address was dated March 16, 1835 (*Niles' Register* 1835, 88).

7.   William N. Bishop was also a land lottery agent (Moulton 1985, 2:740). The Payne-Butrick papers contain an account by Moravian missionary Henry Clauder on how Bishop confiscated Joseph Vann's property and the Springplace mission possessions. He did not refrain from using violence against potential opponents (Anderson et al. 2010, 2:241, 267–68).

8.   These paragraphs and the following are from a memorial sent to the federal government in June 1836, and signed by John Ross, John Martin, James Brown, Joseph Vann, John Benge, Lewis Ross, Elijah Hicks, and Richard Fields. Here again, Oskison slightly altered the original phrasing of the memorial. I restitute in this footnote and the following, or in the main text between square brackets, the original as it was printed in Ross, John, *Letter from John Ross, Principal Chief of the Cherokee Nation of Indians, in Answer to Inquiries From a Friend Regarding the Cherokee Affairs with the United States, Followed by a Copy of the Protest of the Cherokee Delegation* (1836). It was reprinted in Moulton: "Valuable gold mines were discovered upon the Cherokee lands, within the chartered limits of Georgia, and the Cherokees commenced working them, and the Legislature of that State interfered by passing an act, making it penal for an Indian to dig for gold within Georgia [. . .]. Under this law many Cherokees were arrested, tried, imprisoned, and otherwise abused. Some

were even shot in attempting to avoid an arrest; yet the Cherokee people used no violence, but humbly petitioned the Government of the United States for a fulfillment of treaty engagements, to protect them, which was not done, and the answer given that the United States could not interfere. Georgia [. . .] passed an act directing the Indian country to be surveyed into districts. [. . .] Another act was shortly after passed, to lay off the country into lots. As yet there was no authority to take possession, but it was not long before a law was made, authorizing a lottery for the lands laid off into lots. In this act the Indians were secured in possession of all the lots touched by their improvements, and the balance of the country allowed to be occupied by white men. This was a direct violation of the 5th article of the treaty of the 27th of February, 1819. The Cherokees made no resistance, still petitioned the United States for protection, and received the same answer that the President could not interpose. After the country was parceled out by lottery, a horde of speculators made their appearance, and purchased of the 'fortunate draw-ers,' lots touched by Indian improvements, at reduced prices, declaring it was uncertain when the Cherokees would surrender their rights, and that the lots were encumbered by their claims. The consequence of this speculation was that, at the next session of the Legislature, an act was passed limiting the Indian right of occupancy to the lot upon which he resided, and his actual improvements adjoining. Many of the Cherokees filed bills, and obtained injunctions against dispossession, and would have found relief in the courts of the country, if the Judiciary had not been prostrated at the feet of legisla-tive power. For the opinion of a judge, on this subject, there was an attempt to impeach him, then to limit his circuit to one country, and when all this failed, equity jurisdiction was taken from the courts, in Cherokee cases, by acts passed in the years 1833 and 1834. The Cherokees were then left at the mercy of an interested agent. This agent, under the act of 1834, was the notorious William N. Bishop, the captain of the Georgia Guard, aid to the Governor, clerk of a court, postmaster, &c. and his mode of trying Indian rights is here submitted" (Moulton 1985, 1:427–44).

9. From Bishop's quote on, the alterations were minor and could be corrected in the main text. The exclamation mark in the last paragraph is Oskison's.

10. Joseph Vann's story is told in the same memorial (Moulton 1985, 1:433).

11. Moulton (1985, 1:434). The last exclamation mark is Oskison's.

CHAPTER 14

1. These four stories are told in the 1836 memorial quoted in the previous chapter. However, Ross spelled the names differently: Wahka, Atalah Anosta, Sconatachee, and Richard Cheek (Moulton 1985, 1:435–36).

2. Moulton (1985, 1:444).

3. This is from the "Report of Major Davis," written in March 1836, printed in Powell (1887, 284–85). It is reprinted in Rozema (2003, 63–64). Major William M. Davis was appointed by Secretary of War Lewis Cass to encourage Cherokees to enroll for emigration. On March 5, 1837, he wrote Cass about his concerns over the actions of Schermerhorn, and about the manner the treaty was obtained (62).

4. John McLean was appointed at the Supreme Court in 1829. He was a supporter of Cherokee rights (McLoughlin 1984, 307).

5. These quotes are from the speech Everett gave in the House of Representatives on May 19, 1830. The passage in the next two paragraphs should come before this first quote (*Speeches* 1830, 278–79).

6. From "A Letter to a Gentleman in Philadelphia," addressed to Job R. Tyson, reprinted in Moulton (1985, 1:490–503). The quote is in Moulton (1:502).

7. A reference to the event known as Sherman's March to the Sea. In November and December 1864, Union General William T. Sherman led sixty thousand soldiers from Atlanta through Georgia with the purpose to frighten Georgia's civilian population into abandoning the Confederate cause. Sherman's army's determination to wreak havoc was such that some historians deemed Sherman's campaign the first modern "total war." A Georgia woman described the result of the campaign in her region: "The fields were trampled down and the road was lined with carcasses of horses, hogs, and cattle that the invaders, unable either to consume or to carry with them, had wantonly shot down to starve our people [. . .] The stench in some places was unbearable" (quoted in Norton 2012, 420).

CHAPTER 15

1. Eaton (1914, 101).

2. Eaton (1914, 99).

3. From a speech delivered by Henry Clay in the Senate on February 4, 1835 (Colton 1863, 2:225–26).

4. This paragraph and the following are quoted from the memorial sent "To the Senate and House of Representatives" on September 28, 1836 (Moulton 1985, 1:458–61). According to Moulton's transcription, it was "signed by Ross, George Lowrey, Edward Gunter, Lewis Ross, thirty-one members of the National Committee and National Council, and 2,174 others" (1:461). Oskison condensed several passages of the document; the last part of the quote, which is located two paragraphs down the first part, starts with: "The instrument in question is not the act of our Nation; we are not parties to its covenants; it has not received the sanction of our people. The makers . . ." etc. (1:459).

5. Although it is possible Ross sent such a plea to Jackson, he also sent the same one to Martin Van Buren, who took office on March 4, 1837. This quote can be found in a letter recorded by Moulton, and dated March 16, 1837 (1985, 1:480–87). The exact quote is: "Our fate is in your hands—may the God of truth tear away every disguise and concealment from our case—may the God of justice guide your determination and the God of mercy stay the hand of our brother uplifted for our destruction" (1:486).

6. In a letter to Wool, Acting Secretary of War C. A. Harris wrote: "I am instructed to express the surprise of the President that you permitted the council of the Cherokees to remain in session a moment after it became apparent that it was determined to declare the treaty void. This was the contingency contemplated in the letter of the Department of September 3d, in which you were instructed to interfere and disperse such assemblage. If, upon any future occasion, the non-execution of the treaty should be discussed in council, you will immediately close its session. You will inform Mr. Ross that the President regards the proceedings of himself and associates in council as in direct contravention of the plighted faith of their people, and a repetition of them will be considered as indicative of a design to prevent the execution of the treaty, even at the hazard of actual hostilities, and they will be promptly repressed" (Harris 1837, 54). In the same letter, Harris expresses the president's "determination": "'The treaty is to be religiously fulfilled.' No delegation sent to this place with a view to obtain new terms, or a modification of those of the existing treaty, will be received or recognized; nor will any intercourse be had with them, directly or indirectly, orally or in writing" (53).

CHAPTER 16

1. In the letter to Wool quoted before, Harris had written: "You will also inform [Mr. Ross], that if a delegation proceed to the Cherokees west of the Mississippi, for the purpose of procuring their co-operation in an attempt to set aside or modify the existing treaty, or to obtain a new one, the acting superintendent of the western territory will be instructed to enforce the provisions of the 13th section of the intercourse law of 1834, and to employ military aid, if necessary, under the authority of the 23d section" (Harris 1837, 54).

2. These questions were asked the Senate and House of Representatives in the address dated February 22, 1837: "We have asked, and we reiterate the question how have we offended? Show us in what manner we have, however unwittingly, inflicted upon you a wrong, you shall yourselves be the judges of the extent and manner of compensation. Show us the offence which has awakened your feelings of justice against us and we will submit to that measure of punishment which you shall tell us we have merited. We cannot bring to our

recollections anything we have done or anything we have omitted calculated to awaken your resentment against us" (Moulton 1985, 1:472).

3. Eaton (1914, 104).

4. From a report that Wool addressed to his authorities on February 18, 1837 (Royce [1887] 2007, 164).

5. In September 1836, Brigadier General R. G. Dunlap, who commanded the East Tennessee volunteers, declared to his troops: "I forthwith visited all the posts within the first three States and gave the Cherokees (the whites needed none) all the protection in my power. [. . .] My course has excited the hatred of a few of the lawless rabble in Georgia, who have long played the part of unfeeling petty tyrants, and that to the disgrace of the proud character of gallant soldiers and good citizens. I had determined that I would never dishonor the Tennessee arms in a servile service by aiding to carry into execution at the point of the bayonet a treaty made by a lean minority against the will and authority of the Cherokee people" (Royce [1887] 2007, 164).

6. From a letter of J. M. Mason Jr., to Secretary of War, September 25, 1837, quoted in Mooney ([1891] 1992, 128).

7. From a letter of June 30, 1836, to President Jackson. The corrections are based on Mooney's transcription of Major Ridge's letter (Mooney [1891] 1992, 127–28).

CHAPTER 17

1. The following pages are quoted from pages 213 to 243 of the second volume of Featherstonhaugh's (1847) journal. I give precise references in subsequent footnotes and corrections in in the main text.

2. Featherstonhaugh (1847, 213–15). Oskison took "zealous in the cause of the Cherokees" from "I soon found out that every one at the Mission was zealously disposed in favour of the Indians" (213), and the rest of the paragraph from "He said he knew the Cherokees well, and thought they would die on the spot rather than leave their country; but, if it came to that, the whites were the strongest and must prevail. 'Nevertheless,' added he, 'God has his eye upon all that is passing, and at his own time the Cherokees will be avenged'" (215).

3. Featherstonhaugh (1847, 218–19).

4. Featherstonhaugh (1847, 220).

5. Featherstonhaugh (1847, 222).

6. Featherstonhaugh (1847, 222).

7. Featherstonhaugh (1847, 223).

8. Oskison phrased the rest of the paragraph from: "Here we stopped at an Indian tavern kept by a half-breed Cherokee of the name of Bell, one of the

Indians opposed to John Ross and the majority of the nation. They had nothing but some filthy pieces of bad cake to give me made of Indian corn. Upon my asking a Cherokee woman who spoke English why they did not provide themselves with milk and butter, she said 'it was too much trouble to keep cows.' Everything about their house was dirty and disgusting, and I was glad to see the horses brought out" (Featherstonhaugh 1847, 224).

9. From Featherstonhaugh: "The people about were tall, thin, cadaverous-looking animals, looking as melancholy and lazy as boiled cod-fish, and when they dragged themselves about, formed a striking contrast to some of the swarthy, athletic-looking Cherokees. This, no doubt, is to be attributed to their wretched diet and manner of life; for the better class of Georgians, who lead more generous lives, contains many fine-looking individuals. What these parsnip-looking country fellows seem to enjoy most is political disputation in the bar-room of their filthy taverns, exhibiting much bitterness against each other in supporting the respective candidates of the Union and State-rights parties which divide the State, and this without seeming to have the slightest information respecting the principles of either. Execration and vociferation, and 'Well, I'm for Jackson, by—!' were the nearest approach to logic ever made in my presence" (1847, 226).

10. Featherstonhaugh (1847, 229). They were Georgia Mounted Volunteers.

11. Featherstonhaugh. Oskison seems to have based the end of the paragraph on: "The soil being derived from the lower Silurian limestone is very fertile, and certainly I never saw heavier Indian corn than in two or three settlements that we passed, especially at one Young's, about fifteen miles from Spring Place" (1847, 229–30).

12. From Featherstonhaugh, notably: "Crossing the Cooayhallay, we soon found ourselves in an irregular sort of street consisting of huts, booths and stores hastily constructed from the trees of the forest, for the accommodation of Cherokee families, and for the cooking establishments necessary to the subsistence of several thousand Indians" (1847, 230–31).

13. Featherstonhaugh writes: "The expense of feeding this multitude, which was defrayed by the council, was very great. Fifteen beeves were said to be killed every day, and a proportionate quantity of Indian corn used. [. . .] Upon further inquiries, I learnt that Mr. John Ross was the sole director of every thing, that he paid about three hundred dollars a day to the persons who contracted to furnish the provisions" (1847, 236).

14. Featherstonhaugh (1847, 231).

15. Featherstonhaugh (1847, 232).

16. Featherstonhaugh (1847, 233). As Featherstonhaugh was lying down in his hut, "the voices of hundreds of the most pious amongst them who had assembled

at the Council-house to perform their evening worship, came pealing in hymns through the now quiet forest, and insensibly and gratefully lulled me to sleep." The following day, he attended Jones' service, translated by Bushy-head (233). Jesse Bushyhead (1804–44) was baptized in 1830 and he became a Baptist preacher. One of Ross's close supporters, he led a detachment during removal (Anderson et al. 2010, 1:300; Moulton 1985, 1:667, 676).

17. This is what Featherstonhaugh wrote about Evan Jones: "After breakfast I made myself acquainted with Mr. Jones, the Missionary, whom I found to be a man of sense and experience, and who must have received a tolerable education, for he was not even ignorant of Hebrew. He was exceedingly devoted to this nation, having resided a long time amongst them in the mountainous region of North Carolina. The Georgians, and I found most of the other white set-tlers, had a decided antipathy to him on account of the advice he gave to the Cherokees, which had frequently enabled them to baffle the machinations of the persons who were plotting to get their lands. Conscious that he was watched by his enemies, he had become so suspicious of all white men, that from habit he had got a peculiar sinister look" (1847, 234).

18. Featherstonhaugh (1847, 235–36).

19. Feathersonhaugh (1847, 238).

20. Featherstonhaugh: "On my return to our hut, I got into a conversation with our landlord, Mr. Hicks, one of the most intelligent of the Cherokees. He told me, he had once seen some China men at Philadelphia, and that, from the strong resemblance to them in their faces and eyes, he thought it prob-able the Cherokees were descended from that stock. The remark is, at least, founded in fact, for the Cherokees resemble the Tartars very strikingly, both in the general expression of their faces, and in the conformation of their eyes" (1847, 239).

21. Stephen Foreman was appointed assistant editor of the *Cherokee Phoenix* by an act of the Cherokee government dated November 4, 1829. As such, he was "to translate all public documents for publication, from the English into the Cherokee language, and all English news deemed useful for Publication shall also be translated into the same" (*Laws* 1852, 144). He was ordained by the American Board in 1835 (McLoughlin 1984, 339). He was Superintendent of Public Schools in the 1840s (*Constitution and Laws* 1852, 95).

22. Featherstonhaugh (1847, 240–41). Foreman told Featherstonhaugh "amus-ing anecdotes of an agent, named Schermerhorn, who had been appointed by the United States Government a year or two ago, as a commissioner to negotiate with the Cherokees. The man was a sort of loose Dutch Presbyterian Minister, and having taken up the calling of a political demagogue, had been rewarded with this situation by the President, Mr. Van Buren, a Dutchman

also by birth" (240). In fact, Schermerhorn had been appointed by Jackson. The rest of the quote contained in this paragraph is corrected in the text.

23. Lumpkin wrote in 1853: "I was deeply adverse to the policy and views of the Government at Washington, as well as to those of the then Governor of Georgia [. . .] Their plan was to conciliate Ross by money, flattery, and restoring to him, by such conduct, the importance of his former chiefship. I then thought, and I still think, that was the auspicious moment to have divested Ross forever from having further power for mischief, and consummating the ultimate ruin of the Cherokee people. He ought to have been put in strings and banished from the country. Although a large slave holder, Ross was well qualified to have filled a prominent place amongst the New England Abolitionists, or in the Republic of Hayti—and to one of these places I wish to see him emigrate. I deplored the idea of seeing so great a curse planted in the West" (Lumpkin 1907, 2:222). A few pages further, he reprinted notes that he wrote at the Senate, on April 7, 1838, at the request of Secretary of War Joel R. Poinsett and General Scott. Scott was just about to leave for the Cherokee country in order to enforce the removal, and he asked Lumpkin for his "views in regard to the best plan of operations on the part of Gen. Scott, in the discharge of duties which were devolved on him" (2:226–27). He advised that "all propositions coming from Ross should be received and treated as the propositions of a private individual of the Cherokee people, and not as the propositions of a Principal Chief of the Cherokee people" (2:227). In the same document, he described Ross as "the soul and spirit of his whole party, and they will act in accordance with his views. In regard to Ross himself, he is a sagacious, subtle man. Under the guise of an unassuming deportment, his arrogance is unsurpassed. He always takes high ground, and maintains his assumptions with the utmost pertinacity and obstinacy. When he deems it necessary, he maintains the most dignified reserve, and never communicates freely and without reserve even with his best friends. He has the art of acquiring credit for talents and wisdom which he never possessed" (2:229–30).

24. This quote is taken from a "Memorial of the Cherokee Nation" sent to Congress, dated February 22, 1838, and signed "by fifteen thousand, six hundred and sixty-five of the Cherokee nation" (26–27) reprinted in "Further Information Respecting the Aborigines," in the collection of *Tracts Relative to the Aborigines* (Meeting for Sufferings, 1843).

25. Eaton (1914, 109). During a debate about a request from the Cherokees to be naturalized, and thus avoid removal, Wise expressed that, "in his opinion, the Government had just as good a right to make an Indian a citizen, as an Irishman; and if they were made citizens, it would be no disparagement to the

citizens of Georgia. They had now in the city a Georgian, who was Secretary of State; and they had, also, an Indian from Georgia of the Cherokee tribe, named John Ross, who would, at any time, compare in intellect and moral honesty with John Forsyth. He wished to know why such Indians as these were not as eligible to become citizens as the hordes of foreigners from the old world. The Cherokees have assisted in fighting the battles of our country, and had fought side by side with the white man in the struggle for her liberties, and what reason could be assigned why they should not share in its beneficial results?" (*Congressional Globe* 1838, 68).

CHAPTER 18

1. Winfield Scott's address is reproduced in Rozema, where the quote appears slightly differently: "The full moon of May is already on the wane, and before another shall have passed away, every Cherokee man, woman, and child, in those States, must be in motion to join their brethren in the far West. My friends—This is no sudden determination on the part of the President whom you and I must now obey [. . .] I am come to carry out that determination. My troops already occupy many positions in the country that you are to abandon, and thousands and thousands are approaching from every quarter to render resistance and escape alike hopeless. All those troops, regular and militia, are your friends. Receive them and confide in them as such. Obey them when they tell you that you can remain no longer in this country. Soldiers are as kind-hearted as brave, and the desire of every one of us is to execute our painful duty in mercy. We are commanded by the President to act toward you in that spirit, and such is also the wish of the whole people of America. Chiefs, head men, and warriors—Will you then, by resistance, compel us to resort to arms? God forbid! Or will you, by flight, seek to hide yourselves in mountains and forests, and thus oblige us to hunt you down?" (2003, 183–84).

2. Eaton (1914, 113–14).

3. Mooney ([1891] 1992, 130).

4. Quoted in Mooney ([1891] 1992, 130).

5. A very different story about Euchela (or Euchella, Oochella, or U'tsala) was recorded by historians. According to Laurence French and Jim Hornbuckle, quoted by Robert Conley, General Scott sent "Euchella and an armed contingent of Cherokees [. . .] to find and punish Tsali. Euchella's group caught Tsali and, under federal pressure, executed him and all male members of the group with the exception of Tsali's youngest son [. . .] As a reward for his services, Euchella and the rest of his men and their families were allowed to remain east" (2005, 150). According to Hoig, Euchella was persuaded to capture Tsali by William Holland Thomas, a white man who had grown up

Cherokee, and who had secured for Yonaguska's Cherokees an exemption from removal (1998, 264–65). Mooney presents U'tsala as a leader of the refugees from removal, facing a dilemma with Thomas's proposition to help Scott: "His heart was bitter, for his wife and little son had starved to death on the mountain side, but he thought of the thousands who were already on their long march into exile and then he looked round upon his little band of followers. If only they might stay, even though a few must be sacrificed, it was better than that all should die—for they had sworn never to leave their country" (Mooney [1891] 1992, 157–58).

6. Eaton (1914, 117).

7. From "The American Flag," by Henry Ward Beecher.

8. The General Council asked Scott for the permission to manage the removal on July 23, 1838 (Moulton 1985, 1:650–51).

CHAPTER 19

1. The following passages are from a letter that William Shorey Coodey, a nephew of John Ross, wrote to John Howard Payne on August 13, 1840. It is reproduced in Rozema (2003, 133–35).

2. Possibly Chewalookee, a member of the National Council in the 1820s (Anderson et al. 2010, 1:198). Robert Conley writes: "Choowalooka led the eighth wave, leaving on September 14, 1838, and arriving on March 1, 1839, after 162 days. 1,150 people started this trip. 970 finished" (2005, 156).

3. Oskison confuses James Vann and Captain David McNair, who married James Vann's daughter. James Vann is the one that welcomed the first Moravian missionaries and allowed them to build Springplace Mission, when David McNair did offer shelter to Henry Clauder and Nathaniel Byhan in 1831 when Georgia was after missionaries who refused to take the oath of allegiance to the state (Anderson et al. 1:316, 329; McLoughlin 1984, 45–47, 287). David Vann was one of the signers of the Treaty of New Echota (McLoughlin 1986, 450).

CHAPTER 20

1. John Brown, John Looney, and John Rogers were at the head of the Old Cherokees' government, after John Jolly's death, between 1836 and 1839 (Moulton 1978, 109). The John Ross papers contain several letters between them, on the one hand, and John Ross and George Lowrey, on the other hand, over the question of holding a convention marking the official reunion of the Western and Eastern Cherokees in 1839. Brown, Looney, and Rogers argued there was no need since the Western Cherokees' government had been recognized by the emigrants who had arrived under provisions of the

Treaty of New Echota, and had welcomed the late emigrants among them (Moulton 1985, 1:713–31). After the reunion, Thomas Candy and Tobacco Will were members of the National Council (Moulton 1985, 2:24).

2. James M. Bell would side with Stand Watie during the Civil War and would become a prominent figure of the Cherokee Confederates (Moulton 1978, 185). Probably the same Bell was mentioned by Featherstonhaugh as the owner of a tavern he visited and "one of the Indians opposed to John Ross and the majority of the nation" (224). During the 1843 election, Jacob West and his sons George and John, all fierce opponents to the Ross government, were involved in the attack of David Vann and Isaac Bushyhead, both Ross supporters, leaving the latter dead and the former seriously injured. In 1834, John West had been a pro-emigration delegate at Washington (Anderson et al. 2010, 1:145; Moulton 1985, 2:166–67, 176–77; Moulton 1978, 55–56, 136).

3. In 1929, Oskison published what he called, in a brief author's note, a "fictionized biography" of Sam Houston, entitled *A Texas Titan*. Chief Boles, or The Bowl, is also spelled Chief Bowles. For more information on him and the Texas Cherokees, see Mary Whatley Clarke, *Chief Bowles and the Texas Cherokees* (1971). For Mexico's place in Cherokee history, and the "Cherokee Literary Politics" of Oskison and his friend Will Rogers, see James H. Cox (2019).

4. This quote is from a letter to Montfort Stokes, agent for the Cherokees from 1837 to 1842, dated June 21, 1839, in which Ross and thirteen members of the National Committee wrote that "the attempt of a small minority to enforce their will over a great majority contrary to their wishes appears to us to be a course so repugnant to reason and propriety, that it cannot fail to disturb the peace of the community and to operate injuriously to the best interests of the Nation" (Moulton 1985, 1:716).

CHAPTER 21

1. The Act of Union was signed on July 12, 1839. The Constitution was signed on September 6, 1839 (*Constitution and Laws* 1852, 4, 15).

2. Here, Oskison crossed out the following paragraph: "Arbuckle did make one more demand on 'Mr.' Ross for the delivery of the 'murderers,' declaring with all the violent emphasis of which he was capable that they must be taken and punished, and warning Ross that if any trouble resulted from the efforts of his soldiers to capture the guilty Indians, 'Mr.' Ross would be held responsible! Before setting forth on the road to the National Capital, Ross politely reiterated the argument that the United States had no jurisdiction in the matter, and refused to admit that he could in any way be made responsible for Arbuckle's unlawful actions. For the moment, the general subsided."

3. From Commissioner of Indian Affairs T. Hartley Crawford's report to Secretary of War Poinsett, March 30, 1840 (U.S. Congress 1840, 3).

CHAPTER 22

1. John Tyler to Ross, David Vann, and John Benge, September 20, 1841 (Moulton 1985, 2:104–5).
2. Loomis (1859, 269).

CHAPTER 23

1. John Ross to John Stapler, August 14, 1844 (Moulton 1985, 2:238–39).
2. John Ross to E. Jane Ross (his niece), June 18, 1844 (Moulton 1985, 2:210–11). The comment between square brackets is Oskison's.
3. This quote and the following are both from John Ross to Mary B. Ross, July 25, 1845 (Moulton 1985, 2:267–68).
4. Loomis (1859, 270).
5. From a letter to Mary B. Ross and Sarah F. Stapler dated March 23, 1860 (Moulton 1985, 2:435–36).
6. From a letter to Mary B. Ross dated June 6, 1864 (Moulton 1985, 2:583).
7. Here, Oskison crossed out the following paragraph: "Ross had not been able to save for the Cherokees their beloved homeland; his stubborn resistance had been in part responsible for the horrors of the 'Trail of Tears' along which thousands had died; largely because of him, the first years in the west were filled with strife; his people heard him reviled and threatened as a destroyer of peace, and later charged with enriching himself by diverting tribal funds to his own use, yet they always came away from contacts with him crying exultantly, 'Oh-zay-oo! Oh-zay-oo!'"
8. See a reproduction of the painting in the introduction to this volume.
9. Annual Message, October 3, 1843 (Moulton 1985, 2:180).
10. From a letter to Sarah F. Stapler (Moulton 1985, 2:673).
11. Here Oskison crossed out the following lines: "A rich, simple life surrounded him, represented by all gradations of tribesmen from the well educated mixed-bloods to the cabin-dwelling full-bloods of the hills. He was as firmly fixed in the affection and respect of the one as the other."
12. Charles Reese was a private during the war against the Creeks in 1814 (Starr 1921, 42).

CHAPTER 24

1. Oskison does not attribute the epigraph in the original "Unconquerable" manuscript; however it is from Ecclesiastes 9:12.

2. This and the following quotes are from a letter John Ross sent to Cyrus Harris, Governor of the Chickasaw Nation, on February 9, 1861 (Moulton 1985, 2:459–60).

3. The Creek Nation did not actually share a border with the state of Arkansas.

4. Ross quoted governor of Arkansas Henry M. Rector in his reply to him, on February 22, 1861 (Moulton 1985, 2:464–65).

5. This and the following quote are from John Ross to David Hubbard, June 17, 1861 (Moulton 1985, 2:472–74).

6. John Ross to John B. Ogden, February 28, 1861 (Moulton 1985, 2:466).

7. John Ross to Mark Bean et al., May 18, 1861 (Moulton 1985, 2:470–71).

8. Eaton (1914, 180).

9. In a proclamation on May 17, 1861, John Ross told the Cherokees that they "should not be alarmed by false reports thrown into circulation by designing men—but, cultivate harmony among themselves and observe in good faith strict neutrality between the States threatening civil war" (Moulton 1985, 2:469–70).

10. John Ross spells the name of the Creek chief Opothleyahola. In his journal, Stephen Foreman spells the name of the Creek leader "Opothleahotah" (n. d., 2). In an 1866 *Memorial of the Delegates of the Cherokee Nation to the President of the United States, and the Senate and House of Representatives in Congress*, the name is spelled "Opothleyoholo" (1866, 5). Clarissa Confer writes of "pro-Union Creek leader Opothleyahola . . . an elderly Upper Creek spokesman who refused to abide by the treaty signed in July 1861" that created an alliance between the Creeks and the Confederacy (2007, 51–59). For more on Opothleyahola's resistance to the Confederacy and on the pursuit of his band by Confederate soldiers out of the Indian Territory in 1861, see Confer (2007, 59–65). Confer calls this event "the first concerted military action of the Civil War in Indian Territory" (103), and Opothleyahola's followers "the first large group of refugees from Indian Territory" (117).

CHAPTER 25

1. The treaty of alliance to the Confederacy, signed on October 7, 1861, under duress—"the absence of the protection guaranteed to the Cherokee Nation, by the Government of the United States, and the overwhelming pressure of the circumstances which surrounded them, consisting in part of the secession of the States of Missouri, Arkansas and Texas, and the Creek, Seminole, Chocktaw, and Chickasaw Nations, the presence of Confederate troops on our borders, and in our country, etc."—was "revoked and declared null and void by an act of the Council on February 18th, 1863, signed by Lewis Downing, President pro tem of the National Committee, Spring Frog, Speaker of the

Council, William Scraper, Clerk of the Council, and approved on the same day by Thomas Pegg, Acting Principal Chief." An "act for the removal of disloyal men from office" was passed on February 20 and "an Act Emancipating the Slaves in the Cherokee Nation" was passed on February 21 (*Memorial* 1866, 11–12).

2. In contemplating a visit to his home, Rose Cottage, he wrote in a letter to Sarah F. Stapler dated September 22, 1863, that it was his duty to go, "placing my whole trust in that Omnipotent Power who controuls the destinies of the universe—and under whose protecting arm I have been shielded from all harm in the perils, that lay in the pathway of my past life—and with prayers to him for a safe return to my family—I hope to be heard" (Moulton 1985, 2:542).

CHAPTER 26

1. John Ross to Sarah F. Stapler, Steamer Iron City, five miles below Van Buren, Arkansas, August 31, 1865 (Moulton 1985, 2:645–56).

2. John Ross to Annie B. Ross, Fort Smith, Arkansas, September 18, 1865 (Moulton 1985, 2:649).

3. From "Dialogue Between Ross and Dennis N. Cooley," September 15, 1865 (Moulton 1985, 2:646–48).

4. Moulton does not refer to this speech by the delegates. He writes that Ross's speech was followed by "remarks by Elias C. Boudinot in opposition to Ross" (Moulton 1985, 2:648n6).

5. The delegation addressed a memorial to the U.S. government. The *Memorial of the Delegates of the Cherokee Nation to the President of the United States, and the Senate and House of Representatives in Congress* was signed by Smith Christie, James McDaniel, Thomas Pegg, White Catcher, Daniel H. Ross, J. B. Jones, and S[amuel] H[ouston] Benge, on January 24, 1866. As made explicit by the first few paragraphs of this memorial, its main purpose was to protest the establishment of one government over all tribes in Indian Territory: "We learn that a bill has been introduced into Congress, entitled 'A bill to consolidate the Indian tribes, and to establish Civil Government in the Indian Territory.'

"It is our solemn conviction, and the conviction of our people, that if that bill becomes a law, and is carried into execution, it will crush us as a people, and destroy us as a Nation. In hope of averting such a calamity, we beg your consideration of a few facts, which will show our claim on the United States for justice—our claim on them to observe sacredly, all their treaty obligations to us" (1866, 3).

6. Letters from John Ross written there indicate that Joy's was located at the "Corner of 8th St. & Penna. Ave." (Moulton 1985, 2:661).

7. John Ross to Sarah F. Stapler, January 19, 1866 (Moulton 1985, 2:661–63). In the letter and in the *Memorial of the Delegates*, the name of the Cherokee delegate is spelled "White Catcher" (Moulton 1985, 2:662; *Memorial* 1866, 10).

8. John Ross to Sarah F. Stapler, Park Hill, October 28, 1865 (Moulton 1985, 2:652).

9. John Ross to Sarah F. Stapler, April 4, 1866 (Moulton 1985, 2:672–73).

10. Elias C. Boudinot and the other ex-Confederate were probably not official members of the delegation headed by Ross, contrary to what Oskison's phrasing seems to suggest. However, they were also in Washington at the same time. In a letter to Sarah Stapler, dated February 22, 1866, Ross wrote: "The City is full of Indians of various Tribes—among them, Stand Watie & son, Dick Fields & Joab Scales have arrived to be associated, I suppose, with [Elias C.] Boudinot & Wm. P. Adair," the latter probably being the other ex-Confederate Oskison refers to (Moulton 1985, 2:666).

CHAPTER 27

1. Again, Oskison did not include attribution for the epigraph in the original "Unconquerable" manuscript; however, it is from Deuteronomy 6:20–21.

AUTHORITIES

This bibliography was established by Oskison. It is reproduced here exactly as it was found in the manuscript, although it was judged by one of the original reviewers, Grant Foreman, "inadequate in substance and form," and by another, James Hill, "unscholarly" (Oklahoma University Press Collection). References also used by the editor appear again in the editor's reference list, in proper form, and sometimes in more modern references: since Oskison has worked on his biography of Ross, John Ross's letters, for instance, or the Payne papers have been edited in volumes made available and more easily accessible to larger audiences.

I

OF GENERAL INTEREST AND AVAILABLE AT MANY LIBRARIES:

Abel, A. H. *History of Events Resulting in Indian Consolidation West of the Mississippi.* 1906.
  The Indian as Slaveholder and Secessionist.
  The Indian as Participant in the Civil War.
Adair, J. *History of the American Indians.*
Bancroft, H. H. *History of the United States.* Vol. II.
Collier, John, Secretary American Indians Defense Association. *Survey Graphic.* Jan. 1929.
Drake, S. G. *Biography and History of the Indians in North America.* 1857.
Eaton, Rachel Caroline. *John Ross and the Cherokees.* 1914.
Institute for Government Research. *The Problem of Indian Administration.* 1928.
Irving Washington. *A Tour of the Prairies.*
Mooney, James. *Myths of the Cherokees.* 19th Annual Report Bureau of Ethnology, Part I. 1897–8.
Parker, T. V. *The Cherokee Indians.* 1907.
Peters, Richard. *The Case of the Cherokee Nation vs. the State of Georgia.* 1831.
Royce, C. C. *The Cherokee Nation of Indians.* 5th Annual Report Bureau of Ethnology. 1883–4.
Washburn, Cephas (a missionary). *Reminiscences of the Indians.* 1869.

II

NOT GENERALLY ACCESSIBLE, BUT IMPORTANT:

Anderson, Mabel Washbourne. *Life of Stand Watie.* 1915.

"Atticus." *A Vindication of the State of Georgia.* 1827.

Bartlett, Rev. S. C. *Historical sketch of the Missions of the American Board.* 1876.

Barton. *New Views.* 1797.

Bartram, William. *Travels in North America.* 1773–8.

Brown, David (a Cherokee). *Letter to the War Department,* Sept. 2, 1825.

Cherokee Nation. *Laws.* In Cherokee and English. Issued at various times, the earliest in 1826.

Cherokee National Records. Manuscripts, In Carnegie Library, Tahlequah, Okla.

Cherokee Advocate. Tribal weekly newspaper, in Cherokee and English. 1844 ff.

Cherokee Phoenix. Predecessor of Advocate. 1828–34.

Church, Mary Boudinot. *Elias Boudinot. Magazine of History.* Dec., 1913.

Commissioner of Indian Affairs. *The Cherokee Question.* Report to the President. 1865.

Cornelius, Rev. Elias. *The Little Osage Captive.* Edinburgh, 1824.

Couch, Nevada. *Pages from Cherokee Indian History.* 1884.

Featherstonhaugh, G. W. (F. R. S., F. G. S.) *A Canoe Voyage up the Minnay Soter.* London. 1847.

Gentleman of Elvas, The. Hakluyt Society Publications. London. 1851.

Gilmer, George R. *The Georgians.* 1855.

Gude, Mary. *Georgia and the Cherokees.*

Harden, E. J. *Life of (Gov.) George M. Troup.* 1849.

Hawkins, Benjamin. *Journal and Letters* of 1796–1801. Mss. Georgia Historical Society.

Haywood, J. *Natural and Aboriginal History of Tenn.* 1823.

Hicks, Elijah. *Journal* of 1837. Ms. Oklahoma State Historical Society.

Kennedy, John Pendleton. *Memoirs and Life of William Wirt.* Vol. II, Chapters XV–XIX.

Lanman, Charles. *Letters from the Allegheny Mountains.* 1848.

Loomis, A. W. *Scenes in the Indian Country.* 1859.

Lumpkin, Wilson. *Removal of the Cherokee Indians.* 1908.

McKenney & Hall. *History of Indian Tribes of North America.* 1855. 58–70.

Missionary Herald. Files. 1812 ff.

Morse, Jedidiah. *Report to the Secretary of War on Indian Affairs.* 1822.

Nuttall, Thomas. *Journal of Travels in the Arkansas Territory.* 1829.

Payne, John Howard. Collection of material for a contemplated *History of the Cherokees.* Mss. 9 vols. Newberry Library, Chicago. Also *Letters* to N. Y. *Journal of Commerce.* 1841.

Ramsey, J. J. M. *Annals of Tennessee.* 1853.

Ross, John. *Letters and Mss.* In possession of Robert B. and L. C. Ross, Tahlequah, Okla.

Ross Journal. *Historical Magazine.* Oct. 1867.

Ross, Mrs. W. P. *Life and Times of W. P. Ross.* 1893.

Speeches. *On the Passage of the Bill for the Removal of the Indians, Delivered in the Congress of the United States, April and May, 1830.* Boston and New York.

Starr, Emmet. *Early History of the Cherokees.* 1917.

Thompson, Augustus Charles. *Moravian Missions.*

Timberlake, Henry. *Memoirs.* London, 1765.

III

FOR THE RESEARCH STUDENT:

Confederate Statutes at Large.

Congressional Documents. Various serial numbers, 27 to 1,232.

Congressional Globe. Reports of Proceedings of the Sessions of the 23rd to the 31st Congresses.

Gales and Seaton. Register of Debates in Congress. Dec., 1824, to March, 1837.

Indian Office Mss. Records at Washington. Described in Van Tyne & Leland's *Guide to American Archives,* and A. H. Abel's *Bibliographical Guide.*

Official Records of the War of the Rebellion. Series I, Vols. I, II, III, VII, XIII.

Niles' Register. Numbers 4, 6, 14, 16, 26, 36-7-8-9, 40, 41-2.

Richardson. *Messages and Papers of the Presidents,* 1789–1897.

Messages and Papers of the Confederacy, 1861–5.

United States Statutes at Large. Vols. IV, VII, IX.

REFERENCES

Acts of the General Assembly of the State of Georgia, Passed in Milledgeville at an Annual Session in November and December, 1831. 1832. Milledgeville GA.

Adair, James. 1775. *The History of the American Indians: particularly those Nations adjoining to the Mississippi, East and West Florida, Georgia, South and North Carolina, and Virginia.* London: Edward and Charles Dilly.

Anderson, Rufus. 1825. *Memoir of Catharine Brown, a Christian Indian of the Cherokee Nation.* Boston: Samuel T. Armstrong and Crocker and Brewster.

Anderson, William L., Jane L. Brown, and Anne F. Rogers, eds. 2010. *The Payne-Butrick Papers.* 2 vols. Lincoln: University of Nebraska Press.

Atticus. 1827. *A Vindication of the Recent and Prevailing Policy of the State of Georgia, both in reference to its Internal Affairs, and its Relations with The General Government.* Athens GA: G. P. Shaw.

Blackburn, Rev. Gideon, Missionary to the Cherokees, to the Chairman of the Committee of Missions. April 24, 1805. *Assembly's Missionary Magazine, or, Evangelical Intelligencer* (July 1, 1805): 356–57.

Blackburn, Rev. Gideon. 1807. "An Account of the Origin and Progress of the Mission to the Cherokee Indians; in a Series of Letters from the Rev. Gideon Blackburn, to the Rev. Dr. Morse." *Piscataqua Evangelical Magazine* (September 1): 191–94.

Bonnefoy, Antoine. 1916. *The Journal of Antoine Bonnefoy's Captivity Among the Cherokee Indians, 1741–1742.* Edited by Newton D. Mereness. *Travels in the American Colonies.* New York: McMillan.

Boudinot Church, Mary. 1913. "Elias Boudinot." *The Magazine of History* 17, no. 6 (December): 209–21.

Clarke, Mary Whatley. 1971. *Chief Bowles and the Texas Cherokees.* Norman: University of Oklahoma Press.

Colton, Calvin, ed. 1863. *The Works of Henry Clay.* 6 vols. New York: Barnes & Burr.

Congressional Globe. 1838. 25th Cong. 2nd Sess. 6.5 (January 8).

Confer, Clarissa W. 2007. *The Cherokee Nation in the Civil War.* Norman: University of Oklahoma Press.

Conley, Robert. 2005. *The Cherokee Nation: A History.* Albuquerque: University of New Mexico Press.

The Constitution and Laws of the Cherokee Nation: Passed at Tahlequah, Cherokee Nation, 1839–51. 1852. Tahlequah, Cherokee Nation.

Cornelius, Elias. 1824. *The Little Osage Captive, an Authentic Narrative: To which are added some Interesting Letters Written by Indians*. York: W. Alexander & Son.

Cox, James H. 2014. "'Learn to Talk Yaqui': Mexico and the Cherokee Literary Politics of John Milton Oskison and Will Rogers." *Western American Literature* 48, no. 4 (Winter): 400–421.

———. 2019. *The Political Arrays of American Indian Literary History*. Minneapolis: University of Minnesota Press.

Cuming, Sir Alexander. 1731. "Account of the Cherokee Indians, and of Sir Alexander Cuming's Journey amongst them." *The Historical Register* 18, no. 61: 1–18.

DeRosier, Arthur H., Jr. 1972. "Cyrus Kingsbury—Missionary to the Choctaws." *Journal of Presbyterian History (1962–1985)* 50, no. 4 (Winter): 267–87.

Dixon, David. 2005. *Never Come to Peace Again: Pontiac's Uprising and the Fate of the British Empire in North America*. Norman: University of Oklahoma Press.

Eaton, Rachel Caroline. 1914. *John Ross and the Cherokee Indians*. Menasha WI: George Banta Publishing.

Eggleston, George Cary. 1878. *Red Eagle and the Wars with the Creek Indians of Alabama*. New York: Dodd, Mead, & Company.

Everett, Edward. 1831. *Speech of Mr. Everett, of Massachusetts, in the House of Representatives, On the 14th and 21st of February, 1831, on the Execution of the Laws and Treaties in Favor of the Indian Tribes*.

Featherstonhaugh, G. W. 1847. *A Canoe Voyage up the Minnay Sotor; with an Account of the Lead and Copper Deposits in Wisconsin; of the Gold Region in the Cherokee Country; and Sketches of Popular Manners; &c.* 2 vols. London: Richard Bentley.

Foreman, Grant. 1932. *Indian Removal*. Norman: University of Oklahoma Press.

Foreman, Stephen. *Journal and Letters of Stephen Foreman, Cherokee Minister*. The Stephen Foreman Collection, Box F-21. University of Oklahoma Western History Collections.

Forsyth, John. 1830. *Speech of Mr. Forsyth, of Georgia, on the Bill Providing for the Removal of the Indians*. Washington DC.

Fortwendel, Cletus F., Jr. 1996. "Silas Dinsmoor and the Cherokees: An Examination of One Agent of Change." *Journal of Cherokee Studies* 17: 28–48.

Frelinghuysen, Theodore. 1830. *Speech of Mr. Frelinghuysen, of New Jersey, Delivered in the Senate of the United States. April 5, 1830*. Washington DC: Office of the National Journal.

Gaul, Theresa Strouth, ed. 2005. *To Marry an Indian. The Marriage of Harriett Gold and Elias Boudinot in Letters, 1823–1839*. Chapel Hill: University of North Carolina Press.

Gilbert, Bil. 1983. *Westering Man: The Life of Joseph Walker*. New York: Atheneum.

Gilmer, George. 1855. *Sketches of Some of the First Settlers of Upper Georgia, of the Cherokees, and the Author.* New York: D. Appleton and Company.

Grant, Ludovick. 1909. "Historical Relation of Facts Delivered by Ludovick Grant, Indian Trader, to His Excellency the Governor of South Carolina." *The South Carolina Historical and Genealogical Magazine* 10, no. 1 (January): 54–68.

Harden, Edward J. 1859. *The Life of George M. Troup.* Savannah GA: R. J. Purse.

Harrell, Sara Gordon. 1979. *John Ross, the Story of an American Indian.* Minneapolis MN: Dillon Press.

Harris C. A., Acting Secretary of War, to General John E. Wool. October 12, 1836. United States House of Representatives. *Documents of the House of Representatives at the First Session of the Twenty-fifth Congress, Begun and Held at the City of Washington, September 4, 1837.* Washington DC.

Hawkins, Benjamin. 1916. *Letters of Benjamin Hawkins 1796–1806.* Collections of the Georgia Historical Society Vol. 9. Savannah GA: Georgia Historical Society.

Haynes, Robert V. 2010. *The Mississippi Territory and the Southwest Frontier, 1795–1817.* Lexington: University Press of Kentucky.

Haywood, John. 1823. *The Natural and Aboriginal History of Tennessee, up to the First Settlements Therein by the White People in the Year 1768.* Nashville: George Wilson.

Hickey, Donald R. 1989. *The War of 1812: A Forgotten Conflict.* Urbana: University of Illinois Press.

Higginbotham, Mary Alves. 1976. "The Creek Path Mission." *Journal of Cherokee Studies* 1, no. 2 (Fall): 72–86.

Hine, Robert V. and John Mack Faragher. 2000. *The American West: A New Interpretive History.* New Haven CT: Yale University Press.

Hoig, Stanley. 1998. *The Cherokees and Their Chiefs: In the Wake of Empire.* Fayetteville: University of Arkansas Press.

Kappler, Charles J., ed. 1904. *Indian Affairs: Laws and Treaties. Volume II, Treaties.* Washington DC: Government Printing Office.

Larré, Lionel. 2014. *Histoire de la nation Cherokee.* Pessac: Presses Universitaires de Bordeaux.

Larré, Lionel, and LeAnn Stevens-Larré. 2014. "A Mad Narrator as Historian: Sir Alexander Cuming Among the Cherokees (1730)." In *Mad Narrators*, edited by Nathalie Jaëck, et al., 127–46. Pessac: Maison des Sciences de l'Homme d'Aquitaine.

Laws of the Cherokee Nation: Adopted by the Council at Various Periods. 1852. Tahlequah, Cherokee Nation OK: Cherokee Advocate Office.

Loomis, Augustus Ward. 1859. *Scenes in the Indian Country.* Philadelphia: Presbyterian Board of Publication.

Lumpkin, Wilson. 1907. *The Removal of the Cherokee Indians from Georgia.* 2 vols. New York: Dodd, Mead, & Company.

Malone, Henry T. 1956. *Cherokees of the Old South.* Athens: University of Georgia Press.

McClinton, Rowena, ed. 2007. *The Moravian Springplace Mission to the Cherokees.* 2 vols. Lincoln: University of Nebraska Press.

McClinton Ruff, Rowena. 1996. "Notable Persons in Cherokee History: Charles Hicks." *Journal of Cherokee Studies* 17: 16–27.

McKenney, Thomas. 1872. *History of the Indian Tribes of North America with Biographical Sketches and Anecdotes of the Principal Chiefs.* 2 vols. Philadelphia: D. Rice & Co.

McLoughlin, William G. 1984. *Cherokees and Missionaries, 1789–1839.* New Haven CT: Yale University Press.

———. 1986. *Cherokee Renascence in the New Republic.* Princeton: Princeton University Press.

Meeting for Sufferings, ed. 1843. *Tracts Relative to the Aborigines, from 1838 to 1842.* "Further Information Respecting the Aborigines, Containing Extracts from the Proceedings of the Meeting for Sufferings in London, and of the Committees on Indian Affairs, of the Yearly Meetings of Philadelphia and Baltimore, Together with some Particulars Relative to the Seminole War." Second edition. London.

Memorial of the Delegates of the Cherokee Nation to the President of the United States, and the Senate and House of Representatives in Congress. 1866. Washington DC: Washington Chronicle Print.

Mooney, James. [1891] 1992. *History, Myths, and Sacred Formulas of the Cherokees.* Fairview NC: Bright Mountain Books.

Moulton, Gary E. 1976. "'Voyage to the Arkansas': New Letters of John Ross." *Tennessee Historical Quarterly* 35, no. 1 (Spring): 46–50.

———. 1978. *John Ross, Cherokee Chief.* Athens: University of Georgia Press.

———, ed. 1985. *The Papers of Chief John Ross.* 2 vols. Norman: University of Oklahoma Press.

Norton, Mary Beth, et al. 2012. *A People and a Nation: A History of the United States.* 9th ed. Belmont CA: Wadsworth Publishing.

Niles' Weekly Register. April 4, 1835. Fourth Series 12.5: 88.

Oklahoma University Press Collection. Box 9, folder 10. Western History Collections. University of Oklahoma, Norman.

Oskison, John Milton. 1929. *A Texas Titan: The Story of Sam Houston.* New York: Doubleday, Doran, and Company.

———. 1938. *Tecumseh and His Times, the Story of a Great Indian.* New York: G. P. Putnam's Sons,.

Perdue, Theda, ed. 1983. *Cherokee Editor: The Writings of Elias Boudinot.* Athens: University of Georgia Press.

Pesantubbee, Michelene E. 2014. "Nancy Ward: American Patriot or Cherokee Nationalist?" *American Indian Quarterly* 38, no. 2 (Spring): 177–206.

Peters, Richard. 1831. *The Case of the Cherokee Nation against the State of Georgia; Argued and Determined by the Supreme Court of the United States, January Term 1831.* Philadelphia: John Grigg.

Phillips, Joyce B. and Paul Gary Phillips, ed. 1998. *The Brainerd Journal, A Mission to the Cherokees, 1817–1823.* Lincoln: University of Nebraska Press.

Powell, J. W. 1887. *Fifth Annual Report of the Bureau of American Ethnology to the Secretary of the Smithsonian Institution 1883–1884.* Washington DC.

Ramsey, J. G. M. 1853. *The Annals of Tennessee to the End of the Eighteenth Century: comprising its settlement, as The Watauga Association, from 1769 to 1777; A Part of North-Carolina, from 1777 to 1784; The State of Franklin, from 1784 to 1788; A Part of North-Carolina, from 1788 to 1790; the Territory of the U. States, South of the Ohio, from 1790 to 1796; the State of Tennessee, from 1796 to 1800.* Charleston: John Russell.

Ross, John. 1836. *Letter from John Ross, Principal Chief of the Cherokee Nation of Indians, in Answer to Inquiries From a Friend Regarding the Cherokee Affairs with the United States, Followed by a Copy of the Protest of the Cherokee Delegation.* Washington DC.

Royce, Charles C. [1887] 2007. *The Cherokee Nation.* New Brunswick: Aldine Transaction.

Rozema, Vicki, ed. 2003. *Voices from the Trail of Tears.* Winston-Salem NC: John F. Blair Publisher.

Ruskin, Gertrude McDaris. 1963. *John Ross, Chief of an Eagle Race.* Decatur GA: John Ross House Association.

Schwarze, Rev. Edmund. 1923. *History of the Moravian Missions among Southern Indian Tribes of the United States.* Bethlehem PA: Times Publishing.

Smith, James. 1799. *An Account of the Remarkable Occurrences in the Life and Travels of Col. James Smith.* Lexington KY.

Speeches on the Passage of the Bill for the Removal of the Indians, Delivered in the Congress of the United States, April and May, 1830. 1830. Boston: Perkins & Marvin.

Starkey, Marion L. 1946. *The Cherokee Nation.* New York: Alfred A. Knopf.

Starr, Emmet. 1921. *History of the Cherokee Indians and Their Legends and Folk Lore.* Oklahoma City: Warden.

Strouth Gaul, Theresa, ed. 2005. *To Marry an Indian: The Marriage of Harriett Gold and Elias Boudinot in Letters, 1823–1839.* Chapel Hill: University of North Carolina Press.

"Talks between Franklin [state] and the Cherokee Nation." July 31 to August 3, 1786. Franklin (state); Cherokee Indian Nation. *Colonial and State Records of North Carolina.* Volume 22: 655–59. Accessed October 21, 2015. http:// docsouth.unc.edu/csr/index.html/document/csr22-0496.

Thursby, Jacqueline S. 2003. *"Brer Rabbit, Uncle Remus, and the 'Cornfield Journalist': The Tale of Joel Chandler Harris* by Walter M. Brasch, review." *The Journal of American Folklore* 116.459 (Winter): 125–26.

Timberlake, Henry. 1765. *The Memoirs of Lieut. Henry Timberlake.* London.

Troup, George M. to James Barbour. February 17, 1827. *The Examiner, and Journal of Political Economy* 2, no. 14 (February 4, 1835): 212.

United States Congress. 1824. *Message from the President of the United States, transmitting certain Papers Relating to the Compact between the U. States and the State of Georgia, of 1802, etc.* 18th Cong., 1st Sess. 63 (April 2).

United States Congress. 1803. "Arrest of Zachariah Cox by a Governor." 8th Congress, 1st Sess. 361–62.

United States Congress, House of Representatives. April 15, 1840. *Cherokee Indians. Letter from the Secretary of War.* 26th Congress, 1st Sess.

Walker, Robert Sparks. 1931. *Torchlights to the Cherokees: The Brainerd Mission.* New York: MacMillan.

Washburn, Rev. Cephas. 1971. *Reminiscences of the Indians.* Richmond VA: Presbyterian Committee of Publication.

Woodward, Grace Steele. 1963. *The Cherokees.* Norman: University of Oklahoma Press.

Worcester, Samuel to William S. Coodey. April 5, 1830. In Frelinghuysen, Theodore. *Speech of Mr. Frelinghuysen, of New Jersey, Delivered in the Senate of the United States.* Washington DC: Office of the National Journal, 41–44. Reprint in *Cherokee Phoenix*, May 8, 1830.

INDEX

Abel-Henderson, Annie Heloise, xxii–xxiii
Academy at Lovely's Spring, 13
Act of Union (Cherokee), 149, 155, 157, 159, 164, 244n1
Adair, James, 213n22
Adams, John Quincy, 13, 49, 75, 230nn1–2
alcohol legislation (Cherokee), 41, 219n1, 220n5
amalgamation: Cherokee Nation working toward, xxix–xxxvii, 16–18, 32–34, 41–46, 60, 175–76, 200, 209n11, 212n20; controversy among Cherokees regarding, xxxv–xxxvii, 18, 211n18; and cultural integrity, xxxii–xxxiv, 42, 200; economic successes, 46, 67; federal agents on progress toward, 14, 81; George Troup opposing, 225n10; JMO promoting, xxix–xxx, xxxii–xxxiv; JR on process of, xxix–xxxii, xxxiv–xxxvii, 33–34, 48–49, 207n3; missionaries supporting, 18, 36, 85–87, 232n6; progressive Cherokees supporting, 18, 21; as proposed alternative to removal, xxx–xxxii; role of education in, xxxiv, 9, 36–37, 42–45, 48–49, 67, 175, 212n20; and treaty "civilization" policies, 203n6, 204n8, 205n10

amnesty agreements, 154, 155
And Still the Waters Run (Debo), xxi
annuities: Andrew Jackson changing mode of payment for, 83, 89–91; in Treaty of 1817, 36; in Treaty of Holston, 5, 202n5, 205n9; tribal vote on, 90–91, 99; used in removal struggle, 77–78, 80–81, 96–97. *See also* finances/money
Anosta, Atlak (Atalah), 108, 235n1
Arbuckle, General: constitution authorization, 158–59; opposing JR, 147–48, 150, 154–58, 162, 164, 175; responding to Cherokee violence, 153–58, 244n2
Arch, John "Atsi/Atsee," 37, 44, 219n12, 220n8
Armstrong, Francis W., 48, 226n4
Atakullakulla (Ada-gal'kala) "Little Carpenter," 3, 55, 201n4, 206n13
Atticus (Georgia citizen), 63–64, 226n1

Baker, Joseph, 57
Baldridge, John, 68, 227n5
ball games, 2–3
Barbour, James, 94, 233n6
Battle of Horseshoe Bend (March 1814), 25–26, 130, 206n13, 214n10
Baugh, J. L., xxvii–xxviii
Beecher, Harriet, 96
Beecher, Lyman, 96